Teaching as if Life Matters

Teaching as if Life Matters

The Promise of a New Education Culture

Christopher Uhl
with Dana L. Stuchul

The Johns Hopkins University Press
Baltimore

© 2011 The Johns Hopkins University Press
All rights reserved. Published 2011
Printed in the United States of America on acid-free paper
9 8 7 6 5 4 3 2 1

The Johns Hopkins University Press
2715 North Charles Street
Baltimore, Maryland 21218-4363
www.press.jhu.edu

Library of Congress Cataloging-in-Publication Data

Uhl, Christopher, 1949–
    Teaching as if life matters : the promise of a new education culture /
Christopher Uhl with Dana L. Stuchul.
      p.   cm.
    Includes bibliographical references and index.
    ISBN-13: 978-1-4214-0038-9 (hardcover : alk. paper)
    ISBN-10: 1-4214-0038-3 (hardcover : alk. paper)
    ISBN-13: 978-1-4214-0039-6 (pbk. : alk. paper)
    ISBN-10: 1-4214-0039-1 (pbk. : alk. paper)
    1. Holistic education—United States. 2. Learning—United States.
3. Education—Moral and ethical aspects. 4. Values—Study and
teaching—United States. I. Stuchul, Dana L. II. Title.
    LC995.U37 2011
    370.11—dc22   2010039010

A catalog record for this book is available from the British Library.

*Special discounts are available for bulk purchases of this book. For
more information, please contact Special Sales at 410-516-6936 or
specialsales@press.jhu.edu.*

The Johns Hopkins University Press uses environmentally friendly
book materials, including recycled text paper that is composed of at
least 30 percent post-consumer waste, whenever possible. All of our
book papers are acid-free, and our jackets and covers are printed on
paper with recycled content.

This book is a tribute to Chris's mother, Frances C. Uhl,
and to Dana's father, Gary L. Stuchul,
in gratitude for their unconditional love
and for showing us how to LIVE as if Life Matters!

We dedicate this book to our daughter, Katie Diya Uhl,
whose light—as in all children—propels us to Teach as if Life Matters!

—C. Uhl *and* D. L. Stuchul

Contents

Gratitudes

If we are lucky during our years of schooling, we are graced with a remarkable teacher or two—someone able to see the goodness and unique brilliance lying at the core of our being. For me it was Ms. Lucille Bowen and Ms. Stacy Jackson, two English teachers working at Lane High in Charlottesville, Virginia, in the 1960s. Both women were intelligent and joyful—each overflowing with goodwill, each filled with curiosity, each radiating love. Their enduring gift to me was not so much the writing skills they imparted but rather the simple fact that they were able to see that, though I was a mediocre student in terms of test scores, I (like everybody else) had my own unique brand of intelligence and I was worthy of attention. Under their spell I felt seen, accepted, powerful. When they smiled on me, I felt less self-conscious—less a bounded self. At the same time, I saw in them the possibility of being in the world in a whole new way—light and joyful and fully free to pursue my own questions, passions, and stirrings of the heart. In retrospect, these two women were showing me what it means to *teach as if life matters*—what it means to love a student to life!—and for this I am eternally in their debt.

My first teaching job, in 1972, was at Beaumont School, a minimum-security prison for "delinquent" boys in rural Virginia. I was utterly unprepared for this position, never having taken a course in education theory, much less pedagogy. In an attempt to fill this deficit, I used the weeks leading up to my job to read *Teaching as a Subversive Activity*, by N. Postman and C. Weingartner; *Death at an Early Age*, by J. Kozol; *How Children Learn*, by J. Holt; and *Values Clarification*, by S. Simon, L. Howe, and H. Kirschenbaum. In retrospect, I am grateful to these authors; they were my early mentors, helping me to understand the challenges I would face in the classroom, while filling me with enthusiasm for the teaching life.

Since those early days, many other educators (unbeknownst to them!) have shaped my understanding of teaching and the pedagogies I employ in the classroom. I am particularly grateful to Parker Palmer (*The Courage to Teach* and *To Know as We Are Known*), John Holt (*Instead of Education*), Ron Miller (*What Are Schools For?*), Donald Finkel (*Teaching with Your Mouth Shut*), Neil Postman (*The End of Education*), John Taylor Gatto (*Dumbing Us Down*), Rachael Kessler (*The Soul of Education*), Lynn Stoddard (*Redesigning Education*), John Miller (*The Holistic Curriculum*), and Maria Lichtmann (*The Teacher's Way*). These educator/authors have left their imprint on this book insofar as they have provoked me with questions, insights, and challenges.

I am grateful, as well, to the seventy-five undergraduates who took (in groups of fifteen) my teacher preparation course, taught from 2006 to 2010, at Pennsylvania State University. In this course I tested out many of the ideas and practices described in this book. In addition, many of these students were kind enough to offer suggestions for improving the text.

The content and organization of this book further benefited from my collaboration with Jean Forsberg. Jean and I used an early version of this book in 2007–2008 when we co-taught a course for in-service teachers through Penn State's Continuing Education Program. Jean has been an unwavering source of encouragement and support, even creating the painting on this book's cover.

Too, I wish to thank Suzan Erem, Guy LeMasurier, Katherine Hast, Richard Chadek, Gabriela Winqvist, Julia Kasdorf, and Robert Andrejewski for generously reviewing portions of this book and offering suggestions for its improvement.

Finally, I am grateful to Ashleigh McKown at the Johns Hopkins University Press for her professionalism and grace in guiding this book through the publication process and to Julia Smith for her intelligence and care in copyediting. Of course, I take full credit for any and all inaccuracies, as well as for passages revealing my naiveté or ignorance.

—Christopher Uhl

Prologue

This book has been five years in the writing. I began it not fully knowing what compelled me to do so. I certainly didn't have to write it. There was no lucrative contract. My department chair at Penn State was not pressuring me to produce a book. On the surface, I did have a desire to share insights garnered from a lifetime of teaching, but there was something else unspoken inside of me, itching to be released.

My collaborator, Dana L. Stuchul, suggested that I explore this inner itch by simply reflecting on my schooling history. She gave me questions to work with like: What does it mean for you to learn? When have you experienced genuine learning in your life? What's your proof? Who or what have been your teachers? How, if at all, have the things you've learned changed you and how have they influenced your work as a teacher?

With these questions in hand, I went to my writing table. In ritualistic fashion I sharpened my pencil. Then I sat down and I waited. Nothing. I looked out the window. I gazed down at my writing pad. Nothing! Writing has always been a difficult process for me, but this was excruciating. In an attempt to break free, I listened to music, I lit candles, I burned incense. Each of these things had a slight softening effect on me, but still my writing was sluggish and muddled. Then one day I placed a photograph of myself, taken some sixty years ago when I was two years old, on my writing table. Something cracked open inside me. Studying this photo, I was struck by the brightness and trust beaming from my innocent eyes. Was this me? I dug into my old grade-school pictures—first grade, second grade, fourth grade, sixth grade . . . what would I find? As I studied those photos, I noted how the sparkle—the innocence—in my two-year-old eyes seemed to dissolve with time, replaced by a mixture of submission and melancholy. It was as if I was witnessing, through time-lapse photography, a shroud of resignation and sadness descend over me. And it was then that I wondered whether that itch inside me that longed to be exposed was my deep unacknowledged sadness for all those years, growing up, I had spent indentured in classrooms.

In time, I found myself mourning for all that was lost and all that might have been. In effect, I was finally allowing myself to feel a kind of wound lodged inside me. This sense of woundedness, still palpable today, is about how schooling, despite its well-meaning intentions, often diminished my innate autonomy, creativity, curiosity, spontaneity, lightness-of-being, confidence, and more.

Kirsten Olsen in her book *Wounded by School* gives examples of school wounds. As you read her list (19, paraphrased below), consider your own schooling history and how you may have been wounded by these beliefs and feelings:

- the belief that you are not smart, not competent in learning
- the belief that your abilities are fixed and cannot be improved with effort, coaching, intervention, or self-understanding
- painful memories of shaming experiences in school that live on in you as generalized anxiety and a low appetite for intellectual risk taking
- a tendency to classify others, and yourself, into dualistic, reductive categories: "smart/dumb," "artistic/not artistic"
- a generalized loss of pleasure in learning
- and, finally, unprocessed feelings about education and learning that you enact as an adult in your interactions with your own children or students

It is likely that all adults, subjected to American compulsory schooling, who give themselves permission to reflect deeply on their schooling history, will see significant ways in which school has "wounded" them.

Our disinclination, as adults, to do a rigorous retrospective inquiry into our schooling history and wounds is, it seems, a measure of schooling's power to blind us to its impact on our minds and hearts. Admissions such as "Yeah, I hated school," or "Yeah, school was boring," or "I wasn't any good at school" are rarely followed with a critique focusing on how the structure of school or the dominant teaching methods or even the purposes of schooling engender such sentiments in us. Instead, graduates or even dropouts interiorize the inherent flaws in the *system*, making them their own (Illich 1971).

In my case, I confess to experiencing a mixture of naughtiness and giddiness as I began to name my particular school wounds. The naughtiness came from the culturally instilled belief that I had no right to complain about school as an institution. Instead, I should be grateful for the opportunity—the privilege!—I had to go to school. After all, isn't school unquestionably good, and aren't complainers, like me, simply people who didn't measure up in school? In contrast, my giddiness sourced itself in the relief I experienced as I gave myself permission to speak things that I had hitherto been unaware of and/or afraid to speak—things that I was finally recognizing to be true in the depths of my being.

Overall, acknowledging my school wounds—my itch—has served an important purpose, for it has been through naming and mourning these wounds that, in some measure, I have been able to release myself from them.

The Central Purpose of This Book

This book traces its earliest origins to when I created a teacher-preparation course at Penn State for a group of fifteen students with no prior teaching experience. The students were selected from among three hundred who had just taken my "Developing Ecological Consciousness" course. My aim was to prepare these students to teach, single-handedly, a weekly breakout section of that same course the following year.

Normally, students who become teachers spend their entire college careers preparing to do so, and yet I was attempting to prepare them—some might say naively, absurdly, or arrogantly—by means of a solitary three-credit course. Given the immensity of the challenge and the limited time available, I decided to ground my entire course in Parker Palmer's dictum, *We teach who we are*. Specifically, I wanted my students—soon-to-be teachers—to experience themselves as empowered and aligned with life, believing that this, more than anything, would ensure their success in the classroom. Year after year, as I have continued to work with novice teachers in this course, I have come to understand what it means to *teach as if life matters*, as evidenced in this book's six chapters.

Chapter 1: Teaching as if Life Doesn't *Matter: Where We Went Wrong*. There is nothing more precious than *life*. And yet humans everywhere are fouling their environment, rendering planet Earth less able to support life. We are also killing each other—no other species kills its own kind on such a massive scale as Homo sapiens. As a final affront to life, we often hasten our own deaths; through our addictive behaviors, we literally eat, worry, and rush ourselves to death. This chapter exposes how conventional schooling, in spite of rhetoric to the contrary, is *anti-life* insofar as it often separates, even alienates, teachers and students from life. This separation is the problem. The response, elaborated throughout the remainder of this book, is an approach to teaching and learning whose aims differ markedly from those that currently dominate educational discourse and practice. Our intention is to bring life and relatedness out from the educational shadows and silences and into the light . . . in short, to promote *teaching as if life matters*.

Chapter 2: We Are Not Just Brains on a Stick: Relationship with Our Feeling Bodies. To be human is to have a body. Yet, modern schooling generally ignores the body, treating it simply as a conveyance for transporting our brains from place to place. So it is that teachers and students often see their feeling bodies as encumbrances, something that can cause embarrassment and that must be disciplined. However, to *teach as if life matters* is to recognize that our feelings (arising within our bodies) are the "life force" running through us. Feelings and emotions act as catalysts, inviting teachers (and by extension students) to know themselves, the human other, and the world more fully. The principles and practices presented in this chapter illustrate how our feeling bodies have much to teach us, both within and outside the classroom, provided we pay attention.

Chapter 3: Loving the Questions: Relationship with Our Minds. To be human is to have a curious mind. Good teachers are curious. They nurture a relationship with their intellect by asking thought-provoking questions of themselves and others and by creating a question-friendly environment in their classrooms. Such teachers recognize that asking questions is the most potent intellectual tool that humankind has ever developed because questions motivate us to *quest* for knowledge and wisdom. In this chapter, beyond extolling the power of questions to catalyze learning, we showcase a spectrum of approaches that we use to help teachers and students become more skilled in the art of asking questions that truly matter, drawing both into a deeper relationship with their minds.

Chapter 4: Seeing Ourselves with New Eyes: Relationship with Self. Beyond the relationship we teachers have with our feeling bodies and our intellects is the all-encompassing relationship we have with ourselves. Contemporary culture—with its frequent emphasis on judgment, comparison, competition, speed, money, and possessions—often tends to undermine our relationship with ourselves. On top of this, our education system, rather than encouraging introspection and self-knowledge, often promulgates the myth that meaning and happiness come through external sources. The result, for teachers and students, is often a sense of unworthiness and even self-loathing. In this chapter, we share stories about the crippling effects of self-alienation while offering practices for cultivating self-love, both inside and outside the classroom.

Chapter 5: Cultivating Classroom Kinship: Relationship with the Human Other.

A teacher's relationship with her body-mind-self provides the foundation for extending understanding and compassion to the human *other*, particularly to her students. Indeed, as teachers, we have a choice in how we perceive the students who enter our classrooms. We can objectify them, seeing them as empty containers that we must fill with information. Or we can see their unique personhood and convey to them, through our speech and actions, that their interests and feelings and desires matter to us. It is the teacher's communication and listening skills, more than anything else, that determine the quality of her relationships with her students. In this chapter we invite readers to explore how common habits of mind (dualistic thinking, labeling, judging, blaming) create communication styles that lead to separation and dysfunction in our relationships. As an antidote to the status quo, we share the communication approaches and techniques that we use to cultivate kinship in our classrooms.

Chapter 6: We Are Expressions of Everything: Relationship with Earth and the Cosmos. All too often, as modern humans, we live indoor lives, conscripted to a simulacra existence. Tragically, contemporary schooling often fails to recognize our vital connection to the living physical reality that is planet Earth, much less to the generative cosmos that is the ground of all creation. Mired in a human-constructed world, we become separate from vital truths of existence! The relationship that we have to the living Earth and the cosmos changes irrevocably as we awaken to the realization that all beings are made of the same stuff, all part of the same unfolding of "intelligences," all interacting and fitting together like pieces of an enormous tapestry. In this chapter, we offer an array of explorations and practices designed to bring teachers (and their students) into a relationship with Earth and the cosmos marked by affinity and a deep sense of belonging.

A Collaborative Effort

From the early stages of this book's conceptualization to its completion, I was graced to have my colleague and partner, Dana L. Stuchul, serve as a guide, provocateur, contributor, and editor. We are both teachers writing to teachers about the relationships that make up a teacher's life. And not just relationships with our colleagues and students but also the precious relationship each of us has with ourselves, as well as our relationship with Earth—the planet that has birthed us and that sustains us.

Through inquiring into our own pedagogical struggles and through our efforts to make sense of our learning and teaching histories, the purpose for this book became clear—to invite teachers at all levels to join us in placing relation-ship at the center of teaching and learning. Why this focus on relationship? It's simple! Everything that happens—from the level of the cells that constitute our bodies to the mysterious workings of the cosmos that encompasses us—is a story of relationship. Given this formulation, anything that ruptures or undermines relationship is, in effect, anti-life. And it is our contention (based on more than fifty years of combined teaching experience in a variety of school settings) that schools and their dominant pedagogies often do just that—they undermine re-lationship with self, other, Earth, and the cosmos to our collective peril.

This perspective shares much in common with work in the fields of holistic and transformative education. Contemporary holistic educators take issue with the traditional American education agenda (as do we), insofar as it is imposed (compulsory) and largely limited to cognitive pursuits and to ends that con-strict human potential. Rather than restricting education to the cognitive realm, holistic educators aim to create learning environments that nurture the whole person and, in so doing, foster self-actualization (J. Miller 1996, 2006; R. Miller 1997). In a complementary vein, advocates of transformative education seek to create learning environments that challenge young people to question their habits of mind, their beliefs, and their world view so that they might become less controlled by their social conditioning and, ultimately, more self-actualizing. O'Sullivan and Morrell (2002, 18) describe it this way: "Transformative learning involves experiencing a deep, structural shift in the basic premises of thought, feelings, and actions. It is a shift of consciousness that dramatically and irrevers-ibly alters our way of being in the world. Such a shift involves our understand-ing of ourselves . . . our relationships with other humans and with the natural world." Central to both holistic and transformative education is the question, What do humans need to learn to live meaningful lives? The answer, we con-tend, lies in relationship. It is through the cultivation of relationship that we humans find meaning and purpose and discover our place in the family of life.

In the end, to *teach as if life matters* is to ground education in the healing of the fractured relationships we have with ourselves and the world. Insofar as relation-ship is the essence of life, the challenge for teachers is to become relationship masters. This can and will occur, we believe, when teachers have the support and motivation to actively devote themselves to their own self-actualization. In-deed, the best teachers are masters of themselves as well as their subject matter (Schmier 2005). Such teachers offer their students a powerful model of what it means to be fully and authentically human!

The expression of our full humanity is precisely what these times call for. We believe that if human culture is to flourish in the new millennia, teachers will need to become fearless agents of transformation. Nina Simons (2005, 8–9) put this challenge in an educational context when she wrote: "To navigate the wild changes ahead, decrease the violence of this tumultuous time, and shift our civilization's direction, we will need to invest the same authority and value in our relational intelligence and learning as we've previously given to our intellectual development. If we can do that, we will build a contagious energy that will ultimately lead to real healing and restoration . . . of our deep and fundamental interdependence with each other, other species, and the whole interwoven web of creation."

Make no mistake: We teachers *are* especially well positioned to act as agents of transformation insofar as our influence extends, both deep and wide—first to the students in our classrooms and then, as our students step from our classrooms into the world, to society as a whole.

Teaching as if Life Matters

CHAPTER ONE

Teaching as if Life *Doesn't* Matter

Where We Went Wrong

I am a survivor of a concentration camp. My eyes saw what no person
should witness; gas chambers built by learned engineers, children
poisoned by educated physicians, infants killed by trained nurses; women
and babies shot by high school graduates. So I am suspicious of education!
My request of teachers is: help your students to be Human. Your efforts
must never produce learned monsters, skilled psychopaths or educated
Eichmans. Reading, writing, spelling and arithmetic are only important if
they serve to make students more Human.   —H. G. GINOTT 1993

For thirty years I have been a teacher. My content area is ecology. The question
that has guided the majority of my teaching is: How can humans live harmoniously with one another and with the natural world that sustains us? In the 1980s,
it was this question that led me to the Amazon Basin. There, I worked as an ecologist investigating ways to rejuvenate badly degraded Amazonian landscapes.
This question also led me to spearhead the creation of a research institute, the
Amazon Institute of People and the Environment (IMAZON), at the mouth
of the Amazon River, with the avowed purpose of educating policy makers and
citizens in ways that would engender thoughtful stewardship rather than harmful exploitation of Amazonia's natural wealth.

In the early 1990s, my research focus shifted from Amazonia to my home
place—the campus where I taught. Specifically, I wondered about the environmental sustainability (or lack thereof) of Penn State and how this large institution was *teaching*, through omission or commission, about our relatedness to the
natural world. My concern for Earth's ecology also led me to focus on ways of
promoting ecological consciousness, and this, in turn, led me to begin to pay

close attention to the lives of my students. What was going on, I wondered, in the hearts and minds of the young people sitting in my classroom?

At the time, I was perplexed and sometimes even despairing as I encountered young people who seemed to be resigned to following a soul-numbing life script consisting of attending classes, getting a degree, finding a job, paying off loan debt, working at a job for forty-plus years, and then retiring and calling it a life. I wondered if the impoverishment of spirit that seemed apparent in the behaviors and attitudes of many young people, as well as adults, was somehow related to the ever-increasing impoverishment of the environment that I was observing all around me.

I also noted that my own life at that time could be construed as a template for the very impoverishment I believed I was seeing around me. Although I wore the trappings of academic success—I was tenured, highly published, well respected—I was, in a word, insular—largely divorced from myself, others, and the natural world.

This realization left me feeling sad and starved for a new way of being. Call it "crisis," call it "opportunity," call it the rational next step after decades of sporadic reflection—I found myself in the tenacious grip of questions that would have an especially profound impact on my teaching life: How is it that humans learn? What does it mean to "teach"? Does this life of mine as a "successful" college professor represent the full measure of what it means to be human? Does my teaching facilitate the blossoming of my own, as well as my students', fullest humanity? I suspected that the answer was "No." Clearly, the time had come for me to carefully examine my life, my learning, my teaching.

When Teachers Teach as if Life *Doesn't* Matter

There simply is no such thing as anything separate. Nothing, absolutely nothing, exists without being a part of a set or system of relationships. Any attempt to perceive things as separate and apart is an arbitrary and false separation . . . There are no such divisions in life. Life does not create boundaries, we do . . . Hence we create curriculum as if the world were made up of separate parts and we have come to believe the parts, and not the reality of the whole.   —S. CROWELL, R. N. CAINE, AND G. CAINE 1998, 61

Through the years, as I've observed students in classrooms and lecture halls where I teach at Penn State, I've often noticed in their faces signs of resignation, consternation, boredom, restlessness, exhaustion, skepticism, fear, and more. Many appear (at least to me) as souls adrift—anchorless—swept about by the tides of modernity. When I ask my students why they are in college, they usually don't beat around the bush. The dominant, and often exclusive, reason is to get a job. This response reveals how fully many young people (not to mention most adults) inhabit the culturally transmitted narrative that college is a necessary step for survival in a competitive world. "This [narrative] tells us that we are first and foremost economic creatures and that our sense of worth and purpose is to be found in our capacity to secure material benefits" (Postman 1996, 27–28). In light of this narrative, the response to the profoundly important question, "Who are you?" is "I am what I do for a living." This is a severely limiting characterization of what it means to be human.

I wondered what alternative vision—worthy of the work that teachers engage in with learners—might return spirit, love, and possibility to the faces of the young people I was encountering each day. How might these young people, in concert with teachers, become animated in their learning and living? More specifically, how might ideas of what it means to be "human" and to act with "humanity," when married to the study of ecology, yield teaching as if life *does* matter?

In the end, to solve this riddle, I simply needed to pose for myself the question: What is life? My ready response was that "Life is relationship"! Yes, relationship is the essence of life! Imagine my shock as I recognized how antithetical my own teaching was to this truth—that is, how thoroughly my own teaching was anti-relationship—how it was, in fact, an endorsement of all manner of separation! The obvious next question: How might my teaching be, at once, transformed and transformative?

From *Separation Consciousness* to *Relational Consciousness*

Our system of schooling was shaped by a particular worldview; a mechanistic/ technocratic mindset that gave rise to the age of industrial and imperial expansion that began in the mid-nineteenth century. It is increasingly apparent that this historical era has spent its creative energies and is now on the verge of decline.   —R. MILLER 2008, 17

Given the significant ways that human beings now experience separation over their lifespan, it may be that future historians will refer to our current epoch as

"The Age of Separation." The enactment of separation begins at birth. For example, it is likely that your mother was separated from her own innate biological wisdom—relying on so-called experts to deliver you into this world. Then, a few months after birth you may have been placed in a day care center, separated for many hours each day from family and kin. After several years in day care, you were probably enrolled in a school where you were sorted—separated by age, social class, and test scores—and taught that to "know" it is necessary to tear apart, to objectify—in short, to separate from. Then, as an adult, having learned (like most everyone else) that to survive it is necessary to trade your life energy for an abstraction—money—you may have been coaxed to separate yourself from the possibility of doing ennobling work in the service of goodness, beauty, and wholeness. Later in life, once you get up there in years, there is a good chance you will go into a retirement home, separated from the rest of society. Finally, at the moment of death, it may even be that you will be separated from your personal dignity, as the medical establishment transacts your passing.

We all swim in the waters of separation, often without even knowing it. Science, with its emphasis on abstract models and numbers, creates separation through objectification. Religion often cultivates separation by dichotomizing the world—for example, saved versus fallen, good versus evil; social institutions, like the justice, welfare, and education systems, engender separation by cultivating helplessness. Modern technologies create separation by luring us with comfort and efficiency, often at the expense of personal know-how, interdependence, and community.

Outward manifestations of our separation from life abound. Just read the newspapers. We harm and kill each other everywhere, every day, through acts of violence and warfare. We despoil Earth's air, water, and soil—everywhere everyday—mostly with impunity.

And, so, what might we, as teachers, do to respond to these times—how might we educate, in the true sense of the word, namely: to lead young people forth from darkness into light?

We could begin by recognizing that as teachers we are uniquely positioned to be societal change agents. After acknowledging this, we might ask: At this juncture in history, what kind of change is most essential so that our species might not merely survive, but flourish?

Our short answer to this question is that these times are calling us toward a change in consciousness—a comprehensive change in how we understand ourselves—specifically, a shift in our worldview from *separation consciousness* to *relational consciousness.* Václav Havel, the first democratically elected president of Czechoslovakia, affirmed the importance of shifts in consciousness when he said, "If we have learned one thing about this revolution, it is that consciousness precedes being" (in Hart 2003, 196).

Education Myths and *Separation Consciousness*

All that we are is the result of what we have thought.
The mind is everything.
What we think, we become.   —BUDDHA

For much of my professional life I bought into our culture's conventional wisdom around teaching and learning. For example, I believed that (1) learning occurs best within schools and classrooms; (2) learning is best accomplished through direct knowledge transfer from teacher to student; (3) the use of motivational and disciplinary devices (so-called carrots and sticks) enhances learning; and (4) learning occurs best when it is grounded in objectification. These four beliefs (which I now regard as myths) are so commonplace—so widely accepted—that to question them is tantamount to heresy. But question them we must if we are to move toward a new, more life-affirming, paradigm of teaching and learning.

Myth #1. Learning Occurs Best within Classrooms and Schools

Donald Finkel, in his book *Teaching With Your Mouth Shut*, invites readers to think back over their lives with an eye to selecting their three most significant learning experiences and then, in each case, to stop and ask three questions: (1) Did this experience take place in a school? (2) Was a professional teacher involved? and (3) What conditions and factors were involved in bringing about this learning? Finkel observes that "most people's significant learning—the learning that has really mattered . . . did not take place as a result of intentional teaching . . . [And] if a teacher or a teacher-like figure was important to your learning, she was probably doing something different from enthusiastic *telling* . . . Perhaps she got out of your way, gave you the opportunity to make your own mistakes, or failed to rebuke you when you expected a rebuke. But more than likely, no teacher was even present" (2000, 7).

Reviewing my own learning history, it became clear that formal schooling had seldom been an important locus of learning for me. As often as not, my true classrooms and best teachers showed up in daily life. For example, I learned

Portuguese by living in Brazil; I learned sports by getting out on the field; I learned ecology by roaming in the forest, eyes wide open, and by working side-by-side with able mentors; and I learned about the importance and power of listening and expressing feelings forthrightly in the cauldron of relationships. More recently, I have been learning the rudiments of carpentry and farming by apprenticing myself to skilled practitioners in these realms.

As teacher Matt Hern points out, "In a lot of ways, learning is synonymous with living. Learning is something that happens all the time, whether we intend it or not. Learning is what people do. We learn, take in new information, gain new knowledge, pick up new skills and insights constantly" (2003, 65). Tragically, our culture has conditioned us to believe that learning is something that happens exclusively in schools under a prescribed set of circumstances and that *living* is what we do outside of schools. This, of course, is nonsense. Learning and living are inseparable.

My assessment that I had learned very little of lasting benefit through my formal schooling prompted me to begin to think about what was actually happening during the more than twenty thousand hours I spent in school. After all, we are always learning something. Ideally, what we learn is beneficial to us—it makes us more skillful, competent, self-aware, knowledgeable, and humane. But it is also possible to unconsciously absorb lessons that leave us weaker, less confident, less aware of our true nature and potential, and more dependent on others. Consider:

> We are very unlikely to learn anything good from experiences which do not seem to us closely connected with what is interesting and important in the rest of our lives . . . We are even less likely to learn anything good from coerced experiences, things that others have bribed, threatened, bullied, wheedled, or tricked us into doing. From such we learn mostly anger, resentment, and above all self-contempt and self-hatred for having allowed ourselves to be pushed around or used by others, for not having been smart enough or strong enough to resist and refuse. (Holt 1976, 12)

In the end, I was compelled to admit that what I learned during all my time sitting in classrooms was, well . . . *school*—that is, a way of being that, more often than not, undermined my personal agency, creativity, intelligence, and confidence (Gatto 1992). Caught in the spell of *school*, I learned that to be a successful student, the best path was to be: (1) obedient—to follow the rules; (2) quiet—to sit docilely and avoid asking probing questions; and (3) dependent—to wait to

ESCAPING EDUCATION

In the early 1970s I had the good fortune to live for a few years in the Amazon Basin on the banks of the Rio Negro in the village of San Carlos. While there I made friends with people who had had no formal schooling—Getulio, Pedro, Luciana, and Maria. None of them had ever attended school, and yet the men had an encyclopedic knowledge of the plants and animals of the rainforest surrounding their village, while also being accomplished carpenters, hunters, and fisherman. The women, for their part, were accomplished farmers, weavers, midwives, mothers, and healers. These men and women acquired their knowledge and skills in the school of life; they learned by listening, watching, and imitating their fathers, mothers, aunts, uncles, and older siblings. Indeed, there is no scarcity of teachers when it comes to mastering life's arts and necessities.

When I returned to San Carlos in the early 1980s, things had changed. There was a new cinderblock school in the center of town—formal education had arrived! Nowadays the sons and daughters of Getulio, Pedro, Luciana, and Maria spend their days in school.

My friends want a better life for their kids, and they have been led to believe that schooling will provide that. But they harbor doubts. Getulio laments, "My son is learning to read but he doesn't know how to hunt or fish; he doesn't know about the medicinal plants growing in the forest; he doesn't know how to build a house or fashion a dugout canoe, or make a fish trap." Meanwhile, Pedro and Maria watch each evening as their three children rush onto the street to watch the one television set in town. Sadly, it is here that the kids of San Carlos learn about the life of glitter that exists out beyond the village and, by inference, about the seeming backwardness of their parents. (For an elaboration of these ideas, see Prakash and Esteva 1998.)

be told what to do, rather than charting my own learning path. Unknowingly, I was accumulating school *wounds*.

The situation is much the same today. For example, it is commonplace today for grade-schoolers, when asked "what being good means," to respond, "being quiet." And for their teachers to describe a successful classroom as one where the teacher keeps her students on task—that is, where students are doing what the teacher tells them to do. In such contrived settings, students aren't really behaving so much as *being behaved* by their teachers. One troubling result of top-down control is that children's internal decision-making skills do not mature, which is to say that part of their birthright—the experience and responsibility of exercising autonomous choice—is stymied. In sum, cloistering learning activities in schools has the tendency to separate learning from life, contributing to *separation consciousness*.

Myth #2. Learning Occurs Best through Knowledge Transfer

During my early years as a college professor, I taught the same way that I had been taught—I used a standard textbook, I gave lectures, and I administered tests—never stopping to seriously consider whether any significant learning was taking place in my classrooms. Following the dominant teaching algorithm, I was perpetuating a pedagogy absent reflection on its effects.

Then, one day, while interviewing for a job at the University of Michigan I was asked by a graduate student to explain my philosophy of teaching. I was dumbstruck—stilled like a deer caught in headlights. Seeing my befuddlement, the questioner added, "You know, your understanding of how people learn and how this informs your own approach to learning and teaching?" I stammered and mumbled, and it was soon clear that I had nothing worthwhile to say. In truth, though I had been teaching for more than a decade, I hadn't consciously developed a teaching philosophy. And yet I did have a de facto philosophy—the so-called banking model of education. This model is grounded in a set of five beliefs that I had assimilated without ever questioning:

1. Knowledge is a collection of facts that are objectively verifiable and not subject to interpretation.
2. Teaching occurs when facts move (are deposited) from teacher to student by oral transmission or through a text.
3. It is the teacher (credentialed, owing to years of study) who is qualified to transmit these facts.
4. Verifiable learning occurs when the student receives the facts from the teacher, memorizes them, and then passes a test.
5. This teaching and learning takes place in designated locations referred to as "schools."

In this view, information is seen as a resource, education is rendered an industry, and students are viewed as empty "accounts" to be managed by teachers (Freire 1970; Illich 1971; Bowles and Gintis 1976). According to this model, education is centered on a standard curriculum consisting of a body of information that must be *deposited* into students' heads.

The design of education delivery around information transfer has led to an assessment system grounded in tests and grades. Actually, it may be more accurate to say that a culture preoccupied with standards, indices, measures, and numeracy has tended to limit the purview of education to those activities that can be measured through testing. If a student performs well on tests, he is learning, or so we assume. But veteran teacher and principal Lynn Stoddard observes that "grade-point averages only reflect our culture's need to shape students to a common pattern and compare the learning of each child with others" (2004, 100). Indeed, it may well be that, more than anything, grades simply measure a student's ability to play the *game* of school (Pope 2001).

As I considered all this, I realized that curriculum and associated subject matter should be the tools, not the goals, of education. Indeed, the current emphasis on the transmission of a set curriculum confuses ends with means, working against the acquisition of higher-order intellectual skills, not to mention character and self-reliance. Just as with our cash economy, where the mere accumulation of money does not bring satisfaction, so, too, with transmission-based education, the mere accumulation of information does not grant intelligence, much less wisdom or self-actualization. Stoddard goes so far as to assert that transmission-based pedagogy has resulted in "the great brain robbery": "The public school system stole from us—bit by bit—our curiosity. This was done unintentionally, in an effort to make us smart, in an effort to give us knowledge. The result of this is that it robbed each of us of a curious attitude and the chance to acquire personal knowledge, the knowledge that comes from mentally processing new information so that it becomes our own, not knowledge adopted from others" (2004, 76). Elementary school teachers are well positioned to witness "the great brain robbery." A child enters kindergarten, filled with curiosity—bubbling with questions. Then, as the official core curriculum kicks in, often the child's head begins to drop, her shoulders begin to droop, her eyes lose their sparkle . . . until finally, after a few years, the lights go out—the great heist complete. This is the result of adhering to the mistaken belief that significant and worthwhile learning is best accomplished by transferring information from teacher to student. This belief separates, to a significant extent, children from their own capacity to be self-motivated, independent learners.

Myth #3. *Learning Occurs Best When Teachers Use Carrots and Sticks*

The third belief that I absorbed in my schooling and adhered to for many years as a teacher is that learning is hard work. It's not supposed to be fun. You just have to buckle down and do it! Believing that learning was hard work, it was my practice, for many years, to cajole students with both rewards (carrots) and threats (sticks). When I stopped to reflect, I realized that when I myself have been forced or cajoled to "learn" something, I haven't really learned it. Sure, I might be able to pass a test the next day, but give me that same test a year later, and I will most certainly flunk it. What's missing, of course, is desire.

Yes, we all learn best when motivated by desire. Think about it: When we were little we looked around, saw adults walking, and quite naturally wanted to have mobility for ourselves. This motivated us to learn to walk. Likewise, we observed adults making sounds and saw how this caused things to happen, and this created the desire that propelled us to learn to speak—a phenomenal achievement. The same is true for all significant learning. It is the energy of desire that drives the learning process.

Just as kids are motivated to learn how to walk and talk and manipulate numbers for their own real-life reasons, so it is with reading. Dana and I are observing this firsthand with our three-year-old daughter Katie. Several times a day she comes to us with a book in hand and implores us to read to her. Most recently, she has taken to *reading* to herself. Though she is not literally reading, she does carefully turn the pages while she recounts the story to herself. The other day she started singing her ABCs while "reading" one of her books, just like she has heard kids doing on a CD of children's songs. Already she has grasped the connection between letters and the words in the books that she loves. We are not actively teaching Katie to read. Rather, we are simply *setting the table*, being available to her as questions arise, trusting that when she is ready—whether at age four or ten—she'll figure out how to do it. She won't need carrots or sticks; learning is its own reward.

By contrast, when we cajole children to read—all at the same time, in the same way and at the same level—what we get are too many kids who can't read, who won't, who don't or, worse yet, who hate to! In other words, what we get are kids who are separated from their own natural rhythms of development, separated from the emergence of their innate intelligence, curiosity and enthusiasm for learning.

Myth #4. Learning Occurs Best When It Is Grounded in Objectification

In the eyes of the schools I attended, I was an object to be acted upon (the proverbial empty container) as well as an object to be quantified in terms of numbers and grades. Meanwhile, my classmates were objects for me to compete against.

THE ROLE OF DESIRE IN LEARNING

Imagine a twelve-year-old child in America who still hasn't mastered basic arithmetic. Scandalous! Talk about "a child left behind!" And yet in Framingham, Massachusetts, at the Sudbury Valley School, this circumstance would not be a cause for alarm. Indeed, Daniel Greenberg, a teacher at Sudbury, relates how one day a dozen kids between nine and twelve-years-old asked him to teach them arithmetic. Up to that point these kids had seen little need for arithmetic—it had had little relevance in their day-to-day living—but now they wanted to learn it, for reasons important and known to them. Upon hearing their request, Greenberg discouraged them saying, "You really don't want to do this? Your neighborhood friends, your parents, your relatives probably want you to, but you, yourselves, would much rather be playing or doing something else" (1987, 15). But the students insisted and promised to work hard and do all the homework. Greenberg eventually consented, making it clear that he would meet with them for one-half hour on Tuesdays and Thursdays. If they were as much as five minutes late, class would be cancelled; if they missed two classes, no more teaching. "It's a deal," they said. For the text, Greenberg chose a math primer written in 1898 that was chock full of exercises designed to teach basic math skills.

What happened? Here is Greenberg's recap: "Basic addition took two classes. They learned to add everything—long thin columns, short fat columns, long fat columns. They did dozens of exercises. Subtraction took another two classes . . . On to multiplication, and the tables . . . Everyone had to memorize the tables. Each person was quizzed again and again in class. They were high, all of them. They could feel the material entering their bones. Then division—long division. Fractions. Decimals. Percentages. Square roots. They came at 11:00 sharp, stayed half an hour, and left with homework. They came back next time with all the homework done. All of them. In twenty weeks, after twenty contact hours they had covered it all. Six years' worth. Every one of them knew the material cold" (1987, 16–17).

Notice that Greenberg didn't employ sophisticated technologies, innovative pedagogies or the most up-to-date teaching materials. His methods: practice and drill. And these were not exceptional students, just regular kids. Yet, they accomplished in twenty weeks what normally takes six years, and they learned the math "cold."

Greenberg's story illustrates that the critical ingredient for genuine learning is *desire*. Those kids at Sudbury didn't have to be bribed or cajoled or shamed into learning 'rithmetic. They wanted it!

Objectification was reinforced during my graduate-school training in science when I was taught that the way to learn something about a particular plant or animal was to perform an experiment to see how "it" responded. Then, after the experiment I could assess the effect of my manipulation by taking the organism apart, in effect, killing the object of study. Trained as a scientist, I adopted the objectivist approach—believing that it is through measurement and labeling and classifying that I would come to truly know the world.

Over the years I have come to see that numbers and labels are abstractions of reality and that an excessive reliance on naming and measuring tends to deaden my experience of the world. For example, when I first studied botany and zoology, I mistakenly believed that if I knew the scientific name of a plant or animal, I *knew* that organism. This presumption generally had the effect of diminishing my curiosity about the organism I had identified, curtailing the possibility of relationship. In point of fact, all I had learned was a label, an abstraction.

Palmer (1998, 51–52) adeptly captured the logic of objectivism when he wrote: "When we distance ourselves from something, it becomes an object; when it becomes an object, it no longer has life; when it is lifeless, it cannot touch or transform us, so our knowledge of the thing remains pure." Of course, there are times when holding something at arm's length can add an important perspective. However, the institutionalization of objectivism ingrained in our culture and schools can, if we are not careful, reduce the world to a collection of objects, blinding us to the scintillating interconnectedness undergirding reality.

In sum, I am embarrassed to say that much of my teaching life has been spent proffering mindless allegiance to four myths: namely, (1) that learning occurs best in a school setting, when (2) a teacher transfers information to students, (3) employs carrots and sticks, and (4) grounds instruction in objectification. Most educators I meet adhere, often unwittingly, to this same limiting philosophy of teaching and learning. Surely, we can do better.

A New Narrative for Education in the Twenty-first Century

The tumultuous nature of life in the twenty-first century is calling on teachers to reimagine their mission, recasting their purpose as agents of awakening and transformation both inside and outside of schools. In an earlier age it would have been fine for teachers to simply keep on keeping on, but no more. Something new is called for. It is no longer tenable or defensible, much less realistic, for teachers to imagine that someone else is going to fix the system. The fixing will not come from outside. Instead, it must come from within our own hearts and minds. For the system to change, we must change first.

We propose that a new narrative—capable of guiding and inspiring teachers and students—be centered on teaching and learning as if *life* matters. The urgency of teaching as if life matters is self-evident. After all, *life* is what we are! It is all that we have until we don't. It matters very much.

This phenomenon that we call *life* is rife with relationship. If this seems obtuse, consider that the life force animating your body right now is the result of millions of relationships (interdependencies) enacted second by second in your cells, tissues, and organs. That any of us even exists at all is testimony to gazillions of relationships spread out through time and space. We are and we exist in a web of relationships. Nonetheless, the primacy of relationship is often ignored, even undermined, in schools.

But what if relationship was placed squarely at the center of schooling and teaching? What if the essence of learning—the core ingredient of a successful life—was understood in terms of success in life's myriad relationships? Then, we would remember what is self-evident—that getting our relationships right— becoming *relationship masters*—is what a well-lived life is all about. In this reformulation, we would also be challenged to consider that the aim of a genuine *education* is to draw out our full humanity, helping us to create ever-more authentic and caring relationships with ourselves, each other, and the entirety of creation. This vision stands in stark contrast to education in service to blind growth, competition, and consumption that cannot but yield "professional itinerant vandals" (Berry 1987, 50), without knowledge of self or how to live harmoniously with others and the world on which they depend. Such education is more akin to *seduction* (from *seducere*—to lead astray), leading us away from all that serves, honors, and respects life.

So, instead of myopically prioritizing the traditional "3 Rs"—reading, 'riting, and 'rithmitic—we would be wiser, stronger, and safer as a people if we sought to cultivate excellence in an even more basic trio of "Rs"—namely, Relationship with Self, Relationship with Other, and Relationship with Earth. These are "Rs" that offer young people a path to genuine success and fulfillment in life. Absent these Relationship Rs, no amount of inventiveness, wealth accumulation, or technological wizardry will address the myriad social, environmental, and political challenges now confronting humankind.

In the final analysis the curriculum vita (from the Latin meaning "life course") for teachers dedicated to teaching as if life matters is centered on becoming healers—mending separation—fixing the broken, dysfunctional relationships that permeate the fabric of contemporary life. As we teachers heal ourselves, we can model a new way of being that cascades forth into the classroom and society as a whole. Indeed, as Caine and Caine (1997) point out, system transformation begins with teacher transformation.

Wrap-up

A new paradigm of intelligence, based on loving relationships rather than IQ testing, can increase the chances of bringing forth a more respectful and collaborative world. Our very definition of ourselves as thinking beings—homo sapiens—is transformed by a new definition of ourselves as loving beings— homo amans . . . By living in this realm, our creativity is nurtured to come to full blossom and the genius within each of us begins to unfold.

—B. CAMERON AND B. MEYER 2006, 52

Schools are important loci of socialization, and the socialization that occurs in schools is often in lockstep with the dominant culture with its emphasis on competition, materialism, individualism, and speed. We believe that such cultural values are antithetical to the flourishing of life and that the confusion that permeates educational institutions, as well as the anger and anomie evidenced in increasing numbers of students, is not fixable with more technology, more money, more reform, more time in the classroom, or more cleverness.

It is also our contention that the most vexing problem with education in the new millennia is not the size and/or structure of schools, not the qualifications of teachers, not the pedagogy adopted in schools (though obviously these are very relevant and related concerns). Rather, the most vexing challenge has to do with transforming our worldview—our consciousness. Indeed, whether we know it or not, all change begins with a shift in how we see. Specifically, the way forward is to birth a new view of education aimed at cultivating mastery in all of life's relational realms, and we believe that it is up to teachers to lead the way.

In the end, *Teaching as if Life Matters* is an invitation to ground education in love—the energy that creates, fuels, and heals relationships. Nothing else much matters. Love is what we discover ourselves to be once we wake up. And, waking up to our loving relationship to ourselves, to others, and to Earth is the new imperative. In the final analysis, love is the antidote to all that ails and addles us; it is love that transmutes separation consciousness into relational consciousness— love that informs *Teaching as if Life Matters*.

To be sure, love can't be diced and parsed; it can't be taught. But the conditions that lead to the opening and softening of the human heart—for example, a full awareness of how profoundly divided our lives have become, coupled with a capacity to treat ourselves, each other, and Earth with love and kindness—*can* be cultivated. Once the power and primacy of love is recognized, it can be practiced, day-by-day, by teachers loving themselves and their students to life.

Make no mistake: There is an immense hunger in young people for teachers who are love filled—teachers who know who they are; teachers who are grounded and comfortable in their skins; teachers who, because of their own self acceptance, are able to extend full acceptance to their students; teachers who can see the greatness simmering just below the surface in *all* of their students and who understand that they, as teachers, have an important role in the creation of a world of justice, peace, and sanity. In sum, our times are beckoning teachers who have the self-awareness, courage, and wisdom to understand themselves as helpers, healers, facilitators, guides—as people who love!

CHAPTER TWO

We Are Not Just Brains on a Stick

Relationship with Our Feeling Bodies

I have tried many times to think of cognitive tasks that do not involve feelings. So far, I have failed. Try a math problem. Let's multiply 31 and 41. This seems like a case where we use our cognitive brain to make a cold calculation. But how do we know our answer is right? Ultimately, it is a decision based on a belief. We can check out the answer by dividing it back with 31 or 41, and that will increase our confidence, but still that confidence is a feeling. And we won't move on until we have that feeling. Knowing is a feeling. Not only is knowing a feeling, getting to knowing is full of feeling. We feel progress as we do our first step in the multiplication. We feel confidence. But if our answer is challenged, we feel uncertainty—a tiny bit of fear. We feel motivated to prove our answer. And so it goes. Every part of this simple cognitive act seems to be driven or evaluated by a feeling.

—J. ZULL 2002, 73

Aaahh, feelings. Those messy, muddled, mysterious, often distracting parts of us. In their elevated state, we call them *emotions*. And we are a bundle of them. We are them, and they are us—like it or not. Perhaps, growing up, you have *learned* that emotions cannot be trusted, that there are times and places for the having or experiencing of emotions but that schools and classrooms are *not* such places. You may have *learned* that feelings and emotions are hindrances to learning—preventing clear, significant, and lasting learning from occurring. Indeed, if you are like most people, during your schooling years, you learned, through word and example, to separate your knowing and thinking from your feelings, your head from your heart, your mind from your feeling body. How did all this come to pass?

In the West we live with the legacy of René Descartes' dictum, *Cogito ergo sum*—"I think therefore I am." This view negates the body (the seat or home of feelings and emotions) while elevating the mind. In fact, the free and open expression of feelings and emotions is viewed suspiciously by a people and culture doggedly and relentlessly in pursuit of "success"—of "progress"—in the modern techno-scientific sense.

Contemporary schools are ever more narrowly geared toward shaping the intellect alone, with social and emotional learning relegated to being lower-tier goals. Within the early grades, the focus on memorization, reading comprehension, vocabulary expansion, spelling accuracy, and numeracy—reifies the primacy of the mind over the feeling body. At higher educational levels, this primary focus intensifies with the strong emphasis on analysis, objectivity, logic, abstraction, and problem solving. Given this conditioning, it is not surprising that school children often come to see their bodies and associated emotions as an encumbrance—as sources of embarrassment or distraction, requiring discipline.

In most schools and classrooms, the messages young people receive, either explicitly or implicitly, are that feelings and the feeling body *don't* matter. If you are feeling bubbly, calm down; if you are feeling depressed, take a pill; if you are feeling sad, get over it; if you are feeling angry, get yourself under control; if you are feeling afraid, rise above it. In other words, *don't* feel!

It would appear that the requirements of grades and standardized tests, of measuring and quantifying student and school achievement fuel the evident separation between mind and body within schools and classrooms. But might it be that the opposite is more accurate: That our Western heritage—that is, mindbody separation—has yielded an institution (schools), a dominant approach to learning (empty container/banking model), and a perspective on the purposes of learning (instrumentalism) that elevates the former (mind) and minimizes the latter (body)?

The excessive reliance and emphasis on the intellect obscures important sources of information that only the unified body-mind can offer. In fact, according to Goleman (1995), IQ (Intelligence Quotient) contributes, at best, 20 percent to the factors that contribute to success in life. What's more, IQ is fairly static. This means that whatever your IQ was when you were in your teens, it is likely to stay at that same level throughout your life. However, emotional intelligence (EI)—the ability to identify and handle one's emotions, to motivate oneself and to extend empathy to others—can steadily improve over time.

The point is this: The separation of mind and body—that is, the denial of the feeling body—within schools and classrooms constricts learning and is

BEWARE OF EMOTIONS

As a male, I was brought up to regard my emotions as something to keep under cover or at least under control. In school, when I fidgeted in my seat—something I apparently did frequently—I was told to control myself. When I fell and skinned my knee in the schoolyard, I was warned, "Big boys don't cry!" It was as if there was a sign at the entrance of my school saying, "Check your emotions at the door."

I was just a kid, and I wanted to please my teachers. In my kid's head I assumed that my teachers must be right. After all they'd been around a lot longer than me. If they said that expressing exuberance or anger or sadness or fear or pain was unacceptable, who was I to argue! Looking back, now, I understand what was going on. Emotions are energy. When we allow ourselves to feel our emotions, they *move* us; we become enlivened, activated by an inner authority. But school is set up to make us outer directed; it is structured to channel our attention and allegiance toward outer authorities—teachers, institutional rules, textbooks, testing protocols. So it is that young people grow up spending their days in school, learning to face forward, pay attention, follow instructions, and, through it all, to stuff their feelings deep inside. Such a regimen takes an unacknowledged toll—diminishing spontaneity, creativity, exuberance, authenticity, and more.

stultifying to the human spirit. Teachers are particularly prone to this mind-body separation. Why? Because we are the ones who were successful in school. More often than not, we were the ones who followed the rules, jumped through the hoops, and submitted to authority, often at the expense of our full and free emotional expression. Now as teachers, it is no surprise that we are the ones who often continue to create school cultures that view students as merely *brains on a stick* (thanks to J. Macy for this phrasing). However, as Candace Pert, author of *The Molecules of Emotion*, points out, "We have bodies for other reasons than to transport our heads around." Indeed, our bodies are magnificently complex, with their own innate *intelligence*—the result of billions of years of evolution.

Welcoming the body into the classroom starts with teachers. It begins with giving ourselves permission to cultivate a rich, playful, attentive, and loving relationship with our own feeling body. How to do this is what we explore in this chapter.

How Emotions Serve Us

Almost anybody can learn to think or believe or know, but not a single human can be taught to feel. Why? Because whenever you think or you believe

or you know, you're a lot of other people; but the moment you feel, you're
nobody-but-yourself.   —E. E. CUMMINGS 1958, 13

Emotions are our responses to the world around us as well as to our thoughts
and beliefs. To illustrate, imagine Joan, a high school student, waking up in
the morning and realizing that she has overslept and will be late for school.
Worse yet, it's a test day. Immediately, Joan experiences *anxiety* and *frustration*
as she rushes to the bathroom. Preparing to brush her teeth, she notices that her
brother, once again, has failed to put the top on the toothpaste, and she scowls
in *disgust*. Simultaneous with her disgust, Joan experiences a mix of *sadness* and
loneliness because she has the thought that her brother must not respect her, otherwise he would cap the paste. Moving from the bathroom to the kitchen, Joan
looks outside and notices that it is snowing. This prompts a brief rush of *delight*.
But then, realizing that she won't be able to ride her bike to school and that this
will make her even later, she feels outright *despair*. Just then, her brother rushes
in and says, "Guess what? School is cancelled today!" Hearing this, Joan is filled
with *joy*. Then her brother tells her, quite to her *surprise*, that he misses hanging out and suggests that they both go and play in the snow. Suddenly, Joan's
heart cracks open, and she feels *love* for her brother. In the course of a mere five
minutes, Joan experiences ten discrete emotions.

Charles Darwin recognized that the capacity of human beings to experience a
wide range of emotions is critical to our survival. Just as the armor plates of the
armadillo help it survive, so, too, our capacity to feel and express emotions contributes to our survival. Daniel Goleman, drawing on the work of sociobiolo-
gists, explains: "Our emotions . . . guide us in facing predicaments and tasks too
important to leave to intellect alone—danger, painful loss, persisting toward a
goal despite frustrations, bonding with a mate, building a family. Each emotion
offers a distinctive readiness to act; each points us in a direction that has worked
well to handle the recurring challenges of human life. As these eternal situations
were repeated and repeated over our evolutionary history, the survival value of
our emotional repertoire was attested to by its becoming imprinted into our
nerves as innate, automatic tendencies of the human heart" (1995, 4). Obviously,
survival in the life and death sense is crucial. Flourishing into our fullest humanity in all of the roles that each of us assumes throughout our lifetime (student,
partner, parent, friend, colleague, etc.) is also of crucial importance.

If the overriding goal of education is to expand and deepen our capacity for
relationship, as we believe it should be, then it is paramount that educators rec-

ognize that feelings and their associated emotions act as catalysts, inviting us to be and to know ourselves and to know and to be in relationship with each other and the world at large, more fully. Indeed, our feeling body can serve as our most precious lifelong teacher, provided we are willing to pay attention.

Emotional *Non*-Development

Emotions are at the root of everything we do, the unquenchable origin of every act more complicated than a reflex. Fascination, passion, and devotion draw us toward compelling people and situations, while fear, shame, guilt and disgust repel us from others . . . Greed and ambition run beneath the surface of economics; vengefulness and reverence under the veneer of justice.

—T. LEWIS, F. AMINI, AND R. LANNON 2000, 36

When a child is born she is entirely dependent on others for her survival. In most cases it is the mother who sends her infant the first messages about what kind of world she has been born into. Indeed, the way the infant is treated by her mother can have profound and long-lasting effects on the child's emotional expression.

Take the case of a newborn who, quartered in her own room, cries out for several long minutes in the middle of the night before her mother awakens. Imagine that this mother, against her instincts, chooses not to respond to her infant's cries because she has been told by *her* mother that it is best to just let a baby "cry it out." This newborn child receives, in some measure, the message that she is not worth responding to. Of course, it need not be this way. Imagine a baby who sleeps in a crib in the same room with her mother. Hearing her baby's cry, this mother understands that her child is simply calling out—in the only way that an infant can—to be held close, to experience the contact of skin and breath, and to be nourished. This mother knows instinctively that if a baby's needs are not met, a vital link—the bond of trust between child and mother—will be ruptured. She knows, in effect, that responding to her child's cries assures her daughter that she is loved and that expressing feelings is natural and good.

Although parents may extend love unconditionally during the first years of a child's life, at some point, usually around the age of two, they often decide that their child should now begin to conform to societal norms by behaving in a certain way—the child should use the potty, go to bed and eat at prescribed times, refrain from crying in public, and so forth.

From the child's perspective, each new parental prescription or prohibition is bothersome. After all, she has no notion of such social constructs as right versus wrong, acceptable versus unacceptable, polite versus impolite. But now, suddenly, rules are being imposed. It is no wonder that adults often refer to this stage as the "terrible twos," failing to understand that the reason for their child's rebellion is precisely because she is attempting to exercise her autonomy as a means of exerting control over her environment.

Parents often give force to their prohibitions by employing fear. So it is that the two-year-old is warned that she will get killed if she goes out in the road (fear!), or drown if she goes near the creek (fear!), or be bitten by a snake if she ventures into the woods (fear!). Parents also instill fear by withdrawing their love. For instance, the child is punished with a shout, a slap, or a time-out when deemed naughty. In these instances, it is primarily fear of the loss of parental love that prompts the child to obey. Through all this, the child learns that love is conditional—contingent upon adhering to rules and norms established by her caregivers.

One common way that both parents and teachers hinder emotional development in children is by minimizing their emotions. For example, in response to emotional upset, a child might be told, "It's not that bad," or "Stop crying, it's not the end of the world," or "Don't be afraid, you can do it." Such common expressions of consolation and encouragement contradict—and, in effect, invalidate—the child's inner experience. If you doubt this, simply imagine yourself, in an emotionally distraught state, venting your emotions to a friend. The last thing you would want to hear from your friend is, "It's not that bad; there's no reason to be so upset." Children, in a state of upset, have the same need as adults to have their emotional states validated, not trivialized.

Adults also use distraction to undermine the healthy emotional development of children. For example, a child wails because she wants to play outside in the freezing cold, and her well-meaning mom attempts to distract her attention away from outside. Employing distraction is often seen as clever parenting, but in actuality it can be a disservice as it denies the child the opportunity to experience herself as capable of handling her emotions (including disappointment). As Aldort points out, "the rush to distract a child from her hurt or frustration, to compensate for a disappointment, or to minimize the importance of her plight is a response to [the parent's] anxiety, not the child's. [The child] must experience living with emotional storms if she is to master them" (2006, 102).

Often, the net effect of all of this, admittedly well-meaning, emotional in-

KATIE AND THE SALT SHAKER

Unnecessary parental prohibitions can undermine a child's confidence and autonomy. Once, when Dana and I took our then eighteen-month-old daughter Katie to a restaurant, she began to play with the salt shaker. Telling her that she shouldn't touch it would have made absolutely no sense to Katie. She had little idea what salt was or why it would be wrong to shake it onto the table. For her there was just something on the table about the size of her fist that was solid and white with a shiny top. If we were to scold her for touching it, we would be saying, in effect, "When you follow your own inclinations, you will mess things up and make us unhappy." This message would undermine her confidence in her own ability and authority to explore the world. Of course, it is necessary for parents to establish some boundaries when caring for children, but if children are corralled with a multitude of unnecessary prohibitions, they may, due to their fear of losing parental love, lose their precious connection to their own curiosity and inner goodness and, in some measure, *abandon* themselves. When this occurs, it is especially tragic because it is the quality of this precious relationship that each of us has with ourselves that ultimately determines the richness and warmth of all the other relationships in our lives.

terference is that the child is gradually socialized to look to her parent/teacher, rather than to herself, when it comes time to feel and to act. She, in effect, internalizes all the adult messages—all the prohibitions and warnings and dismissals—and develops an "inner critic"—a voice that monitors her actions, judging what is right and wrong to feel and to do. Tragically, this is not her genuine self speaking. Rather, the child's social conditioning is dictating how she *should* feel, think, and behave. So it is that most children, by the time they reach six or seven, *give themselves away*—they become slaves to the beliefs, expectations and wishes of others (Huber 1995b).

Once her internal authority is surrendered, the child becomes a "performer," aligning her speech and actions to the expectations of those around her. If children do this year after year, gradually they lose touch with what they, themselves, are genuinely feeling from moment to moment. They become anything but themselves. Ingrid Bacci, the author of *The Art of Effortless Living*, puts it this way: "If we put restrictions around what feelings we think we're supposed to have, when we're supposed to have them, where and with whom, we end up being pretty confused. That's why the normal state in our culture is a state of diminished feeling" (2000, 111).

This condition of feeling distant and separated from one's feelings is a form of depression. It is telling that the most common treatment for depression is

LONG-TERM CONSEQUENCES OF EMOTIONAL SUPPRESSION

Given enough time, the prolonged suppression of emotion undermines one's very posture, not to mention health. Powerful emotions, like anger, fear, and shame, that are capped and locked inside eventually manifest in our bodies as illness and pain. This has particular relevance for heart disease, the number-one cause of death in the United States. Heart disease doesn't strike people randomly, nor can it be fully attributable to something as simple as diet or even genetic inheritance. Limmer (1995, 31) posits that "a heart attack is literally an attack upon the heart brought about through the inability of an individual to process or feel his or her emotions, especially love." Limmer's point is this: Absent the ability to express our emotions cleanly and forthrightly, our bodies end up serving as a kind of *garbage dump* for our unresolved feelings and unacceptable emotions. While this coping strategy may work for a time, ultimately it is both physically and emotionally crippling.

medication designed to extinguish the feelings associated with depression. A more life-affirming approach, rather than suppressing feelings with prescription drugs, would be to acknowledge that there is a legitimate reason for one's depression and then to allow oneself to *feel* depressed—in effect, to enter into relationship with depression. As Huber (1999) points out, "Our feelings are the most intimate experience we have of ourselves . . . When I stop depressing [my] feelings, I can begin to take care of the parts of me who feel isolated, vulnerable, and afraid . . . All [I] have to do is acknowledge how [I] am feeling and then treat [myself] as [I] would treat a friend who was feeling the same way" (37, 83, and 108).

In sum, the people walking into our classrooms—whether they are 5 or 45—have received a multitude of cultural messages aimed at tamping down their emotional expression—messages with the power to cripple their relationship with themselves and the whole of life. The situation need not be seen as hopeless, however. As teachers, we can befriend our feeling body and invite our students to do the same.

Inviting Teachers and Students to Body-Feeling Awareness

At school we were taught mathematics, reading, and the geography of the world, but few of us were taught much about the geographical mapping of the home we live in—our bodies.   —D. FARHI 1996, XV

Creating environments in schools that are hostile to the cultivation of body awareness and the expression of feelings contributes to the stagnant, lifeless, as well as rebellious atmosphere present in so many schools today. This is of particular concern because of a multitude of observations revealing that young people, worldwide, are increasingly emotionally troubled, lonely, depressed, unruly, impulsive, and anxious (Goleman 1995). The good news is that teachers, through their words and behaviors, can create learning environments that are welcoming to both the mind *and* the body. Our ability to do this is enhanced when we work to cultivate body-feeling awareness within ourselves and our students. In what follows, we offer three examples of how body-feeling awareness can be cultivated within teachers and students alike.

What's Your Emotional History?

It is likely that most, if not all, of us had a much broader emotional repertoire when we were small than we have today. It is social conditioning (as described earlier) that leads us to reign in, or even censor, certain emotions. One way to gain insight into possible limitations in your present-day emotional range is to investigate your emotional history. This can be done by responding to certain open-ended questions such as:

> The emotion that I have the most difficulty expressing is _____.
> It really bugs me when people act like _____.
> It upsets me when I am in the company of someone who _____.
> I hate to feel _____.
> One emotion I wish I could get rid of is _____.
> When I was growing up I learned that it was definitely not OK to
>   feel _____.
> I wish I felt more _____.
> When I am at my best I feel _____. (Huber 1995b)

When I completed this inventory, I became aware, for the first time, that it was not acceptable to feel pride in my family. I also realized that I am happiest when I am playing and joking around, and yet I rarely give myself permission to play because I have been conditioned to believe that I have to *earn* the right to play.

This exploration can lead to insights regarding how gender influences one's expression (or not) of emotion. To explore this for yourself, mark *M* after each emotion in the following list if you mostly associate that emotion with men and *W* if your association is more with women: Anger ____, Jealousy ____, Glee ____, Joyfulness ____, Silliness ____, Gratitude ____, Radiance ____, Agitation ____, Sadness ____, Panic ____, Disgust ____, Surprise ____.

As you consider your responses, you may want to reflect on how the people that you grew up with reacted to these emotions, paying special attention to emotions that you have been socialized to regard as not acceptable, perhaps because of gender. In this vein, Huber reminds us that "It is not true that certain feelings are okay and others are not. 'Okay' and 'not okay' are thoughts. The problem comes when we reject ourselves for what we're feeling. When we put thoughts in charge of feelings we get into trouble" (1999, 36). A good way to begin to step out of "trouble" is to identify realms of emotional expression that have become off-limits and then to give yourself permission to feel all of what you are feeling in any given moment.

What Are You Feeling Right Now?

Not surprisingly, given the pervasiveness of emotional suppression, many people have a difficult time knowing what they are actually feeling, often mistaking their judgments and labels for feelings. How about you? You can test your adeptness by deciding whether a feeling is being expressed in each of the following three statements:

Statement 1. "I feel like you *don't understand* me." What do you think? Although the speaker uses the word *feel*, "don't understand" is not a feeling. Rather, it is a judgment directed toward the other person. The speaker's feeling underneath "I don't understand" might be something like confused, angry, or disheartened.

Statement 2. "You are *hideous*." "Hideous" is certainly a strong word, and it is associated with feelings, but it is a label, not a feeling. The feeling beneath "hideous" might be something like nauseated, disgusted, irritated, or terrified.

Statement 3. "When you don't give me a hug when you come home, I feel *neglected*." How about this one? Can you feel "neglected"? No, "neglected" is an assessment of what the speaker thinks the other person is doing to them. The feeling is likely to be something like lonely, despairing, unhappy, or forlorn. (paraphrased from Rosenberg 1999, 48–49).

A prerequisite for emotional intelligence is the capacity to know what one is feeling from moment to moment. So, as a follow-up to the exercise above, pause and ask yourself: What *am* I feeling in this moment? Do you know? If you're like many people, your tendency will be to immediately go to your head and try to think your way to an answer. In this case, you'll simply be thinking and then talking *about* your feelings, instead of actually *experiencing* them.

To appreciate the difference between *reporting on feelings* versus *having feelings*, quiet yourself and bring your awareness to your breath. Then direct your gaze down to your body and sense what it feels like in your gut. Ask, "What are my actual body sensations down there in my gut?" As you do this, notice when you are thinking instead of feeling and then come back to just feeling, noting the visceral sensations in your gut. Then, when you are ready, move to your chest, and with curiosity, begin to note the body sensations in your chest. Continue in this way bringing your awareness to your throat.

The rationale here is simple: We have our feelings in our body—in our gut, chest, throat, and so on. (This comes as a revelation for many people.) If you can sense how you *feel* in these places, you can then bring your emotions to your awareness. With practice, it will be possible to note subtle shifts in how you are feeling in your body, minute by minute, as you go about your daily activities. For example, when teaching a class, you might notice a slight discomfort arise when you embellish a story (beyond what is true). Or, if a student arrives late, you may note a small contraction in your throat. The point is that minute by minute throughout the day each of us is having feelings in our bodies, and when we have the presence of mind to bring our awareness to these feelings, there is an opportunity to learn something. For example, when you take note of anxiety or nervousness or constriction, you can ask: What's this all about? What's wanting my attention here?

In sum, our feelings and emotions are legitimate for the simple and obvious reason that they are ours! When we criticize ourselves for having certain feelings and emotions, we create a barrier between ourselves and our own life force.

What Your Body Can Teach You if You Listen

Growing up, going through school, we're seldom invited (let alone taught) to be body listeners. But what would taking our feeling body seriously look like? Martha Beck (2001) contends that the energetic and emotional state of our body can act as a kind of guiding compass provided we learn to "read" it. To this end Beck suggests creating a twenty-point scale, going from "minus 10"—a strong negative body-feeling (e.g., feeling trapped, panicked, or knotted up)—through "0"—a neutral body response—to "plus 10"—a strongly positive body-feeling (e.g., feeling free, loose, happy, joyful).

As a way of calibrating or fine-tuning one's personal Body Meter, Beck suggests the "Shackles Test." It's easy to do. Just bring to mind something or someone that you know is wrong for you. It could be a person that sends you running for cover, a radio station that you loathe, someone's behavior that is deeply upsetting to you. Whatever you choose, let the thought of this unsavory thing fill your mind and then pay attention to how you feel in your body, as if you were "reading your own living guts" (Beck 2008, 43). Remember this as your "shackles on" body response—a minus 10 on your Body Meter. Next, think of a person or place or thing that you know to be good for you because it fills you with a sense of well-being, purpose, and/or joy. As you hold this in your mind, pay full attention to how your body feels, and remember this as your "shackles off" body response. This is what it feels like when you are in full alignment with life—a plus 10 on your Body Meter!

Now, consider three things that you plan to do tomorrow and evaluate each one with your Body Meter. For example, perhaps you will begin your day by having breakfast with a good friend who has been away for the past three weeks. You are very happy that you will be with this friend for breakfast, and you mark this as a "plus 8." Next, you plan to get in your car and drive thirty minutes through rush-hour traffic to work. The thought of this commute feels a bit heavy; you don't look forward to it but you've been through it before. You score this as a "minus 2." Once at work, you will spend the day teaching your tenth-grade history class. As you consider this, you detect a distinct tightening in your stomach and a slumping of your shoulders—a "minus 7" on your Body Meter. Suddenly, through the lens of your body, you have the ability to feel, see, and understand the day before you more fully.

Your Body Meter can be used to gauge the vigor and/or dysfunction in all aspects of your life. For example, use it to gauge the vitality (or brokenness) of your relationships to your parents, children, siblings, partner, friends, boss, co-workers. Use it to help you gauge:

- your living situation: How do you feel (from minus 10 to plus 10) about the city/town, neighborhood, and house where you live?
- your job: What do you register in your body when you consider the various aspects of your job?
- your leisure time: What is your body response when you consider things you do in your spare time like watching TV, reading, or exercising?

The point here is that our feeling body offers us navigational guidance, telling us, as nothing else can, how we *feel* about our lives day by day.

The Role of the Body and Feeling States in Effective Teaching

For many years it never occurred to me that the solutions to the teaching difficulties I was having might lie, at least in part, in changing my habits of body (posture, facial expression, gestures, manner of walking, clothing) and/or my feeling state while in the classroom. Then, on a summer day in 2003, a trusted friend, Richard Chadek, taught me something that I will never forget. At the time, Richard and I were sitting on a bench close to the Vietnam Memorial, and I was telling him that I sometimes lacked confidence when presenting novel ideas and exercises to students. Richard immediately asked me if I would act out what I was talking about, using a concrete example. I stood, took a deep breath, and began, inviting an imaginary classroom of students (personified by Richard) to participate in an activity designed to illustrate how social change occurs. When I finished, Richard asked me to observe my posture. In that moment I saw that I was leaning back slightly with my left foot behind my right foot, my knees were locked, my hands were deep in my pockets with fists lightly clenched, my chest was slightly contracted, my shoulders were slumped forward and down, and my head was slightly bowed. Richard suggested that everything about my body presentation suggested that I was resigned to failure! He was right.

Next, Richard guided me into a slightly exaggerated version of the posture I had just been in. I stood with my right foot six inches in front of my left foot, while placing most of my weight on my left foot (so that I was clearly leaning back). Then he instructed me to arrange my body so that my torso and shoulders drooped even more. Finally, he told me to collapse my chest. Once I had settled into this posture (back-down-contracted), he asked me to check how I felt in my body. Did I feel ready to greet the world? Was I filled with confidence and agency? Was I set to launch a new initiative? Ready to warmly greet the next person I met? Hardly! What I felt was weak, fearful, and a bit pathetic.

Finally, Richard invited me to transform my posture by: (1) shifting my weight forward to my right foot; (2) lifting my torso and shoulders up toward the sky; and (3) opening and expanding my chest. The idea wasn't to exaggerate but simply to work within my natural range of movement. Once I had assumed this new posture (forward-up-open), Richard, again, asked me to observe how

I felt in my body. Now I felt bold, engaged, animated. Feeling playful, I experimented, shifting back and forth between these various body positions—that is, forward and back, up and down, open and contracted—checking for differences in my emotional state. I was surprised to note how subtle changes in my body configuration affected my overall sense of ease, well-being, and agency.

Richard concluded our time together in D.C. by asking me which combination (back/forward, down/up, contracted/open) came closest to how I presented myself to the world day by day? In that moment I realized that I mostly knew myself to greet the world from a *back-down-contracted* position. Richard persisted asking, "If you were to put a word to this dominant body position, what would it be?" My word, I realized, was *careful*. However, when I changed my body posture to *forward-up-open*, I felt engaged in the world and my word shifted to *ready* (Uhl 2004). We can all take Richard's teachings into our classrooms to influence our overall state of well-being and to become a more powerful, energized presence for our students.

Since that day in D.C. with Richard, I have been learning more about the importance of attending to the "feeling atmosphere" of my classroom. Goleman (1995) writes about how students *catch* feelings and emotions from their teachers (and vice-versa), in much the same way that you or I might catch a cold from a friend. To illustrate this concept of "emotional contagion," Goleman tells the following story:

> It was an unbearably steamy August afternoon in New York City, the kind of sweaty day that makes people sullen with discomfort. I was heading back to a hotel, and as I stepped onto a bus up Madison Avenue I was startled by the driver, a middle-aged black man with an enthusiastic smile, who welcomed me with a friendly, "Hi! How you doing?" as I got on, a greeting he proffered to everyone else who entered as the bus wormed through the thick midtown traffic. Each passenger was as startled as I, and, locked into the morose mood of the day, few returned his greeting.
>
> But as the bus crawled uptown through the gridlock, a slow, rather magical transformation occurred. The driver gave a running monologue for our benefit, a lively commentary on the passing scene around us: there was a terrific sale at that store, a wonderful exhibit at this museum, did you hear about the new movie that just opened at that cinema down the block? His delight in the rich possibilities the city offered was infectious. By the time people got off the bus, each in turn had shaken off the sullen shell they had entered with, and when the driver shouted out a "So long, have a great day!" each gave a smiling response. (1995, ix)

Just like on that New York bus, teachers often notice mood shifts in their classrooms from day to day. Some days there is a palpable heaviness in the air; other days there is an electric buzz in the room. An aspect of emotional intelligence for teachers is being able to detect when the mood and energy of a class is flat and then to know how to positively change the situation. Particularly challenging is the case where the teacher is feeling depressed or flat on a particular day. One thing I do in this situation is to call to mind a happy, enlivening moment in my life, and, then, I endeavor to "merge" with this moment so fully that I begin to experience that lightness of being once again. As students enter the classroom, I make eye contact, smile, and greet them in some way that feels both genuine and uplifting to me. If I don't know the person so well and find myself struggling, I simply imagine, as I look at them, that glitter—stardust—is raining down all around them, and I smile. Finally, as I carry out these greetings, I choose to believe that during our class today great things will happen.

In this illustration, I am, in effect, creating a kind of *mood virus* in the classroom. Goleman (2006) reports that researchers in Sweden have found that if we simply see a picture of a smiling face it is enough to subtly activate our smile

muscles. More generally, whenever we see a photograph of someone displaying a strong emotion, whether it be happiness, grief, rage, or anything else, our
facial muscles automatically begin to mirror the emotion we are observing, and,
in turn, these subtle shifts in our muscles cause shifts in our feeling state. If you
doubt this finding, simply place a pencil between your teeth, biting down ever
so lightly, and notice how this activates your smile muscles and causes a corresponding subtle, or not so subtle, shift in how you are feeling.

In fact, it is now known, based on recent research in neurobiology, that our
brains are wired with a class of neurons dubbed "mirror neurons." These neurons fire in response to the emotions that the people around us are displaying,
in effect, grafting their emotional life onto ours. It is these mirror neurons that
make emotions contagious, leading us into emotional synchrony with others.
Goleman (2006, 43) puts it this way: "Mirror neurons ensure that the moment someone sees an emotion expressed on your face, they will at once sense
that same feeling within themselves. And so our emotions are experienced not
merely by ourselves in isolation but also by those around us—both covertly and
openly."

The discovery of mirror neurons reveals that, often without our awareness,
we are being influenced by the feeling state of others. It also suggests that,
as teachers, if we exercise our capacity to consciously change our own feeling
states, we can shift the emotional valence in our classrooms. In this reframing,
teachers are likely to be more successful in the classroom if they actively cultivate the feeling state that they long for, rather than expecting external circumstances to create that state for them.

Beck (2008) calls this "beginning at the end." In practice this would mean
meeting your class on the first day of the school year firm in the belief that
your new students already regard you as amazing—that their esteem for you is
so huge that you couldn't possibly take it all in. This may seem like a strange
stance, but simply picture yourself interacting with your students firm in the
belief, from day one, that they adore you. "Can you feel the freedom, the ease,
and the humor that's suddenly available to you? Can you feel yourself starting to
smile without trying? Can you tell that this version of you is way more likely to
get approval and cooperation than the version who's always desperately seeking
it?" (Beck 2008, 8).

If you are skeptical of the power inherent in Beck's "beginning at the end"
strategy, she suggests conducting a simple two-treatment experiment in a public place. For "Treatment 1," fill your mind with thoughts like: "I need these

people to treat me with respect; I need them to think I'm great; I need them to like me." Then, walk into your chosen public space and take note of how people respond to you. For "Treatment 2," wait a day and go back to the same public place, but this time fill your mind with thoughts like: "These people think I'm fantastic; they regard me as intelligent and kind and principled; they are interested in me." As Beck (2008, 8) observes, "If you can keep such [empowering] thoughts in mind, you'll notice that you move differently, talk differently, smile in a different way . . . " and, as a result, people *will* naturally move toward you with warmth and interest and respect. And, of course, the same thing is true in the classroom!

Fear and Love in the Classroom

Of all emotional dispositions, there are two—fear and love—that have extraordinary power to transform the educational process for better or worse. And yet how rare it is to hear educators speak of fear or love, much less explore ways of incorporating these twin pillars undergirding human existence into pedagogy and learning. Too, if fear prevents teachers from *teaching as if life matters*, perhaps it is love that points the way.

Fear: The Emotion That Undermines Effective Teaching and Learning

Fear is the proverbial elephant in our schools and classrooms, the unnamed ether that permeates everything. And yet, with only a few exceptions, fear is something we learn, not something we are born with. For example, little kids aren't burdened with fear-filled thoughts like I don't want to make any mistakes or I don't want to look foolish. If a small child held these reservations, she might never learn to walk (Chopra 2004).

But as children grow, they are conditioned, to varying degrees, to become fearful. As young teachers, Dana and I were only dimly aware of the ways in which fear pervaded schools. Now, we recognize the pervasiveness of fear—in ourselves, in colleagues, in teaching pedagogies, in classroom layout, and, most of all, in students. Fear often lurks beneath student behaviors, disguising itself as indifference, arrogance, obstinacy, withdrawal, obsequiousness, and silence. As Palmer (1998, 45) cogently observes: "Students are marginalized people in our society. The silence that we [teachers] face in the classroom is the silence that has always been adopted by people on the margin—people who have reason to fear those in power and have learned that there is safety in not speaking."

Each semester within her introductory education course, Dana devotes an entire class to the topic of fear. At the beginning of class, she looks around the room and randomly selects seven students to come to the front. She then asks each in turn to state the central thesis of that day's reading. Those chosen don't know that Dana is enacting a drama, pretending to be *scary*. Student 1 begins, falters, and Dana feigns a wince. Student 2 speaks, and Dana, somewhat forcefully, reminds her to be succinct. Student 3 is asked if he has, in fact, read the text. And on the drama continues, each student experiencing the weight of their instructor's perceived displeasure with their responses. Finally, Dana speaks the word "Stop" and explains, to many surprised faces, that "the drama is over."

In the debriefing, students confess to practicing evasion strategies to escape being picked when Dana was deciding who to call to the front. When asked to describe what they were feeling in that moment, students never fail to describe rapid heartbeat, nausea, and sweaty palms. Dana asks her students what was going on inside them as the drama unfolded. They mention how they had forgotten their own answers as they listened to their peers speak, how they couldn't stop watching for Dana's reaction, how they were making promises to themselves to read all future assignments more carefully, and even how they desired to escape the classroom altogether.

Everyone is surprised by the realization that no one in the room conjured a negative judgment of another student—for the quality of a response, for appearance, for anything. Yet, when asked how many normally refrain from making contributions in class for fear of their peers' negative judgments, every hand is raised.

The drama and debriefing reveal to all how pervasive are students' feelings of fear within classrooms. They admit to its power to limit their belief in themselves and in their intelligence, as well as their learning overall.

Over the course of years of schooling, students become accomplished at masking their fear, even from themselves, and nearly always from their teachers and parents. Far worse, they soon learn that being fearful is just the normal state of being within a classroom.

As teachers we are often slow to detect the fear residing in our students because of our own heavy sheath of fear. And of what are we afraid? Of our own irrelevancy, of the possibility of having chosen the wrong profession, of spending our lives on trivia, of ending up feeling like frauds, of the judgment of our students, and of stagnation and burnout (Palmer 1998).

Palmer (1998) contends that the biggest fear that teachers and students share is what he calls "the fear of the live encounter." This fear is nothing more, nothing less, than a fear of *otherness*. For if we allow ourselves to open—really open—to other ways of seeing, knowing, and being, we may have to change, and change is painful. "To avoid a live encounter with teachers, students can hide behind their notebooks and their silence. To avoid a live encounter with students, teachers can hide behind their podiums, their credentials, their power. To avoid a live encounter with one another, faculty can hide behind their academic specialties . . . To avoid a live encounter with ourselves we can learn the art of self-alienation, of living a divided life" (38).

For many teachers, fear of a live encounter is evident in their pedagogy—scripted lectures, question avoidance, testing—and in their mannerisms—for example, poor eye contact, authoritative demeanor, and monotone voice. Indeed, it may very well be that for failure to recognize and embrace our own fears, we remain unable to truly *see* our students. On the flip side, once teachers commit to inquiring into their fears, compassion for and connectedness to their students, rather than condemnation and separation, emerge. Absent fear we gain the capacity to see each student as a person, rather than as a category. Free of fear we no longer rush to fill our students' silences with our own fear-generated speech or coerce them into saying the things that we want to hear.

In sum, it is the prevalence of fear in school settings that creates separation—separation between students and their teachers, between students and their learning, between students and their peers, and even separation from the great expanse of possibility that students' lives inherently hold.

Befriending Our Fears

The idea of befriending fear may seem counterintuitive. But consider: Because fear is an intrinsic part of being alive, resisting fear means resisting life, and if we are not careful the habit of fear avoidance can seep into every aspect of our lives, preventing us from loving well, from cherishing beauty within and around us, from being present in the moment (paraphrased from Brach 2003, 186).

The first place to catch or note fear is in our body, for it is there that we first register fear. When we feel constriction in our throat or tightening in our chest or heat in our cheeks—all indicators of fear—we can choose to lean into these sensations, allowing ourselves to really feel our fear. What might our body be telling us about ourselves—about what lies beneath our fears?

Our breath can be an ally in opening to our fears. We can use it to enter into fear—allowing the sensations of fear to intensify each time we breathe in. On each out breath, visualize the fear beginning to crack apart. In this process, we can exercise curiosity and courage by asking: What does my fear actually look like? How do my sensations of fear change from moment to moment? What color/shape, if any, is my fear? What is my fear asking me to look at? What can my fear teach me about myself, about my worldview, my thoughts and beliefs and priorities?

Here is a concrete practice for befriending feelings of fear. To begin, call to mind something that leaves you feeling fearful. Maybe you are afraid that you are going to lose your job or that you are going to die of a heart attack. Whatever the issue, allow yourself to really go there—seeing yourself on the street without a job or in the midst of a heart attack. Steer into your fear with gusto. Then, take a step back and speak in the first person, saying, "I see that you (your name here) are feeling fear." Continue by allowing your fear to get larger and larger—becoming so large that it fills you up, causing you to expand outward in all directions. Visualize the shockwaves of your fear and upset, radiating out into space. When your feelings of fear can get no bigger, take a breath, pause, and note, paradoxically, the reduced intensity of your fear. Usually, by this time the issue evoking the fear no longer seems so important; your fear and upset may even seem a bit comical (Chopra 2004). By engaging in this practice you will come to more fully understand the old dictum, "There is nothing to fear but fear itself."

Feeling our fears is not easy, admittedly, but as Brach points out, there are rewards for this work: "The other side of resisting fear is freedom from fear. When we stop tensing against life, we open to an awareness that is immeasurably large and suffused with love" (2003, 190).

Ultimately, our fears are grounded in beliefs, especially the belief that we might stand to lose something. For example, take the case of Beth, a hypothetical teacher who fears that she will never master the art of teaching. In exploring her fear, Beth asks herself, "What do I believe I will *lose* if I end my career never having mastered the art of teaching?" Two possibilities come quickly to her mind: First, "I will have lost years of my life to a profession that I failed at"; and, second, "I will have lost my self-respect and self-esteem."

Once the beliefs undergirding her fear are out in the open, Beth can determine if they are true. For example, have years of her life been lost if she fails to become a master teacher? Hardly! Chances are, Beth has grown, learned a lot, and come to see and understand people and society through a much larger lens. What about the loss of self-respect and self-esteem? Though Beth might experience disappointment if she takes the step of ending her teaching career, at the same time, she would be afforded a wonderful opportunity to practice unconditional self-acceptance. Ultimately, to free herself of fear, Beth would have to turn around the limiting beliefs undergirding her fears. A turnaround for Beth might begin with the realization that self-esteem resides within her and is not contingent upon outside achievements or judgments.

In sum, when we, as teachers, open and face our own fears, we provide a model for our students, thereby diminishing the fears that paralyze learning, stunt growing, and undermine relationships.

Facing Down Our Fears by Doing the Impossible

What we are unwilling to experience limits our lives, thereby creating the walls of our own emotional prisons. If we are afraid of failing, we will avoid doing things that are risky even though they might ultimately bring us joy and satisfaction. If we are afraid to make ourselves vulnerable, we will miss opportunities to experience the pleasures of intimacy. Each fear that we give in to diminishes the potential fullness of our lives. By the same token, each fear that we identify and face expands and opens us to life.

For illustrative purposes, here is a story from my own life about breaking through fear to freedom. Imagine the joy denied for one who is afraid to sing. This was my condition for fifty-five years. When I was growing up, my family labeled me "Johnny One Note." As a result, I grew up convinced that I couldn't sing. What led me to attempt the impossible was the unlikely circumstance of moving into a house next to a voice teacher. This neighbor, Heidi, pointed out that virtually everyone has the capacity to sing. I was intrigued. Might I actually be able to sing after all? The possibility of actually singing, by itself, wasn't a sufficient incentive for me to confront my fifty-plus years of conditioning and associated fear. However, the prospect of singing to my mom on her ninetieth birthday did motivate me. So, I enlisted Dana as my coach and began practicing —all the while filled with anxiety, as I imagined singing in the presence of my entire extended family. Soon, to my astonishment, I was actually beginning to nail some of the "Happy Birthday" notes.

When the night of my mom's ninetieth birthday celebration arrived, I was filled with trepidation. Finally, as the evening was winding down, I stood resolutely, faced Mom, who was seated several tables away, and toasted her. Then, I walked over and told her that I was going to sing "Happy Birthday" to her. She laughed and, almost as if on cue, said, "Johnny One Note is going to sing! Impossible." Not deterred, I knelt beside her. Then, taking her hand in mine and holding her teary gaze in my teary gaze, I sang—really *sang*—"Happy Birthday."

I believe that in that act we both attempted the impossible, each of us allowing love to conquer judgment and fear.

Acts like this have a "walking on water" quality. They are miraculous and liberating. Dana and I use this "walking on water" challenge as a classroom assignment. In effect, we ask students to embrace their fear by doing the impossible—that is, by committing a miracle. The actual assignment (inspired by Derrick Jensen [2004]) begins with an examination of how fear operates within our society, our schools, our classrooms, and our own hearts. This sets the stage for the challenge to "walk on water." As a means of getting started, we give students the following open-ended sentences:

If only I had the guts, I would _____ .
If I didn't care what people thought, I would _____ .
If I weren't worried about the future, I would _____ .

Students' responses to these open sentences point them toward how they might "walk on water." In the process of figuring out what to do, it is common for students to detect a "little voice" inside that says "No, not that, I absolutely cannot do that!" We suggest that this "little voice" is actually revealing how they might truly "walk on water."

At the end of the semester, our students tell their "walking on water" stories. Rachel begins by saying that she has never told her mom and dad that she loves them, nor have her parents ever spoken these words. Rachel's "walking on water" project is to speak "I love you" to her parents during a weekend visit. She describes how she fretted and agonized during their first meal together on Friday night. The words "I love you" were trapped in her throat. On Saturday, she waited for the *right* moment; it never came. Then, suddenly, it was Sunday afternoon, and her mother and father were getting into their car to drive home. It was then that Rachel realized that there is no *right moment*, only *this* moment—the present—for her to do what, heretofore, she had deemed impossible to do. So, first to her mother and then to her father, she declared, "I love you." Hearing her words, Rachel's parents embraced their precious daughter. Rachel's story is a *coming out*—a saying "yes" to love and the possibilities—the miracles—that unfold when we muster the courage to do the seemingly impossible.

After Rachel, others step forward with their stories: Sarah tells how she had been led to despise Arabs after her Israeli cousin was killed in the Middle East, but now she has done the impossible—she has befriended an Arab student. Josh, who was freaked out by the sight of blood, "walked on water" by volunteering to donate blood; Sam summoned the courage to tell his parents—both doctors— that he was not going to follow in their footsteps but instead pursue his own passion, music.

This practice of facing our fears is equally important for teachers. Professor Tobin Hart suggests that "for many teachers, facing fear and finding one's own voice . . . may include questioning the top-down demands of testing and curriculum . . . and being honest about what brings education to life and what relegates it to banality" (2007, 166). By way of example, Hart reports that when compulsory testing was mandated for Japanese elementary schools, teachers spoke out against this idea and, ultimately, they refused to obey the new law (overcoming their fear of recrimination). As a result, this testing was eliminated. As this story illustrates, when we, as teachers, have the clarity and fearlessness to *speak our truth to power*, we discover our own power and the freedom that comes with it. So what about you? What would "walking on water" look like in the context of your teaching life?

Love: The Antidote to Fear

Robert Walsh in his book *Essential Spirituality* writes: "What we feel within ourselves we find reflected in our world. If we feel angry, we look out on a hostile world; if fearful, we find threats everywhere. But when love fills our minds, we see a world that yearns to love and be loved" (1999, 71). In this context, to teach as if life matters is to realize that each person—each student—in a teacher's care is following his own evolution as a loving being (no matter how convoluted his path may appear). Our task as teachers is to facilitate that path. Such work as facilitators requires that we teachers step away from judging, blaming, and labeling our students and step into full and loving acceptance of them just as they present themselves, moment by moment.

Our understanding of love and our capacity to love are, to a significant degree, byproducts of the ways that we experienced love growing up. Parents, unintentionally or otherwise, often *teach* their children, through their actions, that their love is conditional. So it is that most of us learned at an early age that maintaining the love connection with our parents was conditional upon our meeting their expectations. Teachers reinforce the conditionality of love when they withhold acceptance and approval from students who fail to meet preordained behavioral and academic performance objectives.

As teachers, our capacity to love our students unconditionally begins with

From an early age most of us were conditioned to believe in the concepts of *good* and *bad*. As a corollary, we were socialized to understand that *good* translates into rewards whereas *bad* receives punishment. As a consequence of this conditioning, as adults, we may fail to recognize that *good* and *bad* are merely cultural constructs, rather than fundamental, enduring and immutable aspects of reality and that seeing the world in terms of good versus bad—acceptable versus unacceptable—short circuits love.

One need only spend some time in the presence of a child to realize that the proposition that humans are bad (or do things that are bad) is preposterous. Go ahead and do it. Observe a child. Do you see badness? Sadly, what we adults so often judge as *bad* is simply the child not conforming to our expectations—not doing what we want, not buckling under to our control. Suppose a child spills her milk or scratches the table or takes a toy from her playmate. Is the child bad in these instances? True, a culture, such as ours, attached to the concepts of good versus bad, judges these acts as bad. But experiment with living within the worldview that none of these acts are bad. Consider that children are simply expressing their natural tendency to explore, discover, and experience the world—their natural tendency to push against limits, to test and to experiment. In this more spacious view, a child who took a toy from a playmate is, nothing more, nothing less than, *a child who took a toy from a playmate.* End of story. Absent the cultural construction *bad,* we would understand that children, adolescents, and, yes, adults sometimes act out of ignorance, not badness. We aren't *good* or *bad*; we are all, given our individual limitations, doing the best we can, minute by minute, given our cultural and biological inheritance. Such a recognition has the potential to free us, as teachers, to extend love, unconditionally, to ourselves and to our students.

cultivating the capacity to unconditionally accept and love ourselves. The problem is that most of us, to varying degrees, have been taught to love ourselves conditionally. If our lives are going well (if we are fulfilling our mind's conditions), we are happy with ourselves. If, on the other hand, we are not living up to our self-imposed conditions, we are dissatisfied with ourselves. And get this: It is often our own interior sense of inadequacy and deficiency that we project out on to our students in the form of harsh judgments and disapproval. Argh!

Given our conditioning, it is no surprise that most of us have taken an underdeveloped understanding of love into our adult lives. When we say, "I love you," what we usually mean is, "I love how you are making me feel right now." In other words, our love for another is often conditioned upon how fully the "beloved" matches and meets our own needs and desires—that is, what he or she does for us. The same usually holds when we say, "I love my students," or, "I love my class."

The fundamental truth about love that most of us, including teachers, never come to fully understand is that it is impossible to truly love someone you need. Instead, you end up using them and manipulating them to get what *you* need, rather than offering what brings the "loved" one to their full expression of personhood. As Byron Katie points out: "When you say or do anything to . . . influence or control anyone or anything, fear is the cause and pain is the result. Manipulation is separation, and separation is painful" (2005, 45). In short, we cannot honestly profess to love another if we rely on him or her for our happiness, for where there is genuine love there are no demands, no dependency, no needs to be fulfilled by the other. Love doesn't seek anything; it is already complete. In this vein, John Wellwood in his book *Toward a Psychology of Awakening* (2002) describes unconditional love as being-to-being acknowledgment that responds not to surface attributes of the other but to the intrinsic goodness of the other's heart. "Arising from our own basic goodness, unconditional love resonates with and reveals the unconditional goodness in others as well. It's as though our heart wants to ally itself with their heart and lend them strength in their struggle to realize the magnificence of their being, beyond all their perceived shortcomings" (253, 254, 257). Imagine yourself as a teacher with the mission of leading each of your students back to a recognition of the truth of their own innate goodness. In this way, your actions would truly exemplify teaching as if life matters.

Given the foregoing, it is apropos to ask: If love is what human beings are called to manifest more and more as they develop from children to adults, then why isn't love a major focus in classroom learning and in teacher preparation? Why aren't our leaders spurring us forward to become more accomplished lovers? And, in the context of teaching, learning, and schooling, why are there not courses, workshops, professional development opportunities, departments, and more, centered on the art, science, and practice of love? Indeed, at Penn State where Dana and I teach, the word *love* is seldom uttered in the classroom; *love* doesn't come up in faculty meetings; our university president doesn't mention *love* in his annual address to faculty and staff; and, of course, one's demonstrated capacity to express and spread love is hardly a consideration in hiring or promotion, much less a criteria for college graduation.

If the teaching and inclusion of love within classrooms, schools, and the hallowed halls of academia is too far-fetched, how much stranger still is the reality that at this time when hatred, fear, confusion, and alienation are so apparent throughout the world, so-called educators maintain reluctance to focus their attention on the very quality or condition that is—we believe—necessary to bring us to peace and wholeness.

Of course, a naysayer may argue that the notion of actually *teaching* love is an impossibility. Yet, as teachers—through our daily actions and dispositions as well as the quality of our presence—we have the opportunity to offer instruction in love each day, if we so choose. Said differently: We can chose to align with Palmer's (1998) dictum, "We teach who we are," and *be* love!

Making a Space for the Loving Heart in the Classroom

To teach as if life matters requires that we take a critical journey—maybe even a life versus death journey—that is only twelve inches in length. It is the journey from our heads to our hearts. For as Saint-Exupéry wrote in *The Little Prince*, "Here is my secret, a very simple secret: It is only with the heart that one can see rightly; what is essential is invisible to the eye" (87).

Whether you choose to acknowledge it or not, your physical heart has been working constantly, beating away, on average, 100,000 times each day, since the moment you were born. But that heart of yours is much more than a mechanical pump! It has its own neural network—its own feeling brain. Your heart-brain has the capacity to actually learn as well as to sense and to feel. Indeed, the heart, more than any other organ in your body, responds to your overall emotional condition and broadcasts this state throughout your body and beyond, thereby affecting your general well-being.

In a very real sense your heart behaves similarly to a transmitter, broadcasting messages day and night. It is your moment-to-moment thoughts and feelings that comprise your heart's broadcast. The effects of these broadcasts are registered in what heart researchers call Heart Rate Variability (HRV). HRV is simply the measure of beat-to-beat variation in heart rate and power. For example, if you were hooked up to a heart-rhythm monitor as you sat reading this text, you would observe that the beat-to-beat variation in your heart is changing constantly. In other words, the amount of blood pushed per heartbeat and the time interval between beats would be varying constantly. Why? Because as you read, you experience different emotions—for example, excitement, worry, confusion, appreciation, boredom—and these emotions, even though at times very subtle, affect your heart rhythm and, by extension, the electromagnetic signal that your heart sends to the cells of your body and out into the space around you. Negative emotions (confusion, worry, frustration) create disharmony and incoherence in your heart's rhythms whereas positive emotions (such as appreciation and affection) create harmonic rhythms and, therefore, balance throughout your nervous system. Simply expressed, your heart rhythm pattern tells your cranial brain what your body feels.

Research at the HeartMath Institute reveals that coherent heart rhythms alter both the body's biochemistry (by reducing the production of the stress hormone cortisol) and the body's immune system (by boosting levels of IgA, an antibody that is a first line of defense against infection and disease). This research also reveals that when your heart rhythm patterns are smooth—that is, when you are relaxed and calm—you think more clearly. However, when your heart rhythms are disorderly, your ability to reason clearly and organize your thoughts is diminished (Childre and Rozman 2005).

These findings prompt two questions. First, what can be done to promote smooth, coherent heart rhythms? Second, how might increased heart awareness and coherence enhance our capacity for love, not to mention our capacity to learn? Researchers at HeartMath have been addressing these exact questions and in the process have developed a battery of simple techniques that can be used to promote heart-rhythm coherence, thereby enhancing physiological and psychological well-being and learning.

One HeartMath technique of relevance for teaching and learning is called Quick Coherence. Coherence, in this case, refers to the clarity of thought and emotional balance that occurs when we train our minds to focus on our heart center. The first step of the three-step Quick Coherence practice is to simply shift your attention away from your mind and, instead, to tune into your heart. This step is named *heart focus.*

To get the idea, pause for a moment and focus your attention on your heart. If this seems confusing, begin by focusing on your left foot. Now, shift your focus to your neck. Finally, focus your attention on your heart. Once your attention is anchored in your heart, the second step is to expand your focus to include your breathing and imagine that you are literally breathing in and out through your heart, slowly, gently. Allow your breathing to be smooth and open, not forced. This calm breathing rhythm modulates your heart's rhythm, making it more coherent, which, in turn, has a powerful soothing effect on your brain. This step is named *heart breathing.*

The third and final step, named *heart feeling,* is to bring to mind something that fills you with a sense of well-being. You might call to mind a person who is exceptionally loving or an activity that always leaves you feeling good inside.

The idea is *not* to think but, rather, to actually reexperience, to the extent that you are able, the good feeling associated with this person or activity.

Through participation in this simple three-step sequence—*heart focus, heart breathing, heart feeling*—all of your body rhythms are brought into greater alignment or coherence by virtue of the fact that your heart is the most potent rhythmic oscillator in your body.

"Attitudinal Breathing" is another HeartMath technique of relevance for teachers. The intent of this practice is to establish or create a specific "heart attitude." The first two steps are identical to Quick Coherence—heart focus and heart breathing. The third step entails selecting a specific positive attitude— like compassion or appreciation—and then breathing this positive attitude in through your heart and out through your solar plexus. The idea is to select an attitude to breathe into the heart that counterbalances or offsets a particular state of disequilibrium that you might be experiencing. For instance, if you have had a difficult start to your day with a colleague or acquaintance and you are feeling upset as you prepare to enter your classroom, you could breathe in calmness or compassion. The key is that you not just think about the quality that you want to cultivate but that you endeavor to imbue your heart center with this feeling state.

How many of us have come to believe that, if we're having a bad day in the classroom—for example, feeling frustrated or upset with ourselves or our students—there is little we can do except suffer through it? However, using these simple practices, it is possible to gradually learn to exert the power necessary to positively shift our emotional states.

These HeartMath techniques are finding ever-wider application in U.S. schools. For example, twenty administrators and ninety human relations representatives from Georgia's DeKalb County school system reported making significant improvements in dealing with stress, conflict resolution, and time management as a result of HeartMath training. And "at risk" students who enrolled in a sixteen-hour HeartMath training course at Palm Springs Middle School in Dade County, Florida, realized significant improvements in work and stress management, as well as improvements in relationships with peers, teachers, and family (HeartMath Research Center 2001).

If education at its best is about expanding awareness and self-knowledge, as well as promulgating health and well-being both locally and globally, then perhaps the cultivation of heart intelligence should be an important component of school curricula. In this vein, consider that the feelings, thoughts, and attitudes of each of Earth's roughly 7 billion human inhabitants (7 billion beating hearts!) contributes to a kind of global consciousness climate. This climate—*coherent or incoherent*—is the atmosphere we are immersed in minute by minute throughout the day. It is broadcast in kind of the way radio signals bring music to us. Sadly, the content of much of contemporary music, television, and film contributes to incoherence, undermining core heart values such as kindness, compassion, and appreciation that contribute to coherence. "Stress (i.e., incoherence) first gets broadcast person-to-person—in homes, schools, offices, and streets. Then—amplified and reinforced through TV, radio, and print media—the stress momentum goes global, reaching billions of people daily" (Childre and Martin 1999, 256–57). In other words, both teachers and students (all of us, really!) are being subjected, in varying degrees, to a *consciousness climate* that creates disharmony and incoherence in our bodies.

Aren't we ready for this madness to end? What better place to start than with the tender human hearts beating away in the schools of the world. Allow yourself to imagine how it would be if a key mission of our schools was to affect the consciousness climate of Earth, moving it away from stress and violence and toward acceptance and love. Specifically, imagine if the tens of millions of people within our schools—teachers, administrators, and students, alike—learned these HeartMath skills and in the process had the opportunity to apply their collective powers to the task of creating world peace. Far-fetched? Maybe. Maybe not. Transcendental Meditation practitioners claim that once 1 percent of a population is meditating, the incidence of conflict in its various guises—war, murders, drug abuse, crime, even traffic accidents—decreases (McTaggart 2007). Such a claim would have been regarded as preposterous one hundred years ago, but now that we are beginning to understand the power of thought and intention to shape reality, this no longer seems far-fetched. In sum, it is time for all of us, beginning with teachers, to consider that perhaps we are in the classroom, first and foremost, to extinguish fear and to grow love.

Extending Love out into the World

Each semester I invite my students to consider how their thoughts, quite literally, are the building blocks of their lives. If they are mired in angry or judgmental or blameful thoughts, their existence becomes small, petty, and enfeebled. If their thoughts are kind and loving, their lives inevitably become more expansive, ebullient, and tender. For this reason alone, the practice described in

LOVING-KINDNESS: A GUIDED MEDITATION

Close your eyes and begin to relax, exhaling to expel tension. Now center in on the normal flow of your breathing, letting go of all extraneous thoughts as you passively watch your breathing-in and breathing-out.

Now call to mind someone you love very dearly. In your mind's eye, see the face of this beloved one. Silently speak his or her name. Feel your love for this being, like a current of energy coming through you. Now let yourself experience how much you want this person to be free from fear; how intensely you desire that this person be released from greed and ill-will, from confusion and sorrow and other causes of suffering.

Continuing to feel that warm energy flow coming through your heart, see in your mind's eye those with whom you share your daily life—family members, close friends, and colleagues, the people you live and work with. Let them appear now in a circle around you. Behold them one by one, silently speaking their names, and direct to each in turn that same current of loving-kindness.

Among these beings may be some with whom you are uncomfortable, in conflict, or tension. With these especially, experience your desire that each be free from fear, from hatred, free from greed and ignorance and other causes of suffering.

Now allow to appear, in wider concentric circles, all beings with whom you share this planet-time. Though you have not met, your lives are interconnected in ways beyond knowing. To these beings as well, direct the same powerful current of loving-kindness. Experience your desire and your intention that each awaken from fear and hatred, from greed and confusion, that all beings be released from suffering.

By the power of your imagination, move out now beyond our planet, out into the universe, into other solar systems, other galaxies. The current of loving-kindness is not affected by physical distances, so direct it now, as if aiming a beam of light, to all centers of conscious life. To all sentient beings everywhere, direct your heartfelt wish that they, too, be free of fear and greed, of hatred and confusion and the causes of suffering. May all beings be happy.

Now, from out there in the interstellar distances, turn and behold your own planet, your home. See it suspended there in the blackness of space, like a jewel turning in the light of its sun. That living blue-green planet laced with swirls of white is the source of all you are, all you've ever known and cherished. Feel how intensely you desire that it surmount the spreading wounds and dangers of this time; direct toward it the strong current of your compassion and prayerful wishes for its healing.

Now slowly approach Earth, drawing nearer, nearer, returning to this place where you are now sitting. And as you approach, let yourself see the being you know best of all . . . the person it has been given you to be in this lifetime. You know this person better than anyone else does, know its pain and its hopes, know its need for love, know how hard it tries. Let the face of this being, your own face, appear before you. Speak your name in love. And experience, with that same strong energy current of loving-kindness, how deeply you desire that this being—you—be free from fear, released from greed and hatred, liberated from ignorance and confusion, and all other causes of suffering. (Paraphrased from Macy and Brown 1998, 188–90.)

Loving Kindness Meditation (from Macy and Brown 1998) deserves a place in our schools. Think of it, if you like, as a kind of Pledge of Allegiance, a commitment to align our hearts with love and kindness. What could be better than that!

I introduce this practice by pointing out that love and kindness are two virtues acknowledged by all people, irrespective of religious orientation, and the same is often true with meditation or contemplation. Indeed, my students at Penn State—even those without any prior contemplative practice—are almost always open to and interested in the idea of meditation. In the rare case where students manifest resistance, I honor this, inviting them to simply observe as others try out this practice.

After they complete this guided meditation, I ask my students to comment on their experience. Many find it deeply moving, but occasionally students admit to being uneasy because they are Christian and associate meditation with Buddhism. I ask these students to consider the beliefs that are clearly etched in the language of this loving-kindness practice, namely:

- We have love in our hearts, like a current of energy running through us.
- Humans suffer from fear, confusion, greed, ignorance, hatred.
- Extending *love* and *kindness* to ourselves, each other, and all other beings is a way of reducing the suffering in the world.

Viewed in this way, loving-kindness meditation could as easily be called a *love prayer*, which is to say that it is ecumenical in its reach. What's more, this practice of extending loving-kindness is a wonderful way to cultivate relationship with the world. Indeed, "loving-kindness works only if it is offered, given away, or shared. We cannot bank love; it grows as we give it away. The more we give it away, the greater our capacity for love. This is how loving-kindness becomes limitless" (Halifax 2009).

Wrap-up

All we have is life to live and our transporting vessel for aliveness is the body.
—D. CONNELLY 1993, 100

The capacity to feel and emote is fundamental to human life. Everything about our biological design—our skin, our senses, our nervous system, our brains—is geared toward letting the world in. Feelings and emotions are what arise as we let the world in (Wellwood 1983). As such, our feelings and emotions act as catalysts inviting us to know ourselves, to know each other, and to know the world. Our feeling bodies offer one of the most relevant curricula imaginable for teaching and learning. They have much to teach us, if we care to pay attention.

However, in most school settings, the idea that a student's body—his feelings and emotions—might serve as an important teacher is threatening, perhaps because it posits that there might be other authorities, besides the teacher, that are worthy of a student's attention. There is a danger is this stance, for when feelings and emotion are excluded from the classroom, students are likely to finish their formal schooling imagining that the only resource available to them, when problems arise, is their thinking. However, thinking, alone, rarely leads to clarity. Instead, thinking minus feeling oftentimes results in a mental quagmire. The quagmire-free path involves befriending our emotions, secure in the belief that, in doing so, we open to our fully integrated selves.

It is high time for classrooms to become *real* places—hospitable places that warmly welcome students' bodies, feelings, and emotions. Indeed, to teach as if life matters is to recognize that feelings and emotions are the life force running through our bodies. When we welcome emotions and feelings into the classroom, we welcome life in.

Pursuing the principles and practices presented in this chapter promotes emotional intelligence, ultimately enhancing the quality of our relationships, our decisions, and our overall life satisfaction. For teachers, it all begins with mustering the courage to "walk on water" by welcoming our own feeling bodies into our classrooms. It is worth the risk.

CHAPTER THREE

Loving the Questions

Relationship with Our Minds

Once you have learned how to ask questions—relevant and appropriate and substantial questions—you have learned how to learn and no one can keep you from learning whatever you want or need to know.
—N. POSTMAN AND C. WEINGARTNER 1969, 23

Imagine you're a teacher whose primary goal is to foster the intellectual development of young peoples' minds. You understand *intellectual development* to mean the capacity of the mind to identify, distinguish, correlate, synthesize, compare, persist, define, reflect, reason, and more. You are committed to fostering this family of intellectual capacities in ways that engender in your students a genuine passion for learning. This is a reasonable vision, is it not? What educator wouldn't want this?

Now consider the status quo pedagogy employed in schools to foster intellectual development:

- Students spend much of their day indoors and seated in rows.
- They listen while a teacher offers instruction or they work individually on tasks derived from standardized textbooks, such as answering questions on worksheets provided by educational publishing houses.
- Sometimes they use Internet-based sources to ferret out information, and on occasion they may participate in a special project or enrichment activity to add spice to the entrenched routine.
- Finally, rounding out this instructional formula, they are routinely compelled to complete a battery of quizzes and tests.

It should be self-evident (though it often goes unnoticed) that there is a clear disconnect in this scenario between ends and means. To be more explicit, the end—fostering intellectual development—is not likely to be achieved using the standardized approaches of mass education.

What is more likely is that as young people progress in their schooling, their curiosity will be tamed and their questioning nature subdued. To the extent that this happens, there is a danger that they will become docile, refraining from seeking answers to the raw questions that bubble up from deep inside them. This danger is illustrated in the following story told by Juanita Brown:

> I am seven-years-old, in the second grade at Orchard Villa Elementary school in Miami, Florida. Mrs. Johnson is my teacher. She is very religious, in the Southern tradition. I am a small child for my age—skinny, lively, inquisitive. I want to know everything about everything.
>
> Mrs. Johnson holds prayers in the classroom each morning. One day, while everyone is praying to God, I start to wonder what God actually looks like. As soon as the class prayers are over I raise my hand and pipe up in my squeaky little voice, "What color is God, Mrs. Johnson?" Mrs. Johnson turns beet red. She is extremely upset. I don't understand why she's so angry. She grabs my arm and hisses, "Young lady, you are going right to the principal's office and we're calling your mother." She marches me to the principal's office, and they call my mother. I sit in there, terrified, until my mother arrives.
>
> There we are—the principal shuffling her papers, Mrs. Johnson, still looking outraged, and me, getting smaller and more petrified by the minute. My mother comes into the room and sits down quietly next to me while Mrs. Johnson recounts the sin I have committed in asking the obviously impudent question, "What color is God?" during school prayers. My mother listens in silence. She looks at the principal behind her big wooden desk, then moves her gaze to Mrs. Johnson, sitting primly next to the principal. Then she looks down at me, cowering in my seat. She puts her arm around me warmly, smiles, looks up at my teacher again and asks, "And what color is God, Mrs. Johnson?"
>
> I was deeply grateful and relieved that day in the principal's office. Had that day turned out differently, perhaps my question asking days would have been over.
> (Brown 2001, 134–35)

Thankfully, one little girl's curiosity—her relationship with her mind—was safeguarded that day. Averted was a mind growing sluggish, sheepish, or sour because of submission to someone else's agenda, someone else's questions.

What about you, dear reader? What has been your school experience around questions? Can you readily call to mind times when your questions, curiosities, and interests were honored in school? If you have trouble locating such instances, you are not alone. Many teachers we talk with confess that they spent much of their time as students studying the "correct" answers to questions posed in a preset curriculum, taking tests to demonstrate their proficiency, and then, more often than not, soon forgetting what they had "learned." Curiosity—the life of the mind—and forthrightly pursuing one's own questions was really not the point.

This is troubling especially in so far as there is a strong tendency for teachers to reproduce in their own classrooms the same behaviors and pedagogies that they were subjected to as students. In this chapter, we explore how all of us— teachers and students alike—might discover anew the opportunities for genuine learning that abound when we cultivate our curiosity and reclaim our innate questioning nature.

Fostering an Appetite for Questions

> Schools do not lack answers, they lack depth. Depth is associated more with
> asking good questions than with having all the answers.   —T. HART 2003, 94

When I ask the students in my freshmen seminar at Penn State to say the first thing that comes to mind when they hear the word *question*, they respond with words like *hard, test, wrong, help*. Strikingly, the word *question* for these eighteen-year-olds is seldom associated with words like *open, curious, discover,* or *delight*. This is to say that their associations with questions and questioning tend to be negative and tainted with fear. I understand where my students are coming from.

Flashback 1. *I am ten years old. There is a test on fractions today. I look at the test sheet and panic. What if I don't know the right answers. What if I fail?*

Flashback 2. *I am twelve, and a policeman knocks at my front door. My mom answers. "Is Chris Uhl your son?" he asks. Mom nods, and I step forward. The policemen looks down at me and says, "I have some questions for you, young man." I swallow hard. I'm in trouble.*

Flashback 3. *I am twenty-nine, and today is my oral examination for my Ph.D. The examining committee can ask any question spanning science and philosophy. For over a year I have been preparing. Will I have the "right" answers? Will I pass? I am nauseated.*

Life experiences like these led me to have negative associations with questions, even to fear them as a means of entrapment and humiliation.

With a bit of reflection it may be possible for each of us to trace our individual attitudes around questions back to events in our childhood. If, as a child, your questions were ignored, or worse, ridiculed, today you may tend to avoid asking questions altogether. Or, if as a child you experienced humiliation when attempting to respond to questions from adults, today you may become tense, fearful, and/or inarticulate in the face of questions from others.

In truth, most of us have been socialized (at home and in school), to varying degrees, to view questions *not* as helpers, pointing us toward understanding and insight, but as hindrances that can trip us up, leaving us humiliated. No surprise then that it is unusual to find an adult, and this includes teachers, who wholeheartedly welcomes and celebrates questions.

Parents and teachers, either knowingly or unknowingly, play a key role in shaping young people's attitudes toward questions. For example, imagine a child riding along in the car with her mom. Looking out the window, the child spots a machine in a field and says, "Mommy, what's that big thing over there in the field?" The mother, regarding her child's question as an annoyance, says, "I dunno," in a tone of irritation.

Replay the scenario with a mother who sees her child's question as a gift. When asked about the big thing in the field, this mother responds, "Hmmm, let's see . . . What's growing in that field, honey?" to which the child responds, "Looks like hay to me." Mom follows with, "So, what's hay used for?" "It's used to feed animals," comes the response. Mom asks about the kinds of animals that eat hay (e.g., horses) and the places where these animals live in winter (e.g., barns) and then poses a question about how hay gets from field to barn (it's cut and baled).

Eventually, the mother guides her daughter back to the original question, asking, "Now, sweetie, having figured out that hay was growing in that field, and knowing what hay is used for and how it gets from field to barn, what do you suppose that machine back there was used for?" The child comes up with the answer and in the process learns that her questions matter and that she has the power to think her way clear through to possible answers! The first mother (the one who responds with an irritated "I dunno") annihilates curiosity and creates fear around questions; the second mother nurtures her child's curiosity, engendering in the child an appetite for questions. (Thanks to Derrick Jensen for providing the framework for this story.)

Loving children's questions is a way of loving children, both in the home and at school. For parents and teachers this means not only being open to children's inquiries but being filled with questions, creativity, and curiosity ourselves. For example, imagine a dad who suddenly pretends that he is a visitor to Earth from another planet. Enacting the part, Dad cocks his head and asks his kids for some help in understanding this strange place called Earth. Then, looking up at the sky, Dad asks:

> "What are those things floating up there?"
> "Clouds!" the kids respond triumphantly.
> "Hmm, What's in them?" asks Dad (the alien).
> "Water!" comes the response in unison.
> "Hmm . . . How did water get way up there?"

And before the kids can formulate a response, Dad follows with more questions:

> "Hey, why are those clouds moving?"
> "And wait a minute, how come that cloud over there is changing shape?"

This was the game Greg Levoy was treated to growing up with his dad. As Levoy recalls, "Entire afternoons could go by as we pondered the mysteries of water and wind and how it is possible that we can know so much and understand so little, that we can live with something everyday of our lives and still never come to know it" (1997, 144).

Fast forward: Young Levoy, brimming with curiosity and filled with questions, is going to school for the first time. Walking there with his dad, the boy finds a beautiful rock and puts it in his pocket. When he gets to school, he proudly presents the rock to his new teacher. She responds, "A rock! Please put that away. We don't bring rocks to school." In effect, the teacher says, "Your rock is not part of today's plan; I am in charge here; I decide what is worthy of attention." Meanwhile, the messages for the boy include: I have done something wrong; cool stuff (like a rock) doesn't belong in school; it is best for me to lie low and avoid any more scolding.

Let's run this scenario again with a different teacher. Arriving to school, young Levoy proudly presents his rock to his teacher. She stops what she is doing and really looks at the rock, fully aware of both the boy—his curiosity—and the rock—its mystery. As she allows the boy's curiosity to touch her, she, herself, becomes excited, and this causes children nearby to gather around to see what's going on. She then invites the kids to observe this rock—its color, its shape (e.g., the curves and jagged parts). In a manner similar to young Levoy's dad, the teacher begins to ask questions: Where did this rock come from? Who made it? Why are rocks so hard? What causes their color? How come there are so many different kinds of rocks? More children gather around. The teacher listens as the children respond to her questions. Soon the children are asking their own questions. A whole hour is spent observing this rock, asking questions, and proposing answers. As a result young Levoy learns that rocks and his curiosity are welcome in school, and little Levoy's classmates learn about the central role of questions in catalyzing learning.

Indeed, often more important than an immediate answer to a question is the message that the question is being taken seriously. In this vein, imagine a teacher who responds to a student's question with: "That's a darn good question—so good that I want to really think about it for a minute before attempting an answer." Or, "I could give you my standard answer to that question, but that answer no longer satisfies me; my thinking has changed and here is why . . . " Or, "I sense an edge of frustration in your question. Before answering, I want to get a better sense of your personal concern for this matter so that I can really speak to you directly." Or, "I truly don't know. What do you think?" Such responses are grounded in the belief that new understanding emerges when we take questions seriously.

Imagine how it would be if your students' interests and burning questions determined the vector of teaching and learning in your classroom and if your job as teacher were primarily to create a curricula that grew out of the questions arising in the learners who joined you each day. Of course, for you to do so would mean according agency to your students and seeing their innate interests and passions as generative—as catalysts for discovery and genuine learning. This would be truly subversive. How? Rather than students being obedient to their teacher's demands, teachers would be in the service of their students' curiosity— a transgressive, even radical, inversion of power.

What would it take for teachers to adopt this view of how teaching and learning best occur? Mostly, it would take cultivating a deep trust in children and young people. Teachers would have to:

- trust that to be human is to have natural curiosity and to possess an innate desire to learn

In his book *From Information to Transformation,* Tobin Hart tells the story of a boy named "Gunner," growing up in the fifties in New Jersey. As a bright, but under-achieving high school student, Gunner was sometimes taken by bus to Princeton University along with other students to attend presentations by the distinguished physicists of the day, including Albert Einstein. Once, in the midst of a particularly dry lecture, one of Gunner's classmates asked the assembled scientists what they thought about ghosts. Two physicists quickly dismissed this possibility on the grounds that there was no hard evidence. That seemed to be the end of it, but then Robert Oppenheimer, famous for his role in developing the atomic bomb, offered a different view, saying, "That's a fascinating question. I accept the possibility of all things." Oppenheimer went on to say that "it is necessary to find one's own required evidence" before accepting or rejecting a possibility. In recounting this event, Hart writes, "For Gunner this was a revelation. Instead of closing down and accepting the world as prepackaged, Oppenheimer's perspective opened it back up to mystery, to the possibility of all things, and to one's responsibility to discover it for oneself. Gunner's way of being began to shift as he came to define himself from the center of his own direct experience" (2007, 131).

This story of Gunner (who went on to become a college professor) is a reminder to teachers to see young people's questions as invitations to dialogue rather than as threats to our authority or opportunities to demonstrate our intelligence. The truth is that embedded in most questions is a whole world of ideas, and when we offer tidy answers to questions, we flatten the world rather than allowing young people to ride their questions and to see where they might take them (Hart 2004).

- trust that students' curiosity is a much better foundation for a curriculum than something imposed from outside
- trust that by slowly giving up control we can create the conditions for genuine learning in our classrooms

Trusting the Children: Question-Centered Learning at Byrd Elementary

Imagine that you are a fifth-grade teacher in a Chicago neighborhood rife with street violence, drugs, and gang activity. It is winter, and the temperature of your school is around sixty degrees. Many of the kids don hats and coats in the classroom; some wear mittens. The windows are filthy and pocked with bullet holes. Your school has no lunchroom, no auditorium. The bathrooms are unsightly, with sinks and toilets that work intermittently, if at all. This was the situation in Room 405, Byrd Elementary, when Brian Schultz signed on to teach fifth grade.

Schultz began his job with the question: What knowledge is worthwhile for ten to twelve year olds who are street savvy but have little book learning? He wondered if centering the curriculum on vital issues that students cared about could bring excitement and meaningful learning to his classroom?

He started by asking his fifth-graders, "What are the problems in this school and in your community?" In no time, the kids were shouting out things like no heat in the classrooms, clogged toilets, drugs, trash everywhere. In an hour the students came up with eighty-nine problems. Then, a girl, Dyneisha, observed that almost everything on their list had to do with the awful condition of their school. She was right.

Years earlier, this inner-city neighborhood had been promised a new school. Although a nearby parcel of land had been cleared, no action had been taken. Schultz saw in the heartfelt responses of these fifth-graders an opportunity to address an intriguing academic question: Could he share authority with his students to solve an authentic community problem in the context of a traditional classroom? Stated differently: Could he and his students trust each other enough to create a genuinely democratic classroom? It was worth a try.

As the school year unfolded, Room 405 became the hub of "Project Citizen" —a comprehensive effort to educate the public about the deplorable conditions at Byrd Elementary and to build support for the construction of a new school. The first question the students faced was: Where to begin? After deliberation, they decided to start by carefully documenting the condition of their school. They did this through photographs, video footage, expository writing, surveys, and the construction of a website (www.projectcitizen405.com/).

Next, these fifth-graders faced the questions: Who do we tell about this problem and how do we tell them? In response they defined their public as the citizens of Chicago—especially members of the school board and city officials— as well as national leaders. They used a variety of techniques to reach their audience, including letters, press releases, invitations, interviews, and petitions.

As Project Citizen gained momentum, Room 405 became a combination think tank and campaign office. No longer was the school day divided into separate periods. Instead, reading, writing, math, and social studies all blended together as students worked earnestly to solve a vital life problem. Day by day, they engaged in reading (studying Jonathan Kozal's *Savage Inequalities* to gain a perspective on their own situation), writing (composing letters, press releases, and e-mails to educate the public), and math (categorizing and tallying responses from surveys to buttress their arguments). In the end, these students, with Schultz's mentoring, created a curriculum based on their needs and desires—a democratic curriculum *of, for,* and *by* the students (Schultz 2008).

What was the upshot of all this? First, some local officials took the students seriously and visited their school. Over time, the physical infrastructure at Byrd Elementary did improve. Perhaps more importantly, going to school, for the first time, became relevant for these kids. As one said, "This ain't school, this is important." As a testimony to this shift, the attendance for Schultz's class rose to 98 percent, and it was not uncommon for students to arrive early, stay late, and even work on days off to, as one student put it, "get the job done." Meanwhile, though Schultz made no effort to "teach to the test," the standardized tests scores of most students improved over the course of Project Citizen. No surprise! As the minds, hearts, bodies, and spirits of young people become engaged in authentic, meaningful activity—as they are trusted—school performance cannot but improve.

The Power of Questions

> If I had an hour to solve a problem and my life depended on the solution, I would spend the first 55 minutes determining the proper question to ask, for once I knew the proper question, I could solve the problem in less than five minutes.   —A. EINSTEIN (WWW.QUESTIONDAY.COM/ALBERT_E.HTM)

Einstein reminds us that a well-framed question can unlock mysteries. Indeed, his Theory of Relativity sprang from a novel question, namely: "What would the universe look like if I were riding on the end of a light beam at the speed of light?" (Vogt, Brown, and Isaacs 2003). In a more mundane vein, it was only when Ray Kroc asked the question, "Where can I get a good hamburger on the road?" that the concept of fast-food restaurants and McDonalds, in particular, was born. Everything we know today arose because people in the past were curious. They formulated questions, and doing so galvanized their interest and determination to find answers.

The power of questions as an educational tool goes far back into history. The great Greek thinker and teacher Socrates didn't give lectures or write books; he taught by asking questions. His questions were crafted to challenge his students to think about their beliefs and, specifically, to explore the assumptions underlying their beliefs. For Socrates, his students' thought was the subject matter—*how* they thought more than *what* they thought. Socrates' questions revealed ways in which his students' thinking was dogmatic, contradictory, and/or erroneous. His approach—to guide students to think about their thinking—was regarded as subversive by the governing elites of his time. Accused of corrupting the minds of young men, Socrates was sentenced to death (Phillips 2001).

What Makes a Good Question?

If questions are so important, then one would expect that we, as teachers, would have a sophisticated understanding of what makes a good one, as well as a proficiency in crafting powerful questions. As part of her Ph.D. research, Juanita Brown asked people what they considered the characteristics of a good question. Culling the responses, Brown concluded that, "a good question is one that matters; it is an attractor for energy and it generates energy; it opens up possibilities . . . It invites deeper exploration . . . It has some personal connection . . . It invites a variety of voices . . . It creates a certain tension, a certain dissonance between [one's] current understanding and something bigger . . . [And finally] A good question has to be able to travel well" (2001, 153–54).

Those who believe in the power of questions to catalyze learning know a good question when they hear it. How about you? How would you assess the following questions?

1. Do you like small towns better than big cities?
2. What's the most difficult thing you have had to do in your life?
3. Why is there so much killing in the name of religion?

Imagine that you are an Olympic judge and it is your job to rate these three questions, on a scale of 1 to 10, in terms of their power to engage the human mind. How would you rate them? For most people, question 1 scores low, question 2 scores intermediate, while question 3 is judged as the most thought provoking, intriguing, and challenging.

The way a question is constructed—is it a "yes/no" (like 1 above), a "what" (like 2), or a "why" question (like 3)—goes a long way to determining its power. Vogt, Brown, and Isaacs (2003, 4) illustrate this by asking readers to rank the words *who, what, when, where, which, why, and how* from more to less powerful. Most people rank these question words as follows:

MORE POWERFUL

(4) Why

(3) What, How

(2) When, Who, Where
(1) Which (yes/no questions)
LESS POWERFUL

To make this relationship between question construction and power more explicit, imagine a teacher who is vexed because one of her students, Dave, repeatedly fails to do his homework assignments. In considering how she might broach this subject with Dave, the teacher comes up with four possible questions in accord with the above ranking:

1. *Yes/No*: Dave, did you complete last night's homework?
2. *When*: Dave, when was the last time you completed a homework assignment?
3. *What*: Dave, what is it about doing homework that is difficult for you?
4. *Why*: Dave, why do you suppose homework has become such an issue for us?

Moving from the "yes/no" (Q-1) through the "when" and "what" (Q-2 and 3) to the "why" (Q-4) question, notice the increasing opportunity for reflection and genuine conversation. Indeed, with the "why" question, Dave's teacher avoids creating an adversarial contest where a loser and winner will emerge. Instead, a desire for understanding and collaboration comes to the fore.

Question-Centered Learning

In most schools today, teaching is organized around disciplines or subjects (e.g., Algebra I, English Composition, American History), and teachers instruct students in specific aspects of these subjects during specified periods each day. Imagine, for a moment, how this predominant curricular organization is experienced by young people. The school day begins, and a child is told that she must learn about numbers. Forty-five minutes later the student must learn (and presumably care) about history. As the day unfolds, a string of subjects will be addressed until the day ends. From the young person's perspective, such disciplinary boundaries cannot but be experienced as arbitrary, even irrelevant, in so far as no one has ever taken the time to offer a cogent rationale for organizing the school day around things called *subjects*.

Donald Finkel points out in *Teaching with Your Mouth Shut* that an entirely different approach is possible:

Teachers can organize their teaching around inquiry rather than the separate disconnected abstractions called "history," "math," or "literature." An inquiry-centered course focuses not on traditional subject matter but on a problem or questions. The subject matter is learned as a tool for working on the problem. [For example,] if we wish to understand why advertising dominates our landscape, we will need to learn some social and economic history . . . [In inquiry-based courses] students learn those parts of traditional subjects they can use to tackle the problem, and no more . . . Such a shift changes everything. (2000, 54–55)

For decades, a cadre of progressive educators, like Finkel, have been experimenting with inquiry-based learning where the role of the teacher is more like that of a midwife—someone who creates the conditions for the birthing of understanding from within students. Such teachers spend much of their time asking questions and listening very carefully *to* students instead of talking *at* them. Rather than prioritizing teacher-student interactions, they seek to encourage student-student question-based problem solving.

Clearly, Finkel's approach challenges the dominant authority structure within today's classrooms. This authority structure is grounded in a set of limiting beliefs that are seldom questioned—beliefs such as:

- Children need to be spoon-fed to learn.
- Young people cannot be trusted with unstructured time.
- Young people aren't interested in the content that they "need" to "know."

These sorts of beliefs prevent teachers from returning control over learning to the only place it ever actually resides—in the hearts and minds of students!

An appreciation and appetite for questions and questioning is innate in humans; asking questions is what we do; it is how we learn. In my freshman seminar I acknowledge this by asking students to think of questions that they would like answers to—questions that are really important to them. In making this request, I assert that they are holding within them important questions—questions worth asking—questions worthy of answers.

To add a touch of intrigue to my request, I hold up a large black suitcase, explaining that my case contains an extraordinary computer that is able to answer any question they might have. (This idea is inspired by Postman and Weingartner 1969.) I then carefully rest the suitcase (actually empty) on a table, while challenging students to fill up an entire page with their burning questions. They set to work, some of them glancing up at the black suitcase from time to time. When they are done, I ask a few volunteers to read their questions. Predictably, some questions are designed to test the powers of my pretend super-computer—for example, What's my mom's maiden name? What did I have for breakfast today? I explain that the cost of operating this one-of-a-kind computer is much too high to waste on questions that already have a known answer. Then I ask each student to put their toughest (most computer-worthy) question up on the blackboard. Here is a sampling:

> What causes love to die?
> What's the most important thing to learn while in college?
> Is it good that people are living longer today than in the past?
> Is war a part of human nature?
> What's the fastest and easiest way to make a lot of money?
> Am I crazy?

I explain that my super-duper computer has trouble answering questions that are imprecise and/or laden with assumptions. The computer needs to know exactly what is meant by the words employed in each question. For example, for the question, "What causes love to die?" the computer needs to know what the questioner means by *love*; that is, what type of love is being conjured? Similarly, what is meant by the word *die*? As worded, the question assumes that love can be extinguished. But maybe that's not true? And what about the word *cause*? Asking, "What *causes love to die*," (rather than "What *are* the causes . . . ") implies that there is just one cause. Further, the very word *cause* assumes causality—assumes that we live in a world where effects are invariably the result of causes. But is this the way the world works or simply a reflection of how we have been conditioned to see the world?

In response to these kinds of prompts, students come to see that a culturally conditioned way of seeing the world is often reflected in the construction of our questions. Specifically, "What causes love to die?" reflects a conception of reality based on singularities—one form of love, one form of death, one cause, one effect.

As students delve deeper into this question, they are set free to expand their thinking and understanding of love, causality, and death. One student comments, "If it is genuine love, it won't die. In fact, for love to die is a contradiction in terms, because if love dies, it wasn't really love in the first place." This prompts another student to confess that, in her experience, "Love can die. It dies if I fail to nurture it. It's like a pansy," she explains, "The pansy is love. If I fail to water it, to care for it, the pansy will die. That's the way it is with me and love."

The women next to her challenges, "You are speaking metaphorically. I get your point, but I am not sure I agree because, though pansies and love may share some things in common, they are not the same." This leads to a short digression on metaphors—What are they and how they can be helpful, but also misleading, in clarifying thought.

Returning to the central question, a woman in her fifties says, in a quivering voice, "My take is different. I had imagined that if someone I loved died, my love would die, but when my mother died, my love did not waiver or diminish. In some ways I am even more intimate with my mother now than when she was alive."

After a long silence, a young man speaks of the death of his love for his ex-girlfriend who left him for another guy. He is unequivocal, "It was *love* and it did *die* and it was my girlfriend's leaving that *caused* it to die." Here is a concrete story—something that most class members can relate to and want to explore further. Questions pop out: Tell me about this love you had for your girlfriend? What was it exactly? How did it leave you feeling about yourself? How did your girlfriend experience your love? How was she changed, if at all, by your love? What exactly is it that has now died in you?

As class members sink deeper and deeper into the topic of love, they forget about the imaginary computer in the black suitcase. They forget they are in school. They have stepped into relationship with their own minds and hearts and with each other.

Through an emphasis on question-centered learning, students come to realize that they are not simply empty containers waiting for their teachers to fill them up with information. To the contrary, their own questions and passions form a foundation from which they can extend and expand their understanding through questioning, observing, reevaluating, and reflecting.

Cultivating a Love of Questions: Six Explorations

Humans have been blessed with a curious nature and placed in a world full of wonderful stuff. Our challenge is not to spoil it all by force-feeding artificial, contrived information into delicate hearts and minds.

—L. STODDARD 2004, 76

Almost a half-century ago Postman and Weingartner observed: "It is staggering
. . . [that] the most potent intellectual tool that man has yet developed—the art
of asking questions—is not taught in school!" (1969, 23). What follows are some
approaches—think of them as "explorations"—that we can use to help ourselves
and our students become more skillful in the art of asking questions while, at the
same time, experiencing the delight that open, creative, question-based learning
can offer. These explorations can be modified in innumerable ways to fit most
any learning context.

Exploration 1. Questions to Create Community

It is the first day of class. You watch as students file into the room. Some know
each other, but most are strangers. As you look from face to face, you are curious to know something about these people, and you want to create a classroom
atmosphere that will allow them to begin to know each other. You pass out slips
of paper and invite each person to create a question for the class by completing
the open-ended sentence: *How many of you* _____? When they are done,
students fold up their papers and drop them into a hat (inspired by Jensen 2004).
Then, the hat goes around, and each person picks a slip and reads the question
on it. The questions might sound something like this:

> How many of you are working while you are in school?
> How many of you have doubts about your major?
> How many of you are in an intimate (sexual) relationship?
> How many of you are considering dropping this class?
> How many of you are vegetarians?
> How many of you have pooped in the woods?
> How many of you like to go out drinking?
> How many of you don't watch television?
> How many of you have parents who are divorced?
> How many of you have had a close friend die?
> How many of you think the world will be a better place in fifty years?

Students indicate a "yes" response to a question by raising their hands. The
teacher may chime in with follow-up questions. For example, observing that
more than half of the class raises their hands in response to the first question,
the teacher might ask: "How many resent the fact that you have to work?"
or "How many feel that the work you are doing is making the world a better

place?" Following the teacher's example, students often begin asking their own follow-up questions.

When I begin a course in this way, everyone usually pays attention and participates. Why? Because it is their questions that are receiving attention and the responses are teaching them things about the other people in the room as well as themselves. As this occurs, barriers begin to ease, and apprehension and loneliness tend to dissolve.

Exploration 2. Observation as the Foundation for Questions

Each fall I teach a field-ecology course for fifteen to twenty upper-class science majors. When I first offered this course, I imagined that the students would be skilled observers and would understand that questions invariably have their origins in observations. But I have noted, year after year, that few of my students have ever been invited to take the time to quiet themselves and patiently observe their surroundings.

The following story underscores the critical link between observations and questions. The year is 1859, and Louis Agassiz is a professor at Harvard. A student named Nathaniel Shaler asks to study under him. To gauge the depth and breadth of the young man's knowledge, Agassiz peppers Shaler with questions. Satisfied, Agassiz places a preserved fish in front of Shaler and instructs him to learn all that he can without, in any way, damaging the fish. Shaler sets to work observing, assuming that the professor will soon return to quiz him. But Agassiz does not return that day, nor the next. It isn't until a week later that the professor finally approaches Shaler to ask what he has learned. Based on his observation of the specimen's shape, mouth and teeth design, scales, fin structure, and so on, Shaler shares his questions and his hypotheses. When he is finished, Agassiz says, "That is not right," and walks away. Undaunted, Shaler goes back to work. To his astonishment, he finds that the more attentive he becomes, the more questions arise and the more he discovers, until in his words, he is learning "a hundred times as much as seemed possible at the start" ("From the Editors" 1997, 2). Such is the power—largely forgotten in contemporary schooling—of sustained observation and questioning.

In the spirit of this story, I sometimes give my students an assignment that links observations and questions called Fifty Questions. The first instruction is simple: Go somewhere! In a sociology course the destination might be a social setting, like a shopping mall or sporting event; in a business course, the target could be a factory or a corporate headquarters. In a teacher preparation course, the setting for Fifty Questions could be an inner-city or suburban school.

In my field ecology course, I introduce Fifty Questions to my students by taking them to a patch of forest on the Penn State campus. Upon arrival I say:

> Simply explore with no particular agenda until you find a place where you feel comfortable and then sit down. Once you are settled, look around and observe your immediate surroundings very carefully. If you find that your attention is drawn to a leaf on a plant, observe that leaf as if you have never seen a leaf before, engaging all your senses. As you observe, questions will arise. In the case of the leaf, your questions might sound something like: Why is this leaf shaped the way it is? Why are the margins of this leaf jagged? What's inside this leaf? Why is the leaf green? What is "green"? When I crush this leaf, what causes that strong smell?
>
> And if it happens that while observing the leaf your attention is drawn to a tiny insect on the leaf's underside, observe the insect, again noting the questions that arise from your observations. Continue in this fashion, closely observing those things that capture your attention.

The idea of this exercise is for each student to write down all the questions that emerge from their present-moment observations, without judging or excluding any questions. As students do this, they realize that they have the potential to generate lots of questions. Indeed, this exercise is a way of inviting us back to our essential nature, which is open and curious.

In thirty minutes of observation, my students easily generate fifty questions. I next prompt them to examine their questions with an eye to spotting trends. For example, some students are surprised to discover that most of their questions are focused on plants; other students observe that it was only their sense of vision that triggered their questions (they have no questions prompted by something that they smelled, heard, tasted, or touched). Still others note that the majority of their questions begin with the word *what* and that they have few *how* or *why* questions.

After making these observations, I ask students to share what they regard as their best question. As a group, we critique each question for clarity and crispness, and, as necessary, we modify questions so that they are free of ambiguity. Once students have produced some examples of clear questions, they consider how their questions could be answered. As the semester progresses they design and carry out their own independent research projects. My job through all this is to trust that they possess the capacity (with a bit of coaching) to make careful observations, ask good questions, and carry out well-designed research. Indeed, they do!

Exploration 3. The Power of Why

There is arguably no more powerful question than "Why?" In fact, the freedom to ask "Why?" may be essential to our common humanity. This is illustrated in the story about Primo Levi, a Jewish man forced to endure a long journey in a cattle car to a concentration camp during World War II. Levi was hungry and very thirsty. Deep into the journey, the train stopped. Spotting an icicle, Levi reached out to break it off. Before he could bring the icicle to his lips, a hulking guard grabbed his arm and snatched the icicle away. Levi looked at the guard and asked, "Warum" (Why [have you done this]?). The guard responded with, "Hier ist kein warum" (There is no "why" here). Reflecting on this incident, Fritz Stern wrote: "This 'Hier ist kein warum' stands against everything that is human and constitutes a form of verbal annihilation" (Stern 2000, 4; Uhl 2004).

The question "Why?" comes from our innate desire to make meaning, to understand, and to exercise our intellect. This question also enables us to improve our surroundings by pooling our individual and collective intelligence. Take an example from the corporate world. Toyota—the world's largest automobile manufacturer—gives credit for its high productivity and quality control to the question, "Why?" Every worker on the Toyota assembly line is taught to analyze problems by asking "Why?" over and over again. "This bolt fell off." "Why?" "Because the thread is stripped." "Why?" "Because it was misaligned with the screw." "Why?" And so on. It turns out that almost every design problem encountered at Toyota can be solved with five "whys" or less (Beck 2001, 162).

Derrick Jensen (2004) provides a way of tapping into the power of *why* through a practice he dubs the Annoying Child. This practice is simple to do. When someone expresses an opinion about something, you ask, "Why do you think that?" When that person responds, you follow with, "And why is that?" and on and on—all the while inviting the speaker deeper and deeper into his own thinking.

This practice can be quite revealing. For example, imagine that you are talking to your colleague, Judith, about the *meaning of progress*, and she declares, "As a society we, in America, are making progress." Realizing that Judith has expressed an opinion disguised as a fact, you ask:

"*Why* do you think we are making progress?"

Judith responds, "We are developing new technologies every day."

You come back with, "*Why* are new technologies a sign of progress?"

After a moment's reflection, Judith answers, "Because new technologies make life easier."

"*Why* is an easy life a mark of progress?" you ask.

She replies, "An easy life means more free time."

"And *why* do you believe that new technologies give us more free time?" you query.

"Well, I don't know . . . I just think this must be true," Judith responds.

By repeating these "why" questions, Judith will eventually begin to uncover some of the underlying beliefs and hidden assumptions that frame her definition of progress.

Employing the Annoying Child practice in the classroom, I've discovered that students—far from being annoyed—are actually drawn in by it. Though they may be a bit uncomfortable at first—similar to trying to bend over to touch your toes after you've been standing upright for a long time—with perseverance they discover that this mind "stretch" teaches them about themselves, about how they think, about their assumptions and disabling beliefs. In effect, they surprise themselves, discovering that thinking can be enjoyable and questioning can be enlivening.

Exploration 4. Using Questions to Promote Critical Thinking

A lot of what passes for thinking in our culture is just mental effort expended to back up opinions that, more often than not, have been formed without much genuine thought. Such self-serving thinking is the foundation of what DeBono (1994) terms the "clash system," where two opposing views fight it out. Western civilization—in its philosophy and in its practice—is mired in this clash system as exemplified by the prevalence of argument, debate, dialectics, and adversarial thinking that pervades our politics, our courts, our business decisions, and our day-to-day living.

In reality, the clash of opposing views rarely yields more enlightened reason or understanding. Rather than serving to contribute to the evolution of thought, the *clash system* only serves to harden each person's point of view. As counterattacks and counterdefenses continue, each point of view grows ever more rigid and unable to develop. Only minimal advances in reasoning and understanding result. That this system should exist somewhere in a culture is valuable, even if marginally. That it should dominate the culture is absurd (DeBono 1994, 85–89, paraphrased).

As an alternative to the clash system, DeBono offers a simple, question-based methodology he dubs PMI (where the *P* stands for "Plus," *M* stands for "Minus," and *I* for "Interesting"). This PMI approach can be useful anytime it's necessary to think something through, either within a group or individually. For example, DeBono describes a time when he asked a group of boys (ages ten and eleven) whether they thought it would be a good idea if each of them received $5 each week for attending school. The boys enthusiastically embraced this idea and immediately began fantasizing about what they would do with this new weekly income. DeBono explained the PMI approach and asked the boys to work in groups to come up with the *P*lus, *M*inus and *I*nteresting points with regard to his $5 proposal.

That the boys could generate Plus points was no surprise. The interesting part came when they took the time to really think about the possible Minus aspects to receiving $5 per week for attending school. Many issues, initially overlooked in their zeal, turned up. For example:

The bigger boys would beat them up and take their money.
Parents would no longer give them presents or pocket money.
The school would raise its prices for meals.
There would be quarrels about the money and strikes.
There was no obvious source of this money.
There would be less money to pay teachers.
There would not be any money for the school to buy a mini-bus.

DeBono reports, "At the end of the exercise the class was again asked if they liked the idea. Whereas thirty-out-of-thirty had previously liked the idea, it now appeared that 29 out of 30 had completely reversed their view and now disliked it" (1994, 13).

DeBono is quick to point out that a PMI is not like a typical listing of pros and cons because the primary purpose of a PMI is to explore possibilities, not to argue. The *Interesting* part of the PMI technique is particularly relevant. A good prompt for "I" is: "It would be interesting to see _____." So, for the idea of giving kids $5 per week to attend school, it would be interesting to see:

- if kids' school attendance would improve
- if basic math skills (counting, adding, making change, etc.) would improve
- how parents would respond to this initiative—for example, if they would let the kids keep the money
- if kids would pool their weekly stipends in order to make large purchases previously unimaginable for them as separate individuals

The key point here is that the PMI approach induces a shift in how intelligence is used. Instead of being employed to muster arguments to support preexisting opinions (the adversarial/debate approach so common in our culture), intelligence in the world of PMI is used to exhaustively and creatively explore new ideas. With PMI there are not right or wrong ideas, only thoughtful responses to provocative prompts.

There is no end to the opportunities for using PMI in the classroom. For example, in a case where one student judges a second student's idea as "stupid," the teacher could ask the first student to do a PMI, with a particular focus on the Positive and the Interesting aspects of the "stupid" idea. With only a modicum of effort, PMI could readily become a central part of classroom culture. Anytime a new idea came up—the school parking lot should be turned into a vegetable garden, students should decide what they want to study in school, homework should be eliminated—students could be invited to perform a PMI. In sum, PMI is a question-based technique that promotes the most important survival skill there is—free and open thinking.

Exploration 5. Lectio Divina: *Using Questions in the Context of Contemplation*

Words matter. The ability to speak, write, and read is a prerequisite for functioning effectively in modern society. But in our culture of information overload, words easily become cheapened—filling up space without inviting thought, much less reflection.

Enter *Lectio Divina*, a form of contemplative reading that originated in monastic communities in the twelfth century. Saint Benedict described it as listening deeply to a text "with the ear of our hearts" (quoted in Lichtmann 2005, 22). It is reading as a meditative activity—as a way to expand consciousness and discern wisdom. This makes it particularly appropriate for consideration by both teachers and students.

The actual practice of *Lectio Divina* entails sitting in contemplation, open to the possibility of being transformed by a text. This requires becoming porous, allowing the chosen text to enter all the way to one's center, and, in so doing, to experience oneself as an open question, ready to receive whatever gifts a text may offer.

Bill Arney, a professor at Evergreen College, uses a secular version of *Lectio Divina* to help his students dig deeply into texts. My somewhat modified version of Arney's *Lectio* format begins with the selection of a text by a teacher or student. For example, recently in a workshop for teachers that I was leading, I choose David Orr's text, "What's an Education for?" which I find to be both provocative and inspiring. The teachers read the text ahead of time and then we gathered in a circle, each holding a copy of Orr's essay on our lap. I invited everyone to sit in silence for several minutes so that we could all have time to reflect on the reading. I asked each person to select and read a one- to three-sentence passage that had moved them. This was followed by another period of silence to reflect on what each person had said.

Then, I invited someone to suggest a passage from the reading that seemed to encompass in content and spirit all the passages that had just been read. Suggestions were made by simply reading a passage—either one that had already been read or a new one—with no elaboration or justification. Sometimes in *Lectio* after just one passage is read, there is agreement that this selection captures the group's sentiments. On other occasions, as happened on this day, it is necessary to read several different passages from the text—each one followed by a silence—until a sense of unity is achieved.

Once we had agreed on a passage, I read it aloud several times, suggesting that we all simply allow the text to brush against us like a soft breeze, paying attention to any images, feelings, emotions, symbols, shapes, tastes, movements, or sounds that bubbled up from inside us. The idea, I explained, is to let the text work on us, opening to how it resonates within us (Hart 2004).

As the silence deepened, I asked the teachers to reflect on the one word or phrase from the passage that was most important for them and to share this word or phrase without any elaboration. Then, the passage was read again, followed by several more minutes of silence during which I suggested that we all listen, individually, for *what the text was saying to us*. In due time, each person shared his or her understanding by completing the open sentence, "The text is telling me _____."

In the final stage of our *Lectio*, I read the passage once more, again followed by silence during which we listened for *what the text was inviting us to do.* Eventually, each person shared his or her understanding by completing the open sentence: "The text is inviting me to _____ ." Our *Lectio* ended as it had begun, with several minutes of silence. (Adapted from Arney.)

Some may worry that providing space for contemplation in the classroom is tantamount to bringing religion or spirituality into school, but contemplation—sitting in silence, looking inward, pondering deeply, observing the workings of the mind—is simply a means of cultivating understanding, even wisdom.

Though I am still in the early stages of exploring *Lectio Divina*, I believe that this practice is a form of devotion to ourselves, to each other, and to something grander than ourselves. My mentor in this exploration, though she doesn't know it, is Maria Lichtmann, professor of philosophy and religion at Appalachian State University. In Lichtmann's view (elaborated in her book *The Teacher's Way*) one of the tasks of a teacher is to "read" the "text" of her student's lives. In this vein, she asks: "What if we [teachers] were to see our students as possessing a *story* that we need to read . . . What if their stories were as real to us as the subjects we teach . . . Then our teaching would become a *lectio divina*, a sacred reading of the stories in our students" (34).

In sum, the question underlying *Lectio Divina* is always, "What am I to learn here?" Thus, in order to participate fully, one has to be ready to be changed by the text. If we, as teachers, are to take Lichtmann's words to heart, we must also be ready to be changed by our students.

Exploration 6. Going Public with Questions: Strategic Questioning

Questions aren't just things to be explored within the confines of the classroom. Once teachers and students are awakened to the power of questions, they can engage people in their cities and towns using an exercise called Strategic Questioning.

Strategic Questioning emerged in the early 1980s when Fran Peavy, then in her fifties, asked herself the question, "What might I do to foster world peace?" With time an answer came—Peavy would *listen*! She left the United States and traveled around the world. Arriving in a new city, Peavy would simply sit on a park bench and post a cloth sign that read: "American Willing to Listen!" All it took was this simple invitation, and people came to sit and talk to her. Peavy mostly listened, but she sometimes offered questions. With time, she discovered that certain types of questions had the power to extend and deepen her listening while also deepening the other person's self-understanding. Eventually, she characterized these powerful types of questions as "strategic" (Peavy 2001).

Strategic questions, according to Peavy, are explicitly designed to help move people away from stuck places in their lives. In other words, they are questions that create movement inside one's heart and mind and, in so doing, usher forth new possibilities.

I was introduced to this practice in a workshop that Peavy led in Seattle in 2001, a short time after the September 11th attacks. After a morning session where Peavy introduced us to the theory and practice of Strategic Questioning, she sent us out in pairs to a nearby shopping mall to ask strangers how their lives had changed since 9/11.

Arriving at the mall, my companion and I mustered our courage and approached a woman who sat on a bench, sipping a soft drink. We introduced ourselves and explained that we were participants in a workshop focusing on questioning techniques. The woman—on a lunch break from the beauty parlor where she worked—agreed to talk with us. In response to our questions about her life since 9/11, she spoke of how she had become a kind of therapist as the angst and fear that her clients were feeling in the aftermath of 9/11 surfaced and gushed out in the relative safety of the beauty parlor. She confided that she enjoyed being useful in this new way. When we asked her what she was learning about herself in this time of turmoil, she spoke of her desire to help others. When we inquired about the kind of service she felt most strongly called to, she became quiet. After a long pause, she smiled sheepishly and said that she might like to teach fifth grade. "I love being around kids," she declared. This led us to ask questions to help her explore what stood in the way of her dream.

We spoke with several other people at the mall that day. Each time we were surprised by the heartfelt quality of their responses to our questions. I since have discovered that it is possible to engage in Strategic Questioning in any setting. For example, while I was writing this chapter, Mike, a recent Penn State graduate in biology, called to talk about his difficulty in figuring out how to take his biology major into the workplace.

My first thought was, "This kid should go to graduate school if he hopes to get a good job in biology" but I resisted the temptation to ask, "Have you considered graduate school?" Why? Because, with that question, I would be saying, in effect, "I, Chris, think you should go to graduate school." I also was careful to avoid "yes-no" questions like "Did you enjoy studying genetics?" because such questions tend to narrow the latitude of response. Instead, I decided to ask Mike more general, open-ended questions like:

What do you value most in life?

As you consider the future, what causes your heart to contract in fear?

What do you understand to be your deepest purpose in life?

Looking back over your college years, what were your most exciting learning moments?

What is the most important thing about being you?

In what ways, if any, does any of this relate to Biology?

Mike talked freely, welcoming these kinds of questions. I simply listened. When I asked him, "What do you most value in life?" Mike became silent. I was tempted to jump in by rephrasing my question, but I have learned that when a question is met with silence, it usually means that it has caused the receiver to turn inward. Though Mike had no answer in that moment, it was possible that, given enough time, this question would take on a life of its own, pointing Mike toward his calling in life.

As my conversation with Mike unfolded, it was clear that he had lots of ideas about what he might do with his life. His stuck place was that he couldn't decide which path to pursue. In truth, I had no idea what was best for Mike. Only he knew that. My part was simply to trust that the answers resided in him. As our conversation continued, I endeavored to ask questions in such a way that energy, thought, and creativity could emerge from within him—questions such as:

What makes this moment of indecision most difficult for you?

What obstacles do you see?

How is this moment similar to other moments of indecision in your life?

What are your biggest fears about making a decision?

What question, if answered, would make a difference in allowing you to move forward?

What support do you need to continue to explore options?

Who might you talk to in your quest for clarity?

Throughout our conversation, I kept my queries simple, avoiding convoluted two- and three-part questions. The ideal question draws no attention to itself; it is like a diver who enters the water without making a splash (Peavy 2001).

Though Peavy calls this practice Strategic Questioning, to be successful, it requires deep listening because a question, no matter how "strategic," goes no-

Consider the possibility that each of us, whether we happen to know it or not, has a unique calling. Theologian Frederick Buechner (1993) describes a life calling as that place "where our deepest gladness and the world's hunger meet."

Here's a way to discern your calling based on three *strategic questions*. To begin, take a piece of paper and make three columns. Then, close your eyes, bring your attention to the heart region in your chest, and breathe deeply. Once you are feeling relaxed, ask the first question: "What are the things in my life that bring me deep joy and lasting satisfaction—things that feed my heart?" Write down whatever comes to mind in the first column.

When you are ready, ask yourself the second strategic question: "What things occurring in my family, my community, my world, cause my heart to ache with compassion?" Allow yourself to settle into this question. As answers come, write them down in the third column.

To conclude your investigation, look over your two lists and ask: "Where are the places where my deepest gladness (column 1) and the world's hunger (column 3) meet?" In the middle column, note down your responses to this question. Don't limit yourself by judging whether your responses are practical or doable. Just let your heart and imagination run free. It is in this middle column that you will get clues to your calling.

where unless the person asking it holds no agenda save the commitment to listen with full attention and an open heart. As Peavy observes, "There are times when we truly listen, usually when we sense ourselves to be in danger. We stop in our tracks, our ears prick up and we listen as if our lives depend on it. The listening required for Strategic Questioning is like that: We need to listen as if someone's life depends on it—because it may" (2001, 9).

When I lead students in Strategic Questioning, I choose a general theme. In an education course the goal might be to engage the public around their relationship with education; in an agriculture course, their relationship with food; in an ecology course, their relationship with their environment. (See guide in the box.) The focus is always on relationship—for example, how people make sense and meaning of education, the environment, history, and so on in the context of their own lives.

After going out in public and engaging in Strategic Questioning, my students usually return to the classroom filled with excitement. Often they are surprised by the openness and thoughtfulness of those they have approached with their questions. As they reflect, they realize, in many cases, that their assessments of the American public are based largely on what they have absorbed through

STRATEGIC QUESTIONING GUIDE ON THE ENVIRONMENT

Getting Started

- Find a partner.
- Go to a public place—library, park, coffee shop, hotel lobby.
- Introduce yourself. Explain that you are taking a class and that this is an assignment.
- Perhaps start with, "There has been a lot in the news lately about the environment. What are your thoughts on the condition of the environment, in general?"
- Next, move into the Background Questions.

Background Questions

Observation Questions—Examples
- What do you read/hear in the media about the environment and what information do you trust?
- What additional information would you like to have?

Analysis Questions—Examples
- What do you think are the reasons for the current state of the environment?
- What effect is all of this having here and around the world?

Feeling Questions—Examples
- What is it about the current state of the environment that most concerns you?
- How does this concern of yours leave you feeling?

Strategic Questions

Vision/Change Questions—Examples
- How would you like the condition of the environment to be addressed?
- What might it take to bring the current environmental situation toward your ideal vision?
- What forces in our society push against this ideal vision?

Support/Action Questions—Examples
- What would it take for you to work on just one piece of your vision?
- What support would you need to take one small step toward your vision?
- What might your first step be?

—Adapted from Peavy 2001

the media, especially television, and that the media does not offer a flattering picture. By going out to meet the "stranger," offering generous questions, and listening with an open heart, students receive an unexpected gift—a more compassionate view of their fellow Americans.

My own discovery—the gift I receive in placing questions and curiosity at the center of my teaching and of students' learning—is that student's possess immense curiosity waiting to be unleashed. Once unleashed, this curiosity acts as a fountain of youth providing life and energy—a healing elixir—to my aging teacher soul.

Wrap-up

> I want to beg you, as much as I can, dear sir, to be patient toward all that is unsolved in your heart and try to love the questions themselves like locked rooms and like books that are written in a very foreign tongue. Do not now seek the answers, which cannot be given you because you would not be able to live them. And the point is, to live everything. Live the questions now. Perhaps you will then gradually, without noticing it, live along some distant day into the answer.   —R. M. RILKE 1993, 33–35

Early in my teaching career, when I would pause during a class to ask students if they had any questions, I did so with ambivalence, tinged with fear. I was afraid because I believed that it was my job as the teacher to have answers to all of my students' questions. If I lacked answers, I feared I would be judged as incompetent. Now, I see it differently. These days, each time I invite my students to speak their questions, I give up my need to control what will happen next, thereby creating space for the unexpected. I understand that to embrace questions is to embrace the unknown.

I am learning that by introducing explorations like those offered in this chapter, it is possible to create a classroom culture that is question friendly. This is no small matter! Questions are the catalysts for learning; they provoke *movement*; they yield *change*.

In the end, the world that we create is determined, to a significant degree, by the quality and boldness of our individual and collective questions. Encouraging students to become fearless questioners means applauding them not so much for the correctness of their answers as for the audacity of their questions.

For teachers, transforming the contemporary classroom's pervasive fear of questions and preoccupation with answers into a school culture that celebrates and delights in questions is a monumental, yet utterly worthwhile, task. The work begins by cultivating the belief that each student has buried, deep inside, important questions that are worthy of attention. Those questions emerge, provided we create a trust-filled climate that is hospitable to questions, a climate that ultimately leads young people to live *their* questions.

CHAPTER FOUR

Seeing Ourselves with New Eyes

Relationship with Self

Don't forget who you really are. And I'm not talking about your so-called real name. All names are made up by someone else, even the one your parents gave you. You know who you really are. When you're alone at night, looking up at the stars, or maybe lying in your bed in total darkness, you know that nameless person inside you . . . Your muscles will toughen. So will your heart and soul. That's necessary for survival. But don't lose touch with that person deep inside you, or else you won't really have sur-vived at all.   —L. SACHAR 2003, 88

As a teacher and ecologist, I've long believed that all the destruction, violence, and hatred scarring the world around us is a direct reflection of the angst, alien-ation, and anger seething within us. In other words, the outer world we create, both individually and collectively, mirrors directly our inner world. In this same vein, I see it as self-evident that the quality of the relationship we have with ourselves is a key determinant of the quality of all the other relationships in our lives. If we see ourselves as flawed and unlovable, our relationships with others will likely be flawed—pocked with blame, complaint, argument, and fear. If we can muster the understanding and courage to behold ourselves as fundamentally good—to see ourselves with unconditional love and self-acceptance—we can create the conditions for dissolving the judgment and fear that contaminates the larger world in which we dwell. Plutarch expressed this view long ago when he wrote: "What we achieve inwardly will change outer reality."

Young people are open to invitations to gaze inward. In my experience, most yearn to be guided into deeper relationship with themselves, with their hearts and passions. They seek a place in the world that is full of meaning and satisfac-tion. But, although they yearn to be happy, to love themselves, there is often little in their lives that has convinced them of their unconditional lovability. Even less has it been demonstrated how each of us can be the source of the very love and acceptance that we long for.

In the end, coming to full-hearted self-acceptance requires seeing ourselves with new eyes, hearing ourselves with new ears, and quieting our minds while opening our hearts sufficiently to allow our essential being to simply be.

As a way of illustrating this "new eyes" perspective, I share with my students the following story told by Martha Beck (2001) about a time in college when she and her artist friends hired models to pose for them.

> Most of the people we got to pose were college students with bodies that matched the social ideal—slender, fit, perfectly proportioned. After all, who else would risk standing naked in a roomful of strangers? And then, one day, we got somebody really different.
>
> She looked well over sixty, with a deeply lined face and a body that was probably fifty pounds heavier than her doctors would have liked. She'd had a few doctors, too, judging from her scars. Shining purple welts from a cesarean section and knee surgery cut deep rifts in the rippled adipose fat of her lower body. Another scar ran across one side of her chest, where her left breast had once been.
>
> When she first limped onto the dais to pose, I felt so much pity and unease that I physically flinched. But we were there to draw her, so I picked up a pencil. As I began to draw this maimed old woman, the most amazing thing happened. Within five minutes, she became a person of absolutely wondrous beauty. She didn't look like a supermodel; she didn't have to. Her body, in and of itself, was as beautiful as a piece of polished driftwood, or a wind-carved rock, or a waterfall . . .
>
> When this perceptual shift happened, I was so surprised that I stopped drawing and simply stared. The model seemed to notice this, and without turning her head, looked straight into my eyes. Then I saw the ghost of a smile flicker across her face, and I realized something else: She knew she was beautiful. She knew it and she knew that I'd seen it. (78–79)

By loving herself unconditionally, this woman demonstrated to Beck and her young artist friends what full-hearted self-acceptance looks like and, in the process, challenged them to restructure their understanding of reality—and of beauty.

The Mood of Unlove

All the most intractable problems in human relationships can be traced back to "the mood of unlove," a deep-seated suspicion most of us harbor within ourselves that we cannot be loved, or that we are not truly lovable, just for who we are. This basic insecurity makes it hard to trust in ourselves, in other people, or in life itself.   —J. WELLWOOD 2006, 4

The mood of unlove that Wellwood describes is pervasive in our culture. It is evident in how we treat our bodies, how we look outside ourselves to praise and material perks for validation, and how susceptible we are to those who would use fear to manipulate our thoughts and actions. Perhaps nowhere is the mood of unlove more poignantly revealed than in the way that we talk to ourselves—that is, in the stream of subvocal speech constantly running through our minds. As a way of illustrating this seemingly ever-present "inner dialogue," imagine the case of Jill, a new college student on campus going to her first fraternity party. Entering the fraternity house, Jill's self talk might sound something like this:

I don't see anyone I know.
My dress is too short.
I'm dressed like a slut.
I really want a beer but if I start drinking I'll get drunk.
I can't control myself.
Ugh (seeing herself in bathroom mirror), my face looks all shiny and goofy.
I feel so out of place.
Maybe I should just leave; no one would notice.
No, I'm going to go over to say hi to Joann and her boyfriend.
Hmmm, Joann acts like she doesn't really want to talk to me.
Why am I so boring?
I always say such stupid stuff.
I'm an outsider here.
I need a drink to calm down.

This kind of mind chatter is probably familiar to anyone who has walked into a party and felt ill at ease. Each of us likely has our own version that occurs in some setting where our feelings of anxiety or insecurity or insufficiency flare up. Yet, chances are that not one of us would ever say to another some of the disparaging things that we regularly say to ourselves. In the example above, Jill likely would never say to a friend, "You can't control yourself," or "You look goofy," or "You're dressed like a slut," or "You say such stupid stuff." In fact, Jill would probably only speak this way to someone she disdained. If Jill were on friendly terms with herself, her self-talk would be kind, supportive, and understanding rather than ridiculing, chastising, and shaming (Huber 2000).

Psychologists estimate that our self-talk averages fifty words per minute or some three thousand words per hour. This mind chatter is composed of a mix of judgments, observations, doubts, fears, hopes, convictions, anxieties, and more (Holden 2005). Calling this chatter "the voice in your head," Byron Katie (2005) reminds us of the intimate relationship, too often unacknowledged and unscrutinized, we have with ourselves: "Wherever you go, whomever you are with, the voice in your head goes with you, whispering, nagging, enticing. When you wake up in the morning, your thoughts wake up with you. They follow you to the bathroom, get into your car when you do, and come back home again with you. Whether or not someone is waiting for you at home, your thoughts will be there waiting for you. Your most intimate relationship is the one you have with your thoughts" (11–13). What is the tone and content of *your* self-talk? Is the voice inside your head like a courtroom, filled with self-judgment and prohibitions, or is it like a cozy living room, suffused with gentleness and hospitality? Loving, or its opposite?

Psychologist and Buddhist teacher Tara Brach refers to the tendency toward self-loathing in Western culture as *the trance of unworthiness*: "When we are in the *trance* [we are] caught up in our stories and fears about how we might fail; we are living in a waking dream that completely defines and delimits our experience of life . . . Inherent in [this] trance is the belief that no matter how hard we try, we are always, in some way, falling short" (2003, 6).

As a quick way of checking whether you have fallen into the trance of unworthiness, take a moment and ask yourself: Do I accept my body as it is? Do I accept my mind as it is? Do I accept my emotions and moods as they are? Am I at peace with myself? Am I free of judgments and jealousy? Is my life good enough just as it is? Am I doing enough? If you answer "No," to these kinds of questions, consider this as a sign that you are caught, to some degree, in the trance of unworthiness (Brach 2003).

An important step in breaking free of this trance is to fearlessly explore how it is that we, to varying degrees, have internalized the message that we're not completely lovable just as we are. Part of the answer may lie in the biblical narrative of original sin. This story, deeply embedded in the Western psyche,

How do you see human beings? Are we essentially evil, fundamentally good, or somewhere in between? What about you? Do you experience yourself as someone who is sinister, malicious, and hateful, or basically sincere, honest, and well meaning?

If you are not sure, consider: What do you do when you see a child fall and cry? Do you laugh or do you experience concern? What about if you hear news that three young people from your local high school went out drinking and were killed in a car wreck? Would you say "it serves them right," or would you feel a measure of sadness? And what about your daily encounters around town and at work? Are you mostly surrounded by evil people or decent people?

Now, go further and call to mind times when you found yourself in a crisis situation and were being called upon to extend help. Did you run away and refuse to help or did you help as best as you were able? If our basic nature were evil, how do you explain the fact that we hear reports, almost daily, about people risking their lives to save a stranger who was drowning, buried in an avalanche, trapped in a burning building, or wounded on a battlefield? Clearly, the evidence of our innate goodness abounds if we care to look.

leads many (even agnostics) to accept, often unconsciously, the proposition that humans are inherently flawed—prone to being bad, lazy, mean, selfish. Rather than passively accepting this view, what happens if you consider the evidence for yourself?

Might it be that our inability to know, deep in our bones, that we are lovable, just as we are, is the core wound that we all carry to varying degrees? Could it be that this wound lies at the root of all the hate and violence that we see in homes, communities, nations, and the world as a whole? If so, what role, if any, might parents and teachers play in mitigating the effects of this wound?

The work of "mitigation" is daunting, no doubt, in so far as it is unusual to find in our culture a young person (or an adult for that matter) who knows herself to be lovable just as she is—who is not trapped in the "mood of unlove." Media messages, parenting practices, and schooling procedures convey the message to kids, in subtle and not so subtle ways, that they are only provisionally, or conditionally, lovable.

Just consider the types of prohibitions and scoldings that a child might hear in a typical day: *No, you must not do that! Listen to me! Stop that right now! Don't speak like that! You should be ashamed of yourself! You are being a nuisance! Get yourself under control! I don't know what I am going to do with you!* Add to this the barrage of TV messages aimed to make kids (as well as adults) believe that they need all manner of nonessential *stuff* to be happy, acceptable, whole.

Hearing this chorus of messages, it is easy for a child to conclude, consciously or otherwise, that: *Something's wrong with me! I am not worthy of love and acceptance just as I am! I have shortcomings that must be fixed if I am to receive the love I want.* In the face of this self-assessment, most children internalize the messages and mandates from the adults in their lives out of fear of losing their approval, love, and support. Some might consider this effective child training, as now the child is behaving as adults expect her to. The tragic effect of this approach, however, is that it severs the child's connection to her authentic inner voice—her genuine self. Rather than looking inside to determine her true feelings and how to act, she becomes conditioned to rely on outside sources, first parents and, later, teachers, for approval. In the act of becoming a "people pleaser," a solid foundation for a wholesome and loving relationship with herself is undermined.

Schooling, coming as it does in the first two decades of a child's life, cannot help but significantly affect, for better or worse, a young person's relationship with herself. There is much about the structure of conventional schooling—the sorting and tracking of students, the testing, the control from above, the overt and covert forms of coercion, the separation from much of what is real and vital—that endangers, rather than nourishes, wholehearted self-acceptance.

As teachers, we have the power to extend unconditional acceptance and affirming love to our students and in the process to help shepherd them toward fuller self-acceptance. There are thousands of stories about the teacher who took the kid who was lost or angry or sullen and turned him or her around. The gift that the teacher offered in such cases was the ability to see through the child's outward façade to the goodness and unique intelligence that invariably lies at the core of each child. But here is the catch: We can only help young people cultivate robust and compassionate self-acceptance to the extent that we, as teachers, are on this same path of self-discovery, self-knowing, and self-love.

Becoming Aware of Our Conditioning

> Although it isn't fun for anyone, most people still manage to go through their entire lives thinking they are fundamentally incomplete and flawed and believing that they must struggle in order for their lives to be of any real value.
>
> —A. CHILDS 2008, 136

The first step in the journey toward self-knowledge involves becoming aware of our conditioning. This is challenging because most, if not all, of what we think, feel, and believe is socially conditioned. Huber offers a window into the origins of our conditioning through this short, guided reflection.

> Imagine the experience of a newborn infant. Imagine not being able to discriminate sights, sounds, smells, and sensation; not knowing what anything is or what anything means or how things go together; and having no idea who people are or what is good, bad, right, wrong, helpful, or dangerous. Picture not only not knowing that you are you, but not even knowing that you are a you. Imagine that there is nothing "other," no one "else." Everything is one big, undifferentiated "this" with no "that," no separation, no spaces, no end of me and beginning of you—just "we." Everything is equal. Everything is the same. All is one. Now, think about your reality, and consider for a moment that everything you have experienced in your life since you were an infant—the entire universe as you know it—is a systematically conditioned program of beliefs and assumptions that you have been taught. (2000, 23)

If you struggle with Huber's assertion, it may be because you, like the rest of us, have been conditioned to be suspicious of the very idea of conditioning. Aren't we Americans free? Actually, if you look, you will realize that we are not nearly as free as we think. The great irony is that we have been *conditioned* to believe that we are free when, in fact, the freedom that we enjoy is often superficial. We are free to go where we please and to choose from among twenty-eight flavors of ice cream, but often our minds are comprehensively shackled with limiting beliefs imprinted on us by our culture. In short, it is likely that freedom in our thinking is partial at best.

Given the pervasiveness of our conditioning, virtually no part of our thoughts are left untrammeled. "You see what you're taught to see, feel what you're taught to feel, hear what you're taught to hear, do what you're taught to do, and believe what you're taught to believe" (Huber 2007, 52). In other words, all our so-called beliefs and values—all of our standards around integrity, honesty, cleanliness, punctuality, generosity, discipline—are the result of our conditioning. One way of exploring conditioning, on a personal level, is to complete a series of open sentences like the following:

I should . . .
It's not OK to . . .
I don't like people who . . .
Having kids is . . .

Work is . . .
What matters most in life is . . .
Money is . . .
People need to . . .
To be happy I need . . .
Rich people are . . .

Our responses to these kinds of prompts are the result of our conditioning. So, for example, if you complete the open sentence, "To be happy, I need . . . " with the phrase "lots of money," this response is born of your conditioning. Of course, once you become aware of this, you can choose to examine your response—your conditioning—by asking questions like: Is it really true that I need lots of money to be happy? Who says so? What about those times when I was happy and almost penniless? (Huber 2000). We need not remain totally at the mercy of our conditioning.

Beneath Your Conditioning, Who Are You?

I am pure Awareness. I have a mind, but "I" am not just my thoughts. I have
emotions, but "I" am not just these emotions. I have a body but "I" am not
just this body. What remains after disidentifying from body, mind, and senses
is our essence of being that is unborn and always present.

—R. MILLER 2005, 65

It is possible to be born, to grow old, and to die without ever engaging, in a sustained way, the question, "Who am I?" In the absence of serious reflection, the default answer will be, "I am simply the sum total of my conditioning." This matters, for if we are stuck for our entire lives with only a shallow understanding of ourselves, then our capacity to love ourselves will be correspondingly shallow, for the simple reason that it is hard to love someone lacking in substance, depth, and authenticity. Absent robust self-love, our capacity to extend respect, acceptance, and love to each other and to Earth—the planet that sustains us—is necessarily compromised.

As a way of exploring this question, "Who am I?" consider the words of philosopher and wisdom teacher Wu Wei Wu.

Why are you so unhappy?
Because 99% of what you think,
And everything you do,

Is for yourself,

And there isn't one. (2002, 7)

Most people understand and go along with the first part of this text—it may well be that 99 percent of what most of us think and do centers on ourselves! But when they come to the final sentence, they often balk. Could it really be that what we normally take for the *self* isn't the *self* at all?

As a starting point for exploring Wu's proposition, make a list of all those things that constitute your personal identity. Begin with the open sentence: "I am _____ ," and then fill in the blank. And then do it again: "I am _____ ," and again: "I am _____ ," and again and again, until you have captured, to your satisfaction, all the facets of who and/or what you understand yourself to be.

Now, if what Wu Wei Wu says is true, then all of what you have written—all that you have been conditioned to believe you *are*—is *not*, in fact, who you are! Let's dig deeper.

Are You Your Possessions?

Children understandably identify with things—my toy, my bike. Over time, my toy becomes my car, my house, my boat. If we are not careful, we end up mistaking our possessions for who we are. This is an easy trap to fall into because from childhood on we are barraged with messages that say, in one way or another, "The best way to ensure happiness is to have lots of cool stuff." In the grip of this belief, it is tempting to try to fulfill our essential needs for community, love, relationship, participation, and meaning by acquiring more and more material possessions.

One way to explore if you suffer from this form of mistaken identity is to make a list of all of your significant possessions, and then to consider the following questions (from Tolle 2005):

- Are there things on your list that you designate with the word *my*? For example, is it "the" car or "my" car? "the" tools or "my" tools?
- In cases where the object is best denoted with "my," how does the possession of that thing leave you feeling with regard to people who lack this possession—e.g., Important? Superior? Guilty?
- How are you left feeling in cases where someone else has a better version of something (e.g., spiffier car) than you?
- Finally, how would it affect your sense of self-worth and well-being if you were to lose one of your prized possessions?

Here is the point: When we speak in terms of "my" house and "my" land (or even "my" classroom) we delude ourselves into thinking that these things are part of who we are. The reality is that these things, appearances aside, have nothing to do with who we are. You are *not* your possessions! If you allow this to really sink in, you will likely experience a sense of expansion and spaciousness. This is the result of breaking free from a socially conditioned deception that keeps you from a deeper understanding of who you truly are.

Are You Your Body?

From an early age, most of us were conditioned to believe that our body is the most essential element of who we are. We easily misidentify our outer appearance for who we are. For example, when you express unhappiness because you are having a "bad-hair day" or because your nose is too big, you are making the mistake of imagining that your body attributes constitute who you are. Wrong! In fact, your physical body—that form that is constantly changing and that will grow old and die—is only you in the most superficial sense.

The essence of your body is not a physical form so much as an intense energy field. At first mention, this may seem a bit odd, even New Age. Yet, it is possible to experience this energy field and in so doing to move from your normal superficial outer-body awareness to a more genuine and substantive inner-body awareness.

If you'd like to explore this idea, simply bring your attention to your hands. Sense the energy, the aliveness, in your hands. Hold your palms facing each other about one foot apart and slowly bring your palms together, alert to the energy field created by your hands as they draw together. After sensing the aliveness in your hands—feeling your "inner hands"—move your attention to your feet, sensing the energy, the aliveness, in both your feet and your hands at the same time. Continue in this way, allowing this sense of inner awareness, inner energy, to extend to your arms, neck, head, and chest. As you do this, you will come to experience your inner body not as your body at all but simply and profoundly as life energy, the bridge between form (the physical body) and formlessness (Tolle 2005).

As you experiment with this way of experiencing your body, your sense of yourself may, again, become more spacious and free. That's the point! We grow into a fuller understanding and acceptance of who we are by becoming free of the limiting ways we have been conditioned to see ourselves.

Are You Your Beliefs?

As human beings, it is difficult to avoid identifying with our beliefs. After all, we have been conditioned to think that our beliefs define who we are. But consider this brief thought experiment: Think of something you believed in the past that you no longer believe today. Now, without that old belief of yours, are you still you—is the essence of your *youness* still present?

Beliefs are nothing more than opinions about things that we are not able to know about through direct experience. Absent our ability to know whether life exists on other planets or if reincarnation occurs or if a supernatural being (e.g., "God") exists, we can formulate beliefs about these things. But we don't need to do this; instead, we could simply dwell in a state of *not knowing*.

Living in a state of not knowing, rather than adhering rigidly to opinions, leads to personal growth and freedom. If you doubt this, consider doing this mini-experiment. When you hear someone expressing an opinion (belief) that you disagree with, pause and catch yourself. Rather than reacting and defending, try simply responding with, "That could be," and, in so doing, letting go of your attachment to your particular viewpoint. There is freedom in this perspective.

A related approach is to identify a strongly held personal position and then to ask yourself: "Would it be theoretically possible for someone to disagree with my position?" If it is possible, then you are dealing with a belief, one among several, perhaps many, other ways of seeing the world. Go further and experiment with literally letting go of your stance, taking note of the feelings—for example, fear, frustration, freedom—that are evoked. Through these kinds of explorations, you will stop confusing your opinions (your stories) with who you are and, in so doing, enter into a less ego-driven, and therefore more loving, relationship with yourself (Tolle, 2005).

Are You What You Do For a Living?

As teachers we run the risk, if we are not careful, of brainwashing our students into believing that success in life is determined by such things as the amount of money one makes, the number of degrees one accumulates, or the prestige of one's job title. None of these things has any direct bearing on genuine success, as spiritual director, Anthony DeMello, explains in the following vignette:

> A small time businessman, 55 years old, is sipping beer at a bar somewhere and he's saying, "Well, look at my classmates, they've really made it."

The idiot! What does he mean, "They made it?" They've got their names in the newspaper? Do you call that making it? One is president of the corporation; the other has become the Chief Justice; somebody else has become this or that.

But who determines what it means to be a success? Being the president of a corporation has nothing to do with being a success in life. You become president of a lunatic asylum and you are proud of it, even though it means nothing. Having a lot of money has nothing to do with being a success in life. *You're a success in life when you wake up!*

All the person striving for "success" is really worried about is what his children will think about him, what the neighbors will think about him, what his wife will think about him . . .

People who made it! Made what? Made asses of themselves. Because they drained all their energy getting something that was worthless. They're frightened and confused, they are puppets . . . They are controlled and manipulated . . . They are constantly tense and anxious. Do you call that human? And do you know why that happens? Only one reason: They identified with some label. They identified the "I" with their money or their job or their profession. That was their error . . .

If I change my profession tomorrow, it's just like changing my clothes. I am untouched. Are you your clothes? Are you your name? Are you your profession? Stop identifying with them. They come and go. (DeMello 1992, 75–76)

DeMello might be judged as ranting, but his words are a refreshing antidote to the myriad ways that our culture conveys a very narrow understanding to young people of what constitutes genuine success.

Success, as commonly understood in our culture—making a name for one-self, coming out on top of the pack—often undermines self-understanding and self-acceptance for two reasons. First, the success seeker allows society, and not his or her own inner compass, to define success; second, he or she defines success as a future event, failing to realize that success is nothing more, nothing less, than successfully being alive in the only moment available to us—the present moment. Consider the social wreckage—the destroyed relationships, neglected children, unethical actions—that lie in the wake of many so-called successful men and women. In the hot pursuit of success, it is easy to forget a very important lesson—namely, that the ends and means are one and the same. So, if we don't engender good will, health, happiness, and well-being in the pursuit of *success*, then the end, too, will be devoid of these essential qualities.

It was perhaps with these qualms in mind that another spiritual teacher,

Thomas Merton, offered this advice to students: "Be anything you like, be mad-men, drunks, and bastards of every shape and form, but at all cost avoid one thing: SUCCESS" (1985, 11). College professor David Orr amplified Merton's ad-monition when he wrote: "The plain fact is that the planet does not need more 'successful' people. But it does desperately need more peacemakers, healers, restorers, storytellers and lovers of every kind . . . It needs people of moral cour-age willing to join the fight to make the world habitable and humane. And these qualities have little to do with 'success' as our culture has defined it" (1994, 12).

The upshot of this questioning into our genuine identity is that we come to understand that though we *have* possessions, bodies, beliefs, and jobs, we are *not* our possessions, *not* our bodies, *not* our beliefs, *not* our job titles, and so forth. In effect, this inquiry allows us to begin to step free of our conditioning, shed-ding the personal and cultural stories that keep us entrapped in the "mood of unlove."

Accepting the Totality of Who We Are

To be nobody but yourself in a world which is doing its best, night and day,
to make you like everybody else means to fight the hardest battle which any
human being can fight, and never stop fighting.   —E. E. CUMMINGS 1966, 13

In the same way that we often over-identify with our surface characteristics (name, occupation, etc.), we also under-identify with, or even remain oblivi-ous to, significant aspects of who we are. The American poet Robert Bly has observed that we humans spend the first several decades of our lives stuffing 90 percent of who we are—the myriad components that constitute our whole-ness—into a long black bag that we drag behind us, and then we spend the rest of our lives attempting to retrieve and bring to light the contents of this black bag so that we might lighten our load. We drag this bag behind us like a literal shadow; it is black because we cannot readily discern its contents, and it is dragged because it is heavy and going through life with it drains much of our vitality (Plotkin 2003).

The contents of this long black bag are those parts of ourselves that make us unlovable to ourselves. In Jungian psychology these disowned parts constitute our "shadow." If we are serious in our pursuit of self-knowledge (a necessary condition for unconditional love and acceptance of ourselves), sooner or later, we will need to face off with our shadow.

Psychologist John Wellwood uses the image of a beautiful castle with thousands of rooms to describe the experience of early childhood and how it is that the shadow is created. As little children, we explore our glorious castle, room by room, giving full expression to each aspect of our unfolding selves. Each room of our castle—each emotion, each quality, each posture, each manner of expression—has its own gift to offer us. At this early stage, the concepts of *good* and *bad* do not exist. Everything simply is as it is; each room, each aspect of self, experienced and accepted just as it is.

Then one day, maybe you were only two years old, someone came to your castle and announced that one of your rooms was deficient and that if you wanted a perfect castle you would need to lock that room. Because you desired the love and approval of that person, you complied. With time others came, and they, too, passed judgment on your castle's various rooms. Some said certain castle rooms were too conservative; others complained that some of your rooms were too bold; others observed that certain rooms were not seen in any other castle, and so forth. Gradually, you locked off more and more rooms, relegating these areas—those essential aspects of yourself—to darkness and shame. Eventually, you were confining your life to just a few of your castle's rooms and even forgetting that those other rooms had ever existed (Wellwood 1996; Ford 1998).

Your castle, with its hundreds of rooms—one containing love, a second honesty, a third hope, a fourth passion, a fifth kindness, a sixth playfulness, a seventh patience, an eighth courage, and on and on—represents the enormity of who you are. Make no mistake, for each room in your castle holding a so-called praiseworthy attribute, there is an adjoining room containing it's opposite. Yes, in your castle exist rooms containing your capacities for hatred, deception, despair, passivity, selfishness, dourness, impatience, timidity, and on and on (Ford 1998).

What's the point of acknowledging in ourselves the presence of qualities such as selfishness, jealousy, deception, and pettiness—qualities that we have been conditioned to abhor? One reason is that in accepting those troubling aspects of ourselves, we give ourselves the gift of freedom. For instance, when I recognize and embrace that there is an aspect of me that I denote as "stupid"—that making mistakes that others might consider as stupid is part of who I am—I give myself the freedom to step out and take risks. If, on the other hand, I block myself off from the possibility of making mistakes, by keeping this aspect of me closed in the "black bag" that I drag behind me, my life may become safer, but it will also become more predictable, pinched, and boring.

There is another even more important reason for embracing the shadowy parts of ourselves, namely: What we refuse to embrace in ourselves, we are prone to project out onto the world in the form of judgment and intolerance. We look out at the world through the lens of our beliefs, assumptions, judgments, and preferences. Everything we see, think, and feel about the world is, really, a reflection of ourselves—of our inner world.

As a way of making this more concrete, imagine opening the newspaper to a story about someone—a criminal—whose actions you find sickening. "How egregious!" you think to yourself. Perhaps you think such a person should be locked away in prison for life. But then you pause and ask yourself: "What kind of adult would commit such a heinous act?" As I reflect on this question, I realize that it would probably be someone who is afraid, insecure, angry, confused, controlling, perverse, and who knows what else. Although I have never engaged in perverse or criminal activities, I can easily recognize times in my life when I have been fearful, insecure, angry, controlling, confused, and, yes, perverse. If I allow myself to go deeper and to imagine how I might behave had I grown up in a chronically abusive environment absent all love, I can't truly know what I would be capable of doing or refraining from doing. The point is not to excuse heinous actions. The point is that if we deny our own individual capacity for cruelty, we will project this denial outward in the form of cruel thoughts, judgments, and actions toward others. Indeed, "what we can't be with in ourselves, won't let us be" (Ford 1998).

None of this is to say that in reclaiming our shadow we should become thieves, bigots, or murderers. In fact, it is precisely when we *don't* acknowledge our shadow that our shadow energies build, sometimes busting outward as violent, even monstrous acts. As Judith (2004, 118) points out, "The greater the repression, the louder our shadow has to yell to be heard and the greater its chance to become demonic."

In sum, our shadow elements are like neglected children. The more we ignore them, the more they act out. By embracing the neglected parts of ourselves, we are able to reclaim the instinctual energies bound up in primal needs and desires. The goal is to evolve from a childish state to a mature state—from throwing temper tantrums to bringing awareness to the gifts contained in our shadow energies. The challenge is to bring the shadow into the light, not to surrender our consciousness to the shadow (Judith 2004). In such a light lies the potential to know and to love ourselves more fully.

Embracing Our Shadow

There comes a time—if we are to develop and flourish as self-actualizing human beings—when we have to unpack our shadow. A good place to start is by making a list of those things that you most love about yourself. Perhaps you love your capacity for compassion or your independence or your wit. Whatever it is, write it down. List as many of your wonderful qualities as you can. Then, next to each of your positive attributes, write down the opposite of that quality. For example, next to compassionate you might put cold-hearted; next to independent, dependent; next to intelligent, stupid; next to fun loving, dour, and so forth. Now, and this is the hard part, open yourself to the possibility that these opposites that you have listed are, in reality, essential parts of you—that they are, in fact, your core shadow qualities.

As a way of taking this further, pay special attention to all those things that other people do that really push your buttons. Ford (1998) suggests imagining that you have hundreds of different electrical outlets affixed to your chest, with each outlet representing a different quality—one outlet for boisterousness, another outlet for aggressiveness, another for kindness, and so on. There are plates over those outlets that correspond to those aspects of yourself that you fully accept. When someone you know exhibits one of these "acceptable" qualities, there is no charge, no electricity; you don't react. By contrast, the charged outlets point to aspects of yourself that you have not fully embraced.

Chances are that there will be a lot of overlap between the things that push your buttons on a daily basis and the list of your core shadow qualities. The reason for this, again, is that "what we find difficult or unacceptable *out there* is, to a significant degree, a projection outward of what we have learned to find unacceptable in ourselves. We want to rid ourselves of that annoying, cantankerous, obstinate, foolish, selfish, overbearing, egocentric, manipulative, lazy, arrogant, stupid individual because when that person is gone, we don't have to be aware of those parts of ourselves" (Huber, 2000, 178).

In my own life, I have discovered, time and again, that anything that pushes my buttons is pointing me toward something about myself that I have not been able to see, much less embrace. Too many times, for example, I have found myself frustrated in conversations that I find lacking depth and intimacy. I have judged these conversations as "boring." One day, I decided to step back and inquire into what this frustration of mine was all about. First, I asked myself, why this feeling? Why frustration? It was then that I realized that I was frus-

There is a Sufi tale about a philosopher who made a special appointment to meet with Nasrudin, a renowned Sufi teacher. At the designated hour the philosopher went to Nasrudin's home, but he was not there. In a fit of anger, the philosopher wrote in chalk the words "stupid oaf" on Nasrudin's door. When Nasrudin returned home, he realized his mistake and went immediately to the philosopher's house to seek forgiveness. Greeting the philosopher, Nasrudin explained, "I had forgotten our appointment but when I saw your name on my door, I remembered immediately."

Not finding Nasrudin at home, the philosopher might have concluded that he had been in an accident or was ill or had been called away by an emergency. Instead, Nasrudin's absence sparked the charged outlet "stupid oaf" on the philosopher's chest. Unable to fully embrace his own "stupid oafness," the philosopher, in effect, projected this judgment onto Nasrudin.

trated because I wanted conversations to have a certain outcome—specifically, I wanted them to leave me feeling engaged, stimulated, excited. I considered if there might be situations in which a person I was talking with might find me to be boring. This question had a jolting quality. Me? Boring to someone else? Could it be? Yes!

In fact, on those occasions when I'm "caught" in a conversation with someone whom I regard as my intellectual superior, I often feel anxious—afraid that I will be unmasked as uninformed and/or ignorant. In these circumstances, my unacknowledged fear leads me to be withdrawn and constricted. In effect, I become the epitome of the *boring* conversation partner that has so often frustrated me. These, days, by recognizing and accepting my own capacity to be boring (especially when I am steeped in fear and insecurity), I am no longer as likely to judge others as boring. Without this judgment, I am left feeling more patient, compassionate, and relaxed in conversation. These open states of mind and heart, of course, create the necessary environment for genuine conversation.

Ford (1998) offers a helpful practice, in cases like mine, where one struggles to fully embrace a shadow characteristic. The practice is done in pairs and involves simply speaking a difficult-to-accept shadow quality to a partner. For me, this would mean saying, "I am boring," to a partner and then listening as my partner affirms, "Yes, Chris, you're boring." We would continue in this back-and-forth exchange until these words and this way of seeing myself—as having the capacity to bore others—no longer held any charge for me. I have found that this simple act of publicly speaking my shadow qualities breaks down, to a degree,

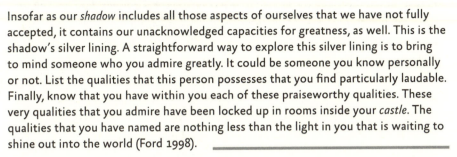

Insofar as our *shadow* includes all those aspects of ourselves that we have not fully accepted, it contains our unacknowledged capacities for greatness, as well. This is the shadow's silver lining. A straightforward way to explore this silver lining is to bring to mind someone who you admire greatly. It could be someone you know personally or not. List the qualities that this person possesses that you find particularly laudable. Finally, know that you have within you each of these praiseworthy qualities. These very qualities that you admire have been locked up in rooms inside your *castle*. The qualities that you have named are nothing less than the light in you that is waiting to shine out into the world (Ford 1998).

my resistance to embracing them and thereby contributes to self-acceptance as well as acceptance of the other. In the act of doing this, the unsavory nature of a shadow quality like boringness begins to dissolve.

In our failure to accept the totality of who we are, shadow and all, we remain mired in the "trance of unworthiness." There is probably no better teacher in the journey to self-acceptance than our shadow. Ultimately, by accepting that we have every aspect of humanity within us, we gain the capacity to extend compassion not only to ourselves but to other people, including, and especially, our students.

Questioning Our *Stories*: A Path to Self-Acceptance

Who would you be without your story?
You never know until you inquire.
There is no story that is you or that leads to you.
Every story leads away from you.
Turn it around; undo it.
You are what exists before all stories.
You are what remains when the story is understood.

—B. KATIE 2002

"Shadow" work leads to personal growth as we come to see the myriad ways that we project our internal dysfunction and suffering onto the outside world. This process is captured in the famous Jewish proverb: "We do not see things as they are but as we are." We go through our days creating stories about the other people in our lives—*My principal doesn't respect me; my students don't care about learning; the other teachers in my school aren't working as hard as I am.* Note how angry, isolated, or disempowered these kinds of stories leave you feeling.

In my work within classrooms and academic settings, I am amazed at how all of us—teachers and students alike—are constantly constructing stories (often with little awareness) and how these stories end up affecting us, for better or worse. Recently, I attempted to illustrate this dynamic to a group of students. It was the first day of class, and I arrived dressed in a coat and tie. I greeted everyone cordially and then offered a no-nonsense synopsis of the course. Then, I asked everyone to simply take a moment to share their initial observations and impressions of me. Though an admittedly unusual request, they obliged, saying, in effect, that I appeared to be a formally dressed, serious, middle-aged male who had taught this course before. Then I left the room (on the pretext that I had forgotten a handout). Outside, I quickly removed my necktie and replaced my sports coat with a black leather jacket. Then I wrapped a red bandana around my head. Returning to the room, I asked the students to once again observe me and share their observations and impressions. Suddenly, in light of my new garb, I was seen as a laid-back, aging, hippie professor who probably smoked weed.

Finally, I asked these students to share how their different stories (growing from their two sets of observations) might lead them to feel and to act. Some students admitted that seeing me in the hippie garb led them to feel anxious, and this feeling, in turn, might provoke them to drop the course. Meanwhile, other students conceded that the hippie outfit created intrigue and left them feeling excited and committed to sticking with the course. On this first day of class, I, in effect, had offered these students a way of understanding themselves by illustrating how their *observations* of my dress quickly morphed into judgments (*stories*) about me. They saw then how their stories affected how they *felt* and, ultimately, how they might *act* (e.g., stick with the course or drop it). It is *story*—an interpretation generated from observations—that is the key component of this sequence: Observation → Story → Feeling → Action. Our stories, once formulated, affect our feelings and actions.

Our stories create our reality both inside and outside the classroom. Recall the student Jill, attending her first fraternity party, whose stories about herself (that she was dressed like a slut, that she was boring, that she couldn't control her drinking, and so on) created a hellish reality for her. However, not one of us, Jill included, has to believe our stories. By questioning our stories—especially those that leave us feeling diminished and stressed—we can come to accept ourselves and to accept life just as it is. Consider this vignette from Byron Katie's book *Loving What Is*:

> Once, as I walked into the ladies' room at a restaurant near my home, a woman came out of the single stall. We smiled at each other and as I closed the door she began to sing and wash her hands. What a lovely voice! I thought. Then, as I heard her leave, I noticed that the toilet seat was dripping wet. How could anyone be so rude? I thought. And how did she manage to pee all over the seat? Was she standing on it? Then it came to me that she was a man—a transvestite, singing falsetto in the women's restroom. It crossed my mind to go after her (him) and let him know what a mess he'd made. As I cleaned the toilet seat, I thought about everything I'd say to him. Then I flushed the toilet. The water shot up out of the bowl and flooded the seat. And I just stood there laughing. In this case, the natural course of events was kind enough to expose my story before it went any further. (2002, 6–7)

For Katie the insight that she could end her personal suffering by simply ceasing to listen to her stressful thoughts (her upsetting "stories") came in a flash, after suffering for many years from chronic depression. One morning she awoke different, feeling joyful. Literally, from one day to the next all her beliefs about how things should or shouldn't be had fallen away. She felt an indescribable delight in everything—in love with life and herself. Then, she noticed that each time she had a new thought, she experienced a feeling—anxiety, fear, well-being, ease, happiness. This simple epiphany led Katie to begin paying careful attention to *all* her thoughts.

At first, she realized that just as her body was being breathed (i.e., breathing occurs involuntarily), she was also *being thought*, in so far as she was subjected to an unceasing stream of thoughts. Katie was particularly interested in catching, in the moment, the occurrence of thoughts that interfered with her wholehearted acceptance of herself and her life just as it was. These thoughts invariably had a complaining quality—something or someone wasn't OK the way it was; it had to be changed, improved, fixed. Rather than arguing with the way her life was presenting itself moment by moment, Katie wondered how it would be if she simply accepted—loved—reality just as it is? In the process, Katie realized that she didn't need to believe everything her thoughts told her. She was not obligated to her thoughts! Could this be true for all of us—that we need not accept everything our thoughts (stories) tell us?

Over time, Katie developed and refined a simple method of self-inquiry that allowed her to examine her thoughts and beliefs and, ultimately, to grow into genuine self-acceptance. An important step in her process of inquiry was to notice that whenever her thoughts were in someone else's *business*, she suffered. Imagine a teacher who has the thought, "My school principal should express his appreciation for me by praising me." The moment the teacher has this thought, she has entered into the principal's business, prescribing what he should be doing.

Going further, this teacher's upset and associated suffering result from her attachment to a thought/story that argues with reality. The simple reality is that her principal doesn't praise her. That's the truth! Extending praise is just not something this principal does; he may offer praise some day, but for now, he doesn't. In acknowledging "what is," the teacher's suffering subsides. Rather than waiting for her principal's praise, the aware teacher returns to her own business, directly offering herself the support and kindness that she longs for. This is self-acceptance in action. As the teacher learns to satisfy her own needs for appreciation, some day she may even gain the security and bigness of heart to acknowledge her principal's efforts—to extend praise to him!

In sum, when you find yourself looking out at the world and seeing problems everywhere, know that this is, very likely, simply a projection of your own inner mental state. Katie (2002) compares this to what happens when the light from a projector (you) shines onto a blank screen (the world) and creates the illusion that there is a piece of lint (a problem) on the screen. In reality, the lint (the problem) is *not* on the screen (it's not out there in the world); rather, the lint is on the lens of the projector (it is in our eye) The problem is in our seeing! Once we realize that the "lint" is actually within us, we can remove it, thereby growing in self-understanding and acceptance.

The Work

Katie (2002) has developed a formal inquiry process that she calls The Work (www.thework.com) for inquiring into stories that separate us from ourselves and from others. The starting place in this process is to bring to mind someone with whom you are upset and then to capture your complaint with this person on paper, using what Katie calls the Judge Your Neighbor Worksheet. This worksheet consists of six questions:

1. Who angers, disappoints or confuses you, and why?
2. How do you want them to change? (What do you want them to do?)
3. What is it that they should or shouldn't do, be, think, or feel?

4. What do you need them to do in order for you to be happy?

5. What do you think of them? Make a list.

6. What is it that you don't want to experience with this person ever again?

In answering these six questions, the person doing The Work creates a series of statements. For example, imagine that you decide to do The Work on Marty, a high school student in your classroom, who is driving you nuts. You sit down with the six questions and rip away:

1. Who angers, disappoints or confuses you, and why? *I am angry at Marty because he doesn't pay attention to me; I am angry at Marty because he talks in class. I am disappointed in Marty because he is not trying.*

2. How do you want Marty to change? (What do you want him to do?) *I want Marty to respect me and listen to me. I want him to put more effort into his assignments. I want him to be more respectful.*

3. What is it that Marty should or shouldn't do, be, think, or feel? *Marty should sit still in his desk and stop looking out the window during class. He should stop talking in class. He should start using his talents and get serious about school.*

4. What do you need Marty to do in order for you to be happy? *I need Marty to pay attention and start applying himself.*

5. What do you think of Marty? Make a list. *I think Marty is self-centered, lazy, disrespectful, and rude.*

6. What is it that you don't want to experience with Marty ever again? *I never want Marty to disrespect me again by not paying attention in class or by disrupting class.*

You may have noted that some of these questions seem redundant. This ensures that the person filling out the worksheet has the opportunity to fully vent his or her upset.

The next step, after responding to the six questions, is to examine each statement by asking four simple questions:

1. Is your statement true?

2. Can you absolutely know your statement is true?

3. How do you react when you think that your statement is true?

4. Who would you be if you were able to reject the truth of your statement?

By way of illustration, let's examine the first statement above—"I am angry at Marty because he doesn't pay attention to me"—in light of these four questions. To make this more realistic, I suggest that, as you read along, you think of someone in your own life who is not paying attention to you and substitute this person's name for "Marty." (I'll substitute "X" here.)

Question 1. Is your statement true? Is it true that X isn't paying attention to you? Don't rush your answer to this question. Go inward and allow your heart to meet your mind: Is it true that X doesn't pay attention to you? Note that "true" doesn't mean "right" or "just" or "good"; it is not a moral assessment. Wait patiently for the truth to come to the surface. The focus is on the facts, on reality. Reality is what's true, what is in plain view.

Question 2. Can you absolutely know that your statement is true? Question 1 (above) is so important that it is asked a second time to coax the "story maker" to really dig deep and be as humble and honest as possible. The mind wants to be right; that's why it holds on so tightly to its thoughts and judgments. But in this case, ask: Can you absolutely know that X doesn't pay attention to you? Are there no examples that you can recall where X did pay attention to you?

Question 3. How do you react when you think your statement is true? This question is an invitation to investigate the cause and effect of thought. A good way to answer it is to make a list of how you react, feel, and treat others, especially X, when you hold as true the statement under investigation. So, how do you react to X when you hold onto the story that he or she doesn't pay attention to you? Your list might include things such as: I distance myself from X; I look away when X talks to me; I talk behind his back; I feel stressed, and so on.

Question 4. Who would you be if you were able to reject the truth of your statement? To respond to this question, it is helpful to imagine that the person you have judged is standing before you. You are looking into his eyes with your *story* about him. As you do so, you temporarily drop your story—your judgment—and, just for a moment you allow yourself to consider how your life would be if you could free yourself from the thought (in this case) that X doesn't pay attention to you. You might note things such as: I would feel light, clear, and happy; I would be willing to listen to X and help him out with his work.

The Work culminates with what Katie calls the "turnaround." This is when we consider that our statements about the other person might actually have something important to teach us about ourselves.

There are several possible turnarounds for the statement: "X does not pay

THE TURNAROUND: A CHANGE OF PERSPECTIVE

When we turn a situation around, we see it in a different light. You can have an embodied experience of what this feels like by simply lifting your right hand above your head and pointing your index finger straight up. Trace an imaginary circle with your finger in a clockwise direction. Continue tracing this circle clockwise while at the same time slowly lowering your arm and hand until you are now tracing the circle at the level of your chest and looking down on it. Even though you have continued to trace the circle in a clockwise direction, as you now look down, the circle will no longer be clockwise, but counterclockwise. While your finger is doing the same thing, your perspective has changed. At first this seems like some sort of trick; we may think that the world—reality—has somehow changed when, in fact, it is only our viewpoint that has changed. Turnarounds are like that. With a shift in perspective, we turn our way of seeing upside down (Kegan and Lahey 2001).

attention to me." The first is: "X *does* pay attention to me." Could this be true? The only way to find out is to pause and review your relationship with X to see if there have been times when X did pay attention to you? In conducting this review, you might discover that X has paid attention to you on many occasions, but there were a few times when you needed X's full and undivided attention and you didn't get it. Your story about X ignoring you is based on these few instances. (It is even possible that you have been replaying these instances over and over in your head, blotting out the truth that X often does pay attention). When the turnaround hits home, there is always a giant BINGO!

A second possible turnaround is: "*You* don't pay attention to X." What about this? Can you think of an instance or two where you weren't being attentive to X? You are certainly not extending kind attention to X if you are judging him, complaining about him, and/or separating from him. So, might this turnaround be as true as, or truer than, your original judgment of X?

A third turnaround is "*You* don't pay attention to *you*?" As you think about this, you might see that, in the context of your relationship with X, your condemning thoughts of X have not helped you. They have caused you to shut down around X and to withdraw from him, which leaves you feeling inattentive toward yourself—stuck in an emotional vortex, distant from yourself. Turnarounds are like mirrors. It is as if our minds, when we are judging others, often get things right, only backwards!

After finishing The Work on this first statement about Marty, the teacher would go on to the second statement, and so forth. In this example, the second statement is "I am angry at Marty because he talks in class." If it is verifiably true that Marty does talk in class, this doesn't mean that you can't do The Work. Rather, it means that you have to look at the unquestioned beliefs below your statement. In this case, your suffering comes not from Marty's talking per se but from your belief that Marty *shouldn't* talk in class. In other words, it is the story that you attach to Marty's talking that causes your suffering. Maybe you interpret Marty's talking as meaning that he doesn't respect you. With this clarity you could then do The Work on the statement, "Marty doesn't respect me," asking the four questions and considering possible turnarounds. Through this process, you might even learn that it is you who doesn't respect Marty. Gulp. Yes, in the end, it is always much more about us than the one we are pointing our finger at.

In sum, though The Work begins by "judging your neighbor," (e.g., the student Marty in our example), the process actually leads us toward accepting and even loving our neighbor and, just as important, to understanding, accepting, and loving ourselves by accepting our part in our upsets. The Work is an invitation to transcend our judgment-infested and conditioned ways of thinking. It is a call to embrace reality just as it is. Undoubtedly, this can be hard to do given all the suffering and strife in our world today. But when we think that things like war, rape, and violence should not exist, we are arguing with reality. These things, horrible as they are, do exist—until they don't! The challenge is to *turn around* our thinking and ask: Can I just end the *war* within me? Can I stop waging *war* and doing violence with *my* stories? If we end the hate and judgment and intolerance that resides in us—if we learn to love ourselves unconditionally— this will be the beginning of the end of war in the world (Katie 2002). Too, with a clear heart and mind, each of us is better equipped to take action beyond ourselves. Who better to lead the way than teachers?

Loving Ourselves by Taking Time to Be with Ourselves

It has become imperative to reclaim stillness, to find a resting place from
the furious pace at which everything is traveling, flowing, and hanging . . .
The faster the world moves "out there," the more important it is for us to
go slower "in here." The still place at the center is . . . the "I" of the storm.
Once we are here, now, present in the stillness, we can begin to comprehend
the swirling energies about us while staying firmly connected to our true and
authentic selves.   —B. CAMERON AND B. MEYER 2006, 36

It seems that the world is constantly pushing us to hurry up—to do more and more faster and faster. So the idea of slowing down—given the responsibilities of family, profession, and community—seems unrealistic and even counterproductive. And if we were to even grant ourselves time to simply *be*, the task, itself, holds challenge. To be still, to be silent, nondoing, unplugged, unavailable except to ourselves—whew! Who could bear such a task?

And, yet, can you imagine loving someone to whom you give neither time nor attention? No way. The path to healing the relationship each of us has to ourselves is paved with time—time to simply be and not do. Levoy (1997) calls such time *hushing* and compares such being to the experience of leaving a busy street and walking into the quiet of a cathedral. There you enter a different realm of time. There is no longer any hurry. You become still. Your mind chatter stops, and a space is created for deeper, more soulful feelings, intuitions, and leadings to arise.

Little in our everyday rounds conjures such a direct experience of solemnity, of calm. Yet, such hushing or contemplation has been recognized across time and space as a way of being that is fundamental to cultivating intelligence and wisdom. It is valued in all the world's wisdom traditions and takes many forms: meditation in Buddhism, contemplative prayer in Christianity, metaphysical reflection in Sufism, and the deep pondering of the Kabbalah in Judaism. Common to these practices is the intention to shake free from routine thought processes and, in so doing, to deepen awareness and self-understanding (Hart 2004).

Scores of empirical studies demonstrate that contemplative practices (in particular meditation), lead to benefits that include reduced blood pressure, improved concentration, expanded compassion, reduced anxiety, relief from addiction, alleviation of pain, improvements in memory, and improved performance in everything from sports and academic test taking to creativity (Murphy, Donovan, and Taylor 1997 in Hart 2004). Still, in our personal lives—and far worse in our school lives—we are mostly unaware of and unpracticed in this important life-sustaining activity.

One way to introduce yourself (or your students) to the practice of hushing is to give the following assignment: Find a quiet place, indoors or outside, and sit for ten minutes doing nothing—not reading, not talking on the phone, not listening to music. Just being! After your ten minutes is up, take some time to write about your experience.

This assignment to "just be" is difficult, especially at first. Some people find it boring, stressful, even scary. To some it even feels like a cruel form of solitary

confinement in that when we face our self, we risk discovering a kind of hollowness lying at the core of our being. For others, such simple "being" feels point-
less, a distraction from important doings that will yield some tangible result.

In actuality, "hushing," or sitting quietly, is an end unto itself. Indeed, to sit
with ourselves, absent all distractions, may be the most important act of self-love
we can enact.

Vietnamese monk Thich Nhat Hanh (1991) offers the following simple
breathing meditation for cultivating relaxation and a sense of groundedness:

> Breathing in I calm my body.
> Breathing out I smile.
> Dwelling in the present moment (in breath)
> I know this is a wonderful moment (out breath).

Reciting these lines while breathing in and out invites presence. Hanh writes,
"It is a joy to sit, stable and at ease, and return to our breathing, our smiling, our
true nature. Our appointment with life is in the present moment" (1991, 10).

Techniques such as hushing, centered breathing, or even a more developed
and disciplined meditation practice are all important in fostering new ways of
being and seeing. It is even possible to create one's own practices. Roger Walsh,
in his book *Essential Spirituality* (1999), has created the following lovely guided
meditation that has the power to give us access to a wise inner teacher, provided
we take the time to stop and pay attention:

> Close your eyes and relax. Imagine yourself in a beautiful place, perhaps your
> favorite beach, mountain, or garden. See yourself there and enjoy the feelings this
> special place evokes. In just a moment you are going to invite into that place an
> extraordinarily wise person. It may be a great spiritual teacher or it may be an un-
> known wise man or woman. Whoever it is, this person will embody qualities such
> as great wisdom, love, and complete acceptance of you just as you are.
>
> Invite this wise person into your place of beauty and introduce yourself. Take
> time to savor the experience of being in the presence of a person of deep wisdom
> and boundless love. What does it feel like to be with someone who understands
> and loves you completely? What fears and defenses melt into nothingness in the
> presence of someone who accepts you just the way you are?
>
> Here is an opportunity to learn and get advice about anything that concerns
> you. Take a moment to think of the questions you would most like to ask. Then
> ask your first question and sit quietly for the answer. There is no need to try to

Each of us was born knowing how to breathe. Observe a baby lying on her back, and you will see a model for good breathing. On the in-breath the child's lungs expand and her belly rises effortlessly; then on the out-breath her belly flattens as her lungs deflate. Remarkably, by the time most young people reach high school they have switched from this natural and healthful belly breathing to chest breathing. Do a check on yourself right now. Take a deep breath. If you are like many people, you will suck your belly in and tighten your abdominal muscles, while lifting and inflating your shoulders and upper chest. In healthy breathing, by contrast, the belly is soft and inflates outward because of the downward action of the diaphragm, while the upper chest stays down.

You can gain greater breath awareness by considering the following questions, while observing your breathing:

Where do you experience your breathing? Chest? Nostrils? Shoulders? Pelvis? Where does your breath originate?
What does your breathing feel like? Smooth? Jerky? Thick? Raspy? Rhythmic?
What about the depth of your breath? Deep? Shallow? In between?

These questions invite us to realize that there is more to observe about our breathing than just an in-breath and an out-breath (Farhi 1996).

make anything happen. Simply relax and allow the wisdom within you to respond. When you are ready, ask your next question, wait for a response, and continue with any further questions.

Next, ask the wise person if he or she has anything to tell you. Again, just relax and wait for an answer. Then ask if there are any questions the wise person has for you.

Finally, ask the wise person if he or she will be available to you in the future at any time you request help or do this exercise. Then express your thanks for the gifts of this meeting.

Now imagine yourself beginning to merge with the wise person so that your bodies, hearts, and minds melt into one. Actually you already are one, because the sage and the qualities such as love and wisdom are creations and part of your own mind.

Feel that you have absorbed the qualities of the wise person and explore the experience. What is it like to be wise? What does it feel like to be fearless and to have no need to defend yourself in any way? What is it like to feel boundless love and care for all people including yourself? And what does it feel like to accept and love yourself completely, just as you are?

After you have savored this experience, gently open your eyes. Try to make the transition slowly and gently so you can bring back the qualities you experienced.

Take a moment to reflect on the fact that these feelings—wisdom, fearlessness, love and acceptance—are not new or foreign to you. They are actually aspects of yourself that you projected onto the wise person. True, these qualities are not fully developed or always accessible to you yet, but they are available and await your attention to grow and flourish. (241–42)

This simple guided meditation reminds us that we have a fount of wisdom within, ready to guide us toward unconditional self-love and acceptance, if only we give ourselves the time and quiet.

In the final analysis, when we search for love outside of ourselves, imagining that others—our family members, our friends, our colleagues, even our students—similarly searching, wounded, and trapped within the "mood of unlove"—can give us the acceptance and love that we so badly want, we cannot but experience sadness and grief. As long as we remain enslaved by conditioning that tells us that we are not lovable just as we are, it won't matter how much love we receive from others, as our focus will always be on the love that is missing rather than the love that is present. It is only as we learn to accept our woundedness in the embrace of our own sweet compassion that we begin to experience our genuine goodness and come to see the pure, absolute, unconditional love that resides both around us and within us. Wellwood (2006, 146) puts it this way: "Just as fish do not see the water around them, so we mostly fail to recognize the ocean of love that surrounds and holds us up. So, all our lives we have been trying to win love, not realizing that great love is right here, freely available."

Wellwood (2006) goes on to offer the following six-step practice for opening up our bodies, hearts, and minds to the living presence of absolute love that permeates the whole of existence.

Step 1. Dwell in your body. Begin by arranging yourself in a comfortable position, either seated or lying down. Then bring your attention to the vital center of your body, located in your belly three fingers below your navel. Breathe into this area, grounding yourself, and feel your strong connection to Earth. Then, extend your awareness up to your heart, the locus of your warmth, your compassion, and your caring nature. Move your attention to the crown of your head, your link to the heavens. In doing this first step you will have arranged your belly, heart, and crown in a line of integrity.

Step 2. Experience your separation from love. Bring your awareness to some specific place in your life where you feel cut off from love. This could be in the context of a particular relationship, or it might be a more generalized feeling of unlove. Allow yourself to experience in your body how this lack of love actually feels. Resist the tendency to let your mind turn all this into a story; just stay with the feeling—emptiness, sadness, despair, fear—whatever it might be.

Step 3. Experience your raw desire to be held in love. Even as you feel the absence of love, allow yourself to feel your desire to be deeply loved just the way you are. Experience the energy of this longing in your body. "This longing is sacred because it is an entry into truth, the truth of your heart as an open channel through which love naturally wants to flow" (Wellwood 2006, 142).

Step 4. Open your heart and crown. Bring your attention to your heart and allow your entire chest region to be filled with the energy of your deep longing to abide in love. In a similar fashion bring your attention to your crown, allowing it to become soft and receptive as you manifest your longing for pure love.

Step 5. Receiving. Embedded in your desire to be deeply loved is your longing to allow love to enter you. So allow your body to be completely receptive to love and then look to see if love—some sense of goodness and well-being—is available right now? Without expectation, simply allow any openness, warmth, tenderness, spaciousness, sweetness, radiance, or equanimity that you feel to permeate your pores and enter your entire being. If you don't feel the presence of love, it is likely that you either didn't feel your separation from love or your desire for love strongly enough.

Step 6. Relaxing into love. As you experience love's presence, allow yourself to melt into it, softening your body boundaries. You don't have to hold yourself up; let love be your ground. "When you let down your defenses and allow love to pour into you, you become one with love, like a sheet of ice melting into the river from which it came. Just as the ice was never separate from the river, so the freezing of the heart has only created a temporary separation from your nature as love" (Wellwood 2006, 147).

Yes, it is only the freezing of our heart that has separated us from the truth of our nature as being goodness and love. In this context, the key to becoming a more loving person—and a compassionate teacher—is to become more permeable to love, to allow love to penetrate us so that we can express it from the inside out.

Loving Ourselves by Learning to *Let Go*

As we have emphasized throughout this chapter, one of life's hardest lessons is that our clinging to opinions, people, places, and things ultimately separates us from ourselves, creating more unhappiness than happiness. We don't have to cling. Indeed, it is through learning to "let go" of our attachments that we move toward deep self-acceptance and genuine happiness.

Here is a simple experiment that you can do right now to get an embodied sense of the freedom and lightness that comes from letting go. The first step is to simply sit in a straight-back chair. Once you are settled, grab on to your chair with both hands, clutching it with all your might. Imagine that a fierce wind is blowing, a wind so strong that it could blow you out of your chair. As you cling to your chair, consider that this is how you hold onto your cherished beliefs and opinions—as if your life depends on them! Take notice of how exhausting and stressful this is. When you can stand it no more, let go of your grip, paying attention to the lightness and ease you experience in your body as you let go. In effect, this is what happens when we let go of our attachments (Tolle 2005).

It is not easy to let go of cherished attachments, but it is possible. You could start by making a list of all the things, all the beliefs, all the concepts, and all the people that you hold dear in your life. For example, if you are in a relationship, put down the name of your partner. In a similar vein, if your job or your religion or money is important to you, put that down. Whatever you hold dear, write it down. Once you have a complete list, pause and hold each item on your list in your mind's eye while saying:

- I don't need _____ (opinion, person, thing, etc.) to be happy.
- This _____ (opinion, person, thing, etc.) is not fundamental to my happiness.
- I can love myself unconditionally without _____ (opinion, person, thing, etc.)

On the surface, this exercise (from Tolle 2005) may seem harsh. It is not. Our journey in life is toward freedom, not toward dependency. So, if you say you don't need your students' acceptance to be happy, this doesn't mean that you withdraw from your students. In fact, when we realize that we don't need another person's love, we discover, paradoxically, that we are more free to love them just as they are, without a sense of obligation and free of manipulation!

More importantly, we discover that we are free to fully love ourselves just as we are. The truth is that we don't "need" anything from anybody. We only think we do when we have abandoned the one relationship that we do, in fact, need—namely, the precious relationship we have with ourselves.

In the end, *letting go* means releasing our attachment to what happens in our lives. Said differently: As we come to unconditionally accept ourselves and others (e.g., our students), we grow in our ability to accept reality just as it comes to us, without conditions. What would it look like, in real life, to let go of attachment to what happens day by day? Here's a story that points the way. As you read it, put yourself in the place of Hakuin, and consider how you would react to the events of this story.

> The Zen Master Hakuin lived in a town in Japan. He was held in high regard and many people came to him for spiritual teaching. Then it happened that the teenage daughter of his next-door neighbor became pregnant. When being questioned by her angry and scolding parents as to the identity of the father, she finally told them that he was Hakuin, the Zen Master. In great anger the parents rushed over to Hakuin and told him with much shouting and accusing that their daughter had confessed that he was the father. All he replied was, "Is this so?"
>
> News of the scandal spread throughout the town and beyond. The Master lost his reputation. This did not trouble him. Nobody came to see him anymore. He remained unmoved. When the child was born, the parents brought the baby to Hakuin. "You are the father, so you look after him." The Master took loving care of the child. A year later, the mother remorsefully confessed to her parents that the real father of the child was the young man who worked at the butcher shop. In great distress they went to see Hakuin to apologize and ask for forgiveness. "We are really sorry. We have come to take the baby back. Our daughter confessed that you are not the father." "Is that so?" is all he would say as he handed the baby over to them.
>
> The Master responds to falsehood and truth, bad news and good news, in exactly the same way: "Is that so?" He allows the form of the moment, good or bad, to be as it is and so does not become a participant in the human drama. To him there is only this moment, and this moment is as it is. Events are not personalized. He is nobody's victim. He is so completely at one with what happens that what happens has no power over him anymore. (Tolle 2005, 199–200)

Hakuin is an exemplar. To gain his degree of detachment, while at the same time being fully engaged in the world is the work of a lifetime. An important starting

It has been said that our unhappiness is determined by the size of the gap between what we have and what we want. In an effort to make this simple formulation more concrete, put a dot on a piece of paper and labeled it "what I have." Then, place a second dot on the paper and label it "what I want." Consider that, in any given moment, the distance between those dots, far or near, is the magnitude of your unhappiness.

Then erase the second dot and place it directly on top of the first dot. In so doing you have created a vision for living with no gap between what you want and what you have. This would mean completely accepting how life presents itself moment by moment—making space for all of it, just like Hakuin. Instead of complaining, judging, or blaming, it would mean meeting the present moment with an unequivocal "Yes!"

How might this play out in everyday life? Imagine waiting for a friend on a street corner. Your friend is late, and you become impatient, thinking, Where is he? He should be on time! Why didn't he at least call to tell me he was running late? How inconsiderate!" In this moment of irritation, the two dots—what you have and what you want—are far apart, and you are experiencing a lot of unhappiness. But imagine that you catch yourself and rather than being in an argument with life, you decide to accept your life exactly as it is presenting itself in the moment. You breathe deeply and say, "Yes," to your situation, realizing, with a smile, that nothing is wrong. Life shows up just as it does, moment by moment. It is never wrong! Freed of your story of how things should be, your mind quiets, and you become aware of the sky, the breeze, your own aliveness. Dwelling in the present moment, you notice, for the first time, the faces of the people walking by; you witness the late afternoon sun lighting the top of a tree; you hear calls of far-off crows. Slowly, you soften, getting a taste of a different way of being in the world. Soon you are no longer frustrated, upset, disappointed, but open, accepting, present, alive.

place is to simply ask—in those instances when you believe that you are receiving unkind or unfair treatment—"Can I say 'Yes' to this?"

Happiness, contrary to our received cultural story, doesn't come from outside ourselves; it arises from our capacity to love our life just as it is, moment by moment—letting go of our stories about how our life "should be." Similarly, love resides as an inexhaustible fount within us. We need only slow down, quiet ourselves, and cast off into the vast river flowing endlessly on.

Wrap-up

The purpose of education is to show a person how to define himself authentically and spontaneously in relation to the world—not to impose a prefabri-

cated definition of the world, still less an arbitrary definition of the individual
himself.   —T. MERTON 1985, 3

Seeing oneself with new eyes, with the eyes of kindness and self-acceptance,
requires dedication, courage, and time. For teachers, the call is to grow, day
by day, into an ever-more compassionate and full-hearted relationship with
ourselves. As this occurs we gain the capacity to act as midwives, guiding our
students toward an authentic and loving relationship with themselves (and by
extension, with others and the world at large). At present, education programs
and policies give little heed to helping teachers, much less students, grow toward self-understanding, self-acceptance, and self-actualization. Contemporary
schooling, more often than not, reinforces the "trance of unworthiness," posit-
ing that a student's worthiness is conditional upon her classroom performance.
So it is that young people become, in a sense, like little Sisyphuses—always
laboring uphill to get the praise, acceptance, and love they desire, only at some
moment to slip back down the love slope, feeling unworthy and unloved.

But what if teachers created the space for young people to explore, to know
themselves, and, in so doing, to discover their unique personhood. Specifically,
what if the messages provided young people by their teachers included:

- You are real and you have a right to be here.
- Your questions matter and deserve consideration.
- You are qualified to have a say in what to learn today and how to
  learn it.
- What you are feeling today and what you have to say are important.
- You are fundamentally good and lovable just as you are.

Such messages bespeak a commitment to see others (and to know ourselves) as
reservoirs of genius, wholeness, and love.

We believe that education is ripe for this new vision that prioritizes self-
knowing and self-actualization. In this new paradigm, students do not depend
on the praise of others to validate their worthiness; rather, their self-esteem
shines forth from their own inner acceptance. *Success*, in this new framework, is
gauged not in terms of one's test scores, college admission, earning power, and
status, but, rather, from one's freedom from the "trance of unworthiness." Self-
awareness, personal growth, and the capacity for love and service on behalf of
the common good become the ultimate goals. This is the change that teaching
as if life matters promises.

One could dismiss this vision with the charge that these matters of person-hood and the heart have no place in schools. But insofar as young people spend the bulk of their growing-up years in schools, there is an unparalleled oppor-tunity for teachers to mentor students in ways that foster self-understanding, healthy self-regard, and personal agency.

Cultivating Classroom Kinship

Relationship with the Human Other

> At this moment in history humans are a dangerously insane and very sick
> species. That's not a judgment. It's a fact. As a testament to insanity, hu-
> mans killed a hundred million fellow humans in the 20th century alone.
> No other species violates itself on such a grand scale. Only a people who
> are in a deeply negative state, who feel very bad indeed, would create such
> a reality as a reflection of how they feel. —E. TOLLE 1999, 66–67

Consider this scene: a high school classroom in a cement-block building in an
urban setting. There is too little natural light, sparse color, and scant evidence
of imagination. The students are seated in rows; some appear bored, others
disgruntled, a few expectant. The teacher enters, clears her throat, preparing to
speak. Just then, her eye gravitates to a student in the back row—the "student
from hell." Here is how educator Parker Palmer (1998, 43) describes his encounter with the proverbial *student from hell:*

> a universal archetype that can take male or female form; mine happened to be
> male. His cap was pulled down over his eyes so that I could not tell whether they
> were open or shut. His notebooks and writing instruments were nowhere to be
> seen. It was a fine spring day, but his jacket was buttoned tight, signifying readiness
> to bolt at any moment. What I remember most vividly is his posture. Though he
> sat in one of those sadistic classroom chairs with a rigidly attached desk, he had
> achieved a position that I know to be anatomically impossible: despite the inter-
> posed desk, his body was parallel to the floor.

My suspicion is that every teacher, no matter the context, has encountered
his or her own student from hell, perhaps many times over. This is the student
whose insubordination, habits, posture, or disposition give us undue consterna-

tion, creating in us disproportionate upset. We tell ourselves that our lives would be better, easier, simpler were it not for this particular student. And, mostly we struggle in vain, unable to learn the big lesson that such a student offers.

The student from hell might be the nervous youngster who can't sit still, the apathetic adolescent whose appearance screams anger, anomie, and disdain, or the cynical college student who judges you and your course as totally bogus. He or she could look like anything, act like anything, but what is almost guaranteed is that most teachers view such students as problems.

Palmer encountered his student from hell while giving a two-day workshop on teaching at a small Midwestern college. After the workshop he agreed to give a guest presentation in a political science course, thinking that this would give him an opportunity to showcase his teaching skills. Everything was going fine until Palmer spotted that student from hell lurking in the back of the classroom.

Palmer became obsessed with this particular student, directing all his efforts toward engaging him. The harder Palmer tried, the more the young man seemed to withdraw. Meanwhile, the other twenty-nine students in the class disappeared utterly from Palmer's awareness. When the class was over, Palmer was humbled by his own ineptitude. He wanted simply to escape and put the whole catastrophe behind him.

Of course, schoolteachers don't have the luxury of simply putting any catastrophe behind them. The next day, they must confront the catastrophe, deal with the student whose hellishness has created their nightmare. Yet, what exactly is the teacher to do? What is her aim, her intention? To restore order? To reclaim authority? To remove the problem student?

Before flying home, Palmer had one final obligation—to attend a dinner at the home of the college president. When the dinner was over, a van arrived to take Palmer to the airport. With relief he put his bags in the back and hopped into the passenger seat. When he turned to greet the driver, he beheld, much to his chagrin, the student from hell from earlier that day.

Palmer's trip to the airport would last an hour. At first they rode along in silence, but after a time the young man asked if they might talk. In their conversation, Palmer learned that this fellow lived with a father who ridiculed his attempts to get a college education, telling him to drop out, settle for a job in the service sector, and call it a life. The student confided that his resolve around college was fading day by day, and he asked Palmer if he had any advice.

Through this remarkable encounter Palmer came to realize that many of "the silent and seemingly sullen" students in teachers' classrooms are neither hellish nor "brain-dead." Rather, they are full of fear, confusion, and/or feelings of isolation. These "problem" students mask their fears and vulnerabilities, opting instead for a "go to hell" stance or "I don't need you" posture.

When I consider that passivity or seeming indifference on the part of my students might have nothing to do with my stories about them and everything to do with fear—mine and theirs—my understanding of my work as teacher shifts. A "way" emerges—a path where hearts and minds can meet, one where no "other" exists, only another human being struggling to become more fully himself. In light of this, my own posture shifts, becoming relational where once it was oppositional.

Rather than avoiding, overlooking, or casting aside so-called problem students, what if teachers gravitated toward them, in the hope of helping them find their voice? What changes in our hearts—in our classroom practices—would be required? It was no accident that the student in Palmer's story appeared sullen when sitting passively in the classroom. But in a different setting, behind the wheel and in charge of taking Palmer to the airport, this young man was able to enter into relationship with Palmer—that is, to find his voice, his agency. The lesson for teachers: To avoid "othering" students and to find ways to put them "behind the wheel."

In our fear-induced judgments of students—that they have no voice worth hearing, no experience worth valuing, no passion worth honoring—not only do we fail to fulfill our duty, we do violence. Imagine how it would be to live under a different set of assumptions about the student from hell. What if we adopted the belief that such a student (and all people really) is an extension of ourselves—that he is me and I am him? What if we viewed each young person as whole, complete, brilliant—each a manifestation of the love and life force that animates existence? Such a way of seeing the "other" would acknowledge our profound interrelatedness, thereby leading us *toward* relational consciousness and *away from* separation consciousness. A necessary first step in enacting this shift in consciousness is to understand how it is that we have become mired in separation in the first place.

Busting Free of Separation Consciousness: Four Frames

On a recent trip with the students in my field ecology class, I decided to bring along a snack consisting of nuts and raisins, grapes, and a few cookies. I set these goodies on a long picnic table, and then I asked the students to find a straight stick about the length of their arm. When they returned with their sticks, I gave each of them two rubber bands and instructed them to use these to secure their stick to their right arm so that they could no longer bend that arm. Next, I invited them to sit at the table and partake in the food, with one proviso—that they hold their left arm behind their back and use only their right arm for eating. They laughed, knowing this was a game, and then they set about eating their snack. Unable to bend their eating arms, some tried to throw the food up in the air and catch it in their mouths, others sheepishly put their mouths to the table and vacuumed up snippets of food. None of this was very easy or pleasant. Noting that they were becoming more frustrated (and hungry) by the moment, I suggested that there was a way of transforming the living hell of *separation consciousness* into the enchanting heaven of *relational consciousness*. That's all it took. In no time they were using their straight arms to extend food to each other. This was a "heaven on earth" experience as everyone received twice over—once when each received food from a classmate and a second time when each extended food to another. The point, of course, is that how we perceive reality—as heaven (relation-based) or as hell (separation-based)—can determine our behavior and our happiness.

Whether we choose to acknowledge it or not, to be alive is not to be separate, it is to be in relationship. There is a rapidly growing body of scientific research revealing the ways that we humans are profoundly interconnected to one another, to all life, and to the cosmos that has *birthed* us. Yet, we live within a national culture that often reinforces and encourages the view that each of us is a separate encapsulated ego. Here, we explore four *frames* for viewing how social conditioning separates us from each other, along with four corresponding ways of cultivating relational consciousness.

Frame 1. Dualistic Thinking Creates Separation

Those born in the West *inherit* at birth a way of thinking that engenders separation and objectification. This mode of thinking is called *dualism*. Dualistic thinking has a long history. For instance, in Genesis we read about a "God" who is separate from the world and who creates man in his own image, a creator separate from and above the rest of creation.

It was Aristotle who formally presented dualism as a worldview. Everything in the world, according to Aristotle, was either one way or the other: black or white, true or not true. Aristotle called this the "Law of the Excluded Middle." It could just as easily have been called the "Law of Separation."

But neither thought nor reality is constituted of opposites. As Targ and Hurtak point out, "Our usual black-and-white dualistic frame of mind almost inevitably creates suffering for ourselves and others because we seriously misperceive
reality, polarizing it into incommensurable opposites and therefore we experience delusion" (2006, xx).

In her book *Raising Your Emotional Intelligence*, Jeanne Segal offers a nice exercise (offered in modified form below) for determining the degree to which one
might be entrapped in and limited by dualistic thinking. It is simple to do. Just
look over the pairs of words below and decide which word in each pair belongs
in the Superior column and which one in the Inferior column. Give it a try.

Word Pairs	Superior	Inferior
Humans—Nature	_____	_____
Clean—Dirty	_____	_____
Rich—Poor	_____	_____
Young—Old	_____	_____
Me—You	_____	_____
Mind—Body	_____	_____
United States—China	_____	_____
College—High School	_____	_____
Right—Left	_____	_____
Masculine—Feminine	_____	_____
Good—Bad	_____	_____
Mental—Physical	_____	_____
Intellectual—Emotional	_____	_____
Light—Dark	_____	_____
Reason—Passion	_____	_____
Generous—Selfish	_____	_____

If you completed this exercise quickly and tended to put the first word in each
pair in the Superior column and the second word in the Inferior column, chances
are that you are deeply steeped in dualistic thinking. If, on the other hand, this
exercise took a long time to complete and you had a difficult time deciding
where to place concepts, your manner of thinking tends toward nondualism—it
is more porous, less black and white.

A person caught within the frame of dualism will be confined in his thinking
to only two alternatives—either this or that, male or female, religion or science,

Republican or Democrat, good or bad. The net effect on one's thought is a lack of creativity and spontaneity because one's thinking is "in the box"!

Freed of dualistic constructs, we are able to embrace reality simply as it is. In this more spacious world, rather than science versus religion, we see science and religion as complimentary ways of knowing; rather than mind versus body, we see mind and body as two sides of the same coin; rather than rationalism versus intuition, we appreciate that both are needed for understanding (Kumar 2002). In short, where there was once separation, now there is connection and relatedness.

Transcending Dualism—From Me versus You to WE

Even though we humans have been using language for tens of thousands of years, we are still beginners when it comes to using speech creatively to resolve differences. Typically, when a disagreement arises, both parties talk past each other as they lay out their positions and present their demands. For example, a teacher, unhappy with her working conditions, goes to her principal and demands a change. The principal might assume a defensive posture, pass the buck, or stall for time. Stuck in this face-off, the two miss an opportunity to create a relationship built on trust, mutual respect, and a shared vision.

Imagine how things would change if the teacher were to regard her principal not as someone separate from her whom she has to oppose but as a colleague with whom she is fundamentally united. In other words, what if she understood that she and her principal form a WE—a unique entity existing outside of the typical *me versus you* duality—a unity that isn't static but dynamic and constantly evolving. Then, the teacher might approach her principal, saying something like: "I believe that WE are both satisfied with my work here and that WE share a loyalty to each other. At the same time the working conditions, as I am currently experiencing them, do not allow me to fulfill my broader commitments to my entire class, my colleagues, and this school. So what is possible here for US? How can WE find a solution? How can WE make this work?" Speaking in this manner, the teacher avoids pushing her principal into a reactive, defensive position, while at the same time creating the space for the two of them to work side by side to find a mutually satisfying solution.

Rather than constricting possibility, a WE approach expands what is possible. No longer is life lived as a zero-sum game where some win and others lose. As Zander and Zander point out, "the practice of the WE gives us a method for reclaiming 'The Other' as one of us. Traditional methods of resolving conflict, all

DIVIDING THE WORLD INTO "THIS" AND "THAT"

Marshall Rosenberg, author of the book *Nonviolent Communication,* advises: "Never put your BUT in someone's face." Why? Because responding to someone else's speaking with "but" often creates separation—it divides the world into *this* and that. To appreciate Rosenberg's point, try adopting the practice of substituting the word "and" for "but" in your speech for one day. This simple substitution creates space for understanding by inviting multiple perspectives. For example, consider how you would feel hearing: "I heard what you said, BUT I disagree with you on this issue . . ." versus "I heard what you said AND I have an additional way of seeing this . . ." With the simple substitution of *and* for *but,* we can take a step toward creating a *both-and* world—a world of possibility and connection and a step away from today's *either-or* world characterized by dualism and separation.

the I/You approaches, tend to increase the level of discord because they attempt to [only] satisfy the dichotomous positions people take, rather than providing the means for people to broaden their desires. I/You methods deprive people of the opportunity to wish inclusively. They do not give people the chance to want what the story of the WE says we are thirsting for: connection to others through our dreams and visions" (2000, 186–87). This WE approach can be practiced whenever and wherever disagreements arise. Central to WE consciousness is the realization that what exists—what is real—is WE. Indeed, the reality is that WE are massively entangled with each other: physically—sharing the same molecules as we breathe, energetically—influencing each other's energy fields, and psychically—affecting each other's thoughts. When we, as teachers, act from the perspective of WE, we shift from the consciousness of disconnection and separation to the consciousness of relationship and interdependence.

Frame 2. Labels and Judgments Create Separation

I was well into my teaching career when I realized that the meaning I ascribed to labels (words) like *university, teacher,* and *student* was the result of my conditioning and, as such, might be restricting my understanding of my life's work. This realization happened spontaneously one day as I walked from my home to the Penn State campus. It hit me: "Penn State" was just a mental construct; there was no "Penn State"! The illusion of "Penn State" persists only insofar as people agree to call a collection of buildings, sports teams, academic pursuits, and financial transactions "Penn State."

Arriving to campus that day, I saw that what I had been calling *Penn State* was, more accurately, a gathering place for all sorts of people—with a wide range of concerns, questions, desires, and ambitions—to pursue learning and engage in all manner of creative pursuits. When I dropped the label *Penn State*, suddenly the whole scene became more interesting and more filled with possibility. Why? Because prior to this shift, I had perceived "Penn State" as a largely heartless, soulless, monolithic entity. That narrow depiction (grounded in dualistic thinking) left me feeling separate—that is, at odds with the very institution in whose employ I served. It was as if I had imagined that I worked in an impersonal "factory" only to realize suddenly that I was dwelling in a "garden of delight."

The same thing happened when I experimented with dropping the label *teacher*, which I had theretofore affixed to myself. Labeling myself as *teacher* limited my imagination and creativity because, through my own schooling, I had been conditioned to understand both *teacher* and *teaching* in narrow and constricting ways—that is, as a series of prescribed behaviors enacted by one person to induce learning in other people. Similarly, I saw that my conditioning around the label *student* restricted me from seeing the innate mystery and magnificence of each being who walked into my classroom. Finally, arriving to my office that day I realized that even my associations (social conditioning) around the word *office* were largely negative, constricting, lifeless. I decided to create new, more enlivening labels to describe my work life. I did this by simply substituting the word *studio* for *office*, *seekers* for *students*, *healer* for *teacher*, and *Garden of Delight* for *Penn State*. I was a healer, going to my studio in the Garden of Delight to work with seekers.

Insofar as labels affect our perceptions, they do make a difference. In classrooms, the use of labels like dyslexic or ADD (Attention Deficit Disorder) can lead teachers to confuse a student's behavior with his personhood. If a teacher says things like "Joey is dyslexic," the implied judgment is that there is something wrong with Joey. However, "dyslexic" has nothing to do with *who* Joey is! A more accurate, label-free way of speaking would sound like: "Joey sometimes mixes up his letters when he reads." This orientation helps to see that Joey *has* a challenge or difficulty rather than coming to believe that Joey *is* the difficulty (Cameron and Meyer, 2006).

Though some might argue that labels empower rather than limit people—to the extent that a person can associate his challenges with some "verifiable" condition—the dark side of this empowerment is a more entrenched separation through language that focuses on distinction, difference, and deficiency. Again, to look at another through the label *ADD* or *dyslexic* or any other label for that matter (e.g., poor, child of single parent, unmotivated, disruptive) is to risk con-

LABELING EINSTEIN

Albert Einstein had the symptoms of someone with severe Attention Deficit Disorder (ADD). Einstein was four when he began to speak; he didn't learn to read until he was seven. If Einstein had been born today, he would have been saddled with an array of labels and likely compelled to take prescription medication to help him better fit into society (Bryson 2004). In "fitting Einstein into society," one shudders to think what insights and knowledge might never have surfaced within the genius Einstein.

fusing the person with the label—that is, to give primacy to the diagnosis rather than the person.

Not only do labels limit how we see others, they can profoundly affect how we see ourselves. For example, as I entered my fifties, I realized that, from an early age, I had been socialized to believe that when someone gets to be sixty they are really old and that *old* means diminished, needy, and faltering. Recognizing that this conceptualization of the aging process was likely to be a self-fulfilling prophecy, I asked myself: What if I were to shift my definition of aging from decline—a steady erosion of vigor and health—to development—a steady increase in awareness, sensitivity, compassion, and wisdom? In short, what if I were to subscribe to the idea that older is often better—that *ageing* can lead to *sage-ing* (Schachter-Shalomi, 1995)? In sum, labels and judgments affixed to people or phenomena are like boxes that confine and restrict perception. They simplify, reduce, and ignore the fullness and truth of the person, entity, or experience that is labeled.

Transcending Judgment: The Labeling Game

Each semester, Dana and I use a role-play known as the Labeling Game to powerfully illustrate the destructive effects of judgments and associated labels in classroom settings. Requiring about twenty minutes to enact, the role-play begins with five volunteers sitting in a circle in the middle of the room. The volunteers are asked to converse about something of general interest. After about five minutes (once the conversation has had sufficient time to develop), the facilitator calls for a time-out. The volunteers close their eyes while the facilitator affixes a paper message on each person's forehead: "Praise Me," "Criticize Me," "Ignore Me," "Make Fun of Me," and "Interrupt Me." The volunteers open their eyes and resume talking with each other.

The ensuing conversation is at once hilarious and disturbing. What is clear is that, try as they might, the five can't conduct a genuine conversation because of the crippling labels that are operating in the circle. After a time, each volunteer has a good idea of what label he/she is wearing. We all know what it feels like to be ignored, made fun of, interrupted, criticized, or praised.

The richness of this exercise comes in the debriefing, when class members respond to questions such as:

What was the point of this exercise?
What might it reveal about labels and judgments in the classroom?
What happened after the labels were placed on the volunteer's foreheads?
What invisible messages/judgments do you put on the foreheads of your
    classmates in this room?
If you could, what message (label), would you *like* to have affixed to your
    own forehead?

On the final question, student sentiments are similar: Mary Beth wants to be seen; Doug wants people to listen to him; Gary wants to be respected. In one way or another, we all want to feel like we matter. But our judgments close us off from each other, preventing us from meeting the Other as an infinite surprise. The take-home message is that our judgments exist only in our minds; we think they are real, but they are simply mental constructs that separate us from one another.

Frame 3. Blaming and Complaining Create Separation

Teacher's lounges sometimes serve as complain and blame centers. While teachers may experience a superficial sense of connection and belonging when they drop into complaint mode, the long-term effect of these negativity echo chambers is to create dissatisfaction and disempowerment.

The conscious act of turning complaints inside out—of expressing what we stand *for* as opposed to what we stand *against*—is one means for creating a more harmonious, more empowered, reality. For example, imagine the teacher who complains to a friend: "The teachers I work with are always gossiping behind each other's backs." Insofar as this teacher is *against* gossiping, she must be *for* open, honest, forthright communication. By turning her complaint inside out and expressing what she stands for, this teacher would help create integrity and peace in her school (Kegan and Lahey 2001).

Complaining is especially dispiriting because it often has blame embedded within it. Rather than complaining and blaming, we can, if we choose, take responsibility for what has happened or is happening. No matter what the issue may be, we must recognize that we, in some sense, contribute to it and that we therefore also have the power to participate in creating a new and satisfying outcome! By consciously abstaining from the "complain and blame" game, teachers (and all people) use their language to build bridges, rather than walls. This is inspiriting.

As a way of exploring this possibility, take a situation in your life where you are complaining and blaming someone or something for a problem you are experiencing. Reflect on the situation with emphasis on how you are a victim and how the other person or thing is to blame for your misfortune. Now, take this same situation and, rather than pointing the blame away from yourself, take responsibility for what has happened to you. Specifically, consider the question, "How did I create this?"

By way of example, it used to really bug me when a student had the audacity to doze off in one of my classes. In these instances, I, unwittingly, became a *victim*, self-righteously *blaming* the offending student for rudeness and/or a lack of seriousness. Then one day I stopped to consider the question: How did I create this? What was my part in my student's dozing behavior? This reflection led me to acknowledge that I can sometimes be boring, especially when I speak in a monotone and/or *talk at* students rather than employing pedagogies that invite them into relationship with the subject. Beyond this, I realized that simply by participating in the institution of schooling—a system that by its very nature is hierarchical—I was imposing my will (in subtle and not so subtle ways) on my students and that one of the ways that a student can resist this imposition is to go to sleep. These realizations led me to accept responsibility for dozing students. They also led me to feel a measure of gratitude toward these students insofar as they were offering me direct, embodied responses to my teaching. Beyond gratitude, I was even able (sometimes) to experience respect and admiration for the dozing student because he had the good sense and courage to respond to his body's call for sleep, rather than to force himself to stay awake simply for appearance's sake.

Nowadays, I choose to see dozing as a call for help from a struggling student—a call to oppose my conditioning as teacher-cum-distant authority—and to respond with decency, compassion, and trust.

Transcending Complaint and Blame: I Am Pointing at Myself

Imagine what it would be like to live in a world where there, literally, was no "other." That's right, no one to blame or complain about! This would mean acknowledging that all those things *out there* in the world that upset us are, in some measure, *in* us. For me it would mean coming to realize that, in a very real sense:

> I *am* the bombs dropping on innocent people.
> I *am* the pilot dropping the bombs.
> I *am* the soldier in the foxhole.
> I *am* Saddam Hussein.
> I *am* the murderer, the thief, the rapist . . .
> I *am* all of this. (inspired by Thich Nhat Hanh)

In thinking and speaking in this way, I challenge myself to imagine a world without the blame and complaint that inevitably leads to separation. A world where all of us, though we may appear as separate, like distinct whitecaps on top of waves, are part of the same singular sea of being stretching out below those whitecaps. In this view, "two" is an illusion—a way of describing an underlying oneness, like the two sides of one hand.

Precisely because we have been conditioned to see ourselves as separate from each other, we struggle with the proposition that we are all one, all part of one indivisible whole. Of course, as we look out at the world, it certainly seems like each of us is separate from the person next to us, but perceptions often can and do betray reality.

There is a powerful exercise that I share with teachers who wish to experience firsthand their degree of oneness with each other. It is simple to do. Find a willing partner and sit face to face. Take some deep breaths to relieve any tension and then look into each other's eyes. Gaze with openness, curiosity, and sweet appreciation. Do this without speaking for several minutes. The intent is to simply see and feel the other, free of judgment, seeing through your heart into the other's heart—perceiving the goodness, innocence, and mystery in this other.

You will likely experience a lot of anxiety, especially at first. Why is it so hard for us simply to "be" in the presence of another? Might the answer be that we believe, deep down, that if we are not performing—not doing something, such as talking, in this case—then we are somehow not acceptable, not worthy?

In the debriefing following this exercise, participants frequently report that once their self-conscious stage passed, they were suddenly able to see the beauty and pure goodness in the eyes of their partner, and this, in turn, led them to see their partner, not as "other" at all, but as inextricably connected to themselves.

This reiterates what sages, ancient and modern, have said—namely, we can only see/know ourselves through the eyes of another. In fact, the Latin word from which our word *pupil* is derived, *pupila*, contains this very connotation—that one comes to know herself through the reflection of herself that she receives within the other's eye.

Frame 4. Fear Creates Separation

It is April 2005. I am going through the security checkpoint at the Baltimore airport. I put my daypack on the conveyer belt. Then there is a commotion. The operator of the x-ray machine sees what looks like a knife in my bag. FEAR! He calls over his supervisor, and they open my bag to discover a small paring knife in a little red case. Three more security personnel come over. Suddenly, I am being treated as a suspected terrorist. FEAR! This is serious. The blade length is measured with precision. I am told that if it had been a quarter-inch longer, I would have been fined several thousand dollars, and federal police would have been called to the scene. In the midst of this turmoil, I pause to really look at my little paring knife—a gift from my sister. It resides in my daypack because I sometimes hike in the mountains near my home. On these mountain walks, I use this knife to slice fruit, cut cheese, sharpen my pencil, cut string, and any number of other things. For me this cutting blade is a daily companion, akin to a watch or a pen or a cell phone. But now, suddenly, in our post-9/11 world, my treasured gift has become a potential instrument of terror—a fearsome object that could be used to enact some horrific deed. In that instant when my paring knife was transformed into an instrument of terror, I, too, was transmuted from a fellow American to a "national security threat."

The tendency to "other" is grounded in an almost instinctual fear of that which is different. Whatever the parameters of our individual lives, we come to regard our own beliefs, values, and habits of being as right, best, and proper. This means that if you were brought up in the city, raised Protestant, and fed meat and potatoes, it is likely that you will regard someone who was brought up rural, Muslim, and vegan with suspicion—you will be predisposed to "other" her.

The subculture of most schools is grounded in othering. Walk into any school, and you will likely see evidence that there is a clearly delineated *in-group*. I remember back to my high school days and all the effort I expended in my high school days to be accepted by the in-group. By my junior year, I had finally made it. I played on the varsity basketball team and was a member of the

Key Club and Student Council. My friends were all "cool"; the girls I dated, all cute. I ignored the majority of the kids in my class—those who weren't cool. In the final months of my senior year, I became aware of Marilyn, a fellow student in my composition class. Marilyn, heavyset and nerdy, was very much in the out-group. I was attracted by the interesting things Marilyn had to say in class and wanted to talk to her, but I didn't approach her because I was afraid of what the in-group would think of me.

Rather than turn a blind eye to the *in-group/out-group* phenomenon in our schools, what if group aggregation became a serious topic of inquiry? What better way to have a conversation about our fear of otherness than by talking about what is real, present, and bubbling just below the surface of students' lives. This is precisely the approach that two colleagues of ours, Sam Richards and Laurie Mulvey, have taken at Penn State. These two sociologists wondered: What would happen if students of diverse racial/ethnic backgrounds were to sit down, in groups of eight to twelve, and simply talk about their personal experiences around race? From this seed question, they created the Race Relations Project (www.racerelationsproject.org). The genius of this project is that it is not designed to convince participants of anything; there is no party line, no political correctness police. Rather, the agenda is simply to create the conditions wherein participants can explore and articulate their own thinking, experiences, and beliefs around race, difference, and otherness.

The actual conversations are facilitated by peers whose role, in the Socratic tradition, is to ask questions and provide occasional prods, coaxing participants to go deeper. In this way the participants give voice, sometimes for the first time in their lives, to their perceptions, assumptions, and feelings around race. Such judgment-free opportunities to meet each other and to be seen and heard can be immensely illuminating. As Mulvey points out, "We don't really know what we think until we have the opportunity to voice it." The Race Relations Project offers a template for how schools across America might give students permission to speak their truth about the beliefs and fears that divide and separate us.

Transcending Fear: The Practice of Truthspeaking

Each fall I teach a freshman seminar at Penn State. On the first day of class I explain that the purpose of the seminar is to reflect on and discuss a collection of essays centering on contemplative education and relational consciousness. I make it clear that the quality of our intellectual exchanges will be crippled should any one of us arrive unprepared. To signal that we are there to learn from each other, I arrange the chairs in a circle. As a final homey touch, I have coffee, tea, and hot chocolate available.

Fast forward. It is the third week of the semester, and after everybody is settled I say, "Raise your hand if you have carefully done the reading for today." Only six of the twenty students raise their hands.

I am "seeing red." Then, I remember to breathe. Ten seconds: "These students are a bunch of lazy good-for-nothings!" Breathe! Twenty seconds: "How dare they come to my class unprepared!" Breathe! Thirty seconds: "Maybe they're not lazy?" Breathe! Forty seconds: "What is really going on here?" Calming myself further, I am able to acknowledge that the simple reality—the truth—in this moment is that most of these folks, for whatever reason(s), have not done the reading. Then, I ask myself, "How can I align myself with life, just the way it is presenting itself, in this very moment?"

I look up and take some time to really see these young people who have gathered with me. My irritation drains away as I behold each person. Etched in their faces I perceive apprehension, exhaustion, fear, sadness, as well as expectancy, enthusiasm, curiosity, and openness.

Absent rancor, I explain that a fruitful discussion of the reading, in my experience, necessitates that each of us be fully prepared. Since this is not possible, I reassign the reading for our next meeting and ask to be contacted ahead of time if anyone is not able to complete the reading. Everyone nods their consent.

Then, I return to silence and ask myself, "What is possible in this moment?" What are the opportunities hidden in what seems like a train wreck? It is then that I see that this crisis is a golden opportunity to practice being real with each other or, in Parker Palmer's language, to overcome our "fear of a live encounter."

I begin by forthrightly telling my students what was going on for me (sharing how I saw "red," sharing my anger and disappointment) after I learned that only six of them had completed the reading. They listen, eyes wide open. After all, it is unusual for a teacher to make himself vulnerable like this. I confess that my anger was so big at first that I couldn't decide whether to yell at them or simply leave the classroom—I was caught in a classical *fight versus flight* moment. Beyond all this, I confess my various responses—anger, frustration, disappointment, confusion—were tinged with the fear that I was not worthy to be a teacher.

Then, I ask if they would be willing to talk about what got in the way of their completing this reading assignment? Specifically, I ask that they go below surface responses like, "I didn't have time," and dig more deeply into their truth—

into what their decision to skip the reading was really all about. In effect, I am inviting them into the practice of *truthspeaking*.

I wait, knowing that it takes time to find one's authentic truth. Eventually, Martin speaks of how he is overwhelmed by college. Noting that Martin is only talking to me, I pull my chair back from the circle and ask him to say more about what "overwhelmed" feels like. He hesitates and then confesses, "It feels scary, like I am sinking." Silence follows. Soon Stacy speaks about her lostness and loneliness at college. Everyone is leaning forward. For the first time in the semester, I begin to see who has been in the room. Especially, I become aware of each person's fundamental need to be seen, appreciated, understood, cherished. By speaking what is true for me on this day—modeling how to speak candidly about my own fear of failure—I create a space for everyone to be real. Truthspeaking is the path toward deeper, more meaningful relationship, both with ourselves and each other, once we decide to allow fear to hold us captive no more.

As we teachers learn to identify and root out the causes of separation (dualism, judgment, blame, and fear) from our own lives, we will join others in catalyzing a shift from separation to relational consciousness and, in so doing, have the joy of participating in the formation of a more sane, just, and compassionate world.

Learning to Speak the Language of Peace

What word made flesh are you today?
What words might you put forth in the service of the world?

—D. CONNELLY, 1993

As emphasized throughout this book, our labels and beliefs and mental constructs create the filters through which we see, understand, and make meaning of the world. In effect, we "word" the world with our words, and in our speaking we have the opportunity to use words in ways that engender relationship or separation.

Nowhere is the potential for learning the language of relationship riper than within schools. Recent research reveals that the capacity to speak openly and honestly, especially in moments of conflict, is a vital life skill in the work environment and at home. Thus, if teachers became masters at modeling the language of common values rather than the language of difference; the language of

THE PRACTICE OF TRUTHSPEAKING

Teacher and writer Tamarack Song, in his book *Sacred Speech: The Way of Truthspeaking,* characterizes "truthspeaking" as stating "clearly and simply what one thinks and feels. There is no judgment or expectation, no disguise of humor or force of anger. The manner of speech is sacred, because it wells up from the soul of our being rather than from our self-absorbed ego" (2004, i).

Song contends that all of us know how to truthspeak. We simply have forgotten it. We get derailed from truthspeaking anytime we get tangled up in shame and guilt and pleasing others and judgment and competition and control and fantasy and regret—which is to say much of the time! Truthspeaking is particularly difficult because we have been conditioned—in our families, through the media, and in our schools—to believe that we must dilute our personal truth in order to be accepted by others. So it is that we run the risk of losing touch with what we hold to be true. And as we separate from our own hearts, we necessarily become more separate from others.

cooperation rather than the language of contest and competition; the language of compassion and kindness rather than the language of intimidation and fear; the language of empowerment rather than the language of coercion and punishment, just imagine how our young people and the world they construct would be transformed!

Marshall Rosenberg has developed just such a "language" of relationship. His method, named "Nonviolent Communication," is based on decades of research and experimentation into forms of speaking and listening that enable people to stay connected to their compassionate nature—that core part of a person's heart that enables him to be in relationship to both himself and another.

If within our core we are essentially compassionate, asks Rosenberg, why is it that so much of the way of relating between and among people is violent? He contends that "violence comes because of how we were educated, not because of our nature. We have been educated [socially conditioned] to believe that we are basically evil and selfish . . . We have learned to think in terms of moralistic judgments of one another. We have words in our consciousness like right, wrong, good, bad, selfish, unselfish, terrorists, freedom fighters. And connected to these judgments is a concept of justice based on what we deserve. If you do bad things, you deserve to be punished. If you do good things, you deserve to be rewarded" (2005, 18).

This way of understanding reality is so deeply embedded in our culture that we barely have the capacity to question it, much less to see its comprehensively debilitating effects on our hearts and minds. In this vein, psychologist O. J. Harvey reported that the frequency of words that judge and classify people found in a given country's literature is positively correlated with the incidence of violence in that country (1961, as cited in Rosenberg 1999). Of course, the idea that with our language we can do violence is not new. What is fresh and timely is the possibility that the way we use language could actually enhance our compassionate nature and contribute to creating peace among us.

The entree into Rosenberg's work comes in recognizing that each of us is a bundle of needs. We all share the need to eat, to express gratitude, to cry, to cultivate friendships, to be respected and trusted, to bond with others, to experience beauty, and so on. Problems arise when these essential needs go unmet—a frequent occurrence in most peoples' lives.

Absent an awareness of our essential needs lying below our many surface wants, we will unavoidably go dead, similar to a baby who will die if its fundamental needs aren't met. Once we understand this, we can begin to develop ways of meeting our core needs directly, instead of slipping into manipulation or conditioned behaviors that undermine our integrity and life purpose.

Now here is the key point: Nonviolent Communication is based on the premise that we, as humans, have an innate desire to meet each other's needs. Do you believe this? Read it again: We, as humans, have an innate desire to meet each other's needs! Think about it. Call to mind something you have done in the last week that made life better for someone else. Take a minute. Now, as you recall that act of yours, register how you felt? If you are like the overwhelming majority of people on Earth, you felt good! It's essentially universal: Human beings enjoy meeting each other's needs. In fact, there is probably nothing that gives us such deep and full satisfaction as helping each other. Our needs serve as the great connectors, linking us to one another, but *only* if we are able to effectively communicate our needs. This is a skill central to Nonviolent Communication.

In sum, Rosenberg's thesis has two parts: (1) an awareness and clean expression of one's genuine needs grows out of compassion for oneself and, at the same time, invites a compassionate response from the other; and (2) compassionate responses (growing out of our innate compassionate nature) have the power to transform our households, classrooms, and communities.

Nonviolent Communication: The Basic Model

To acquaint people with Nonviolent Communication (NVC), Rosenberg distinguishes between two ways of speaking. One he refers to as "violent" and,

ADDICTIONS: CONFUSING NEEDS AND WANTS

It is when we get fixated on a surface *want* that fails to meet a genuine *need* that addictions develop. For example, if we are not able to get the love that we *need,* we might *want* to eat a pint of ice cream every evening to fill the void we feel inside. Or if our fundamental *need* for human interaction is not met, we might *want* to spend hours and hours watching television each evening, experiencing a kind of pseudo community on the screen. In these examples, the wants (ice cream and television) are, actually, expressions of deeper unmet needs. Such wants can become addictions because no matter how much we indulge in them, they can never fill the emptiness we feel inside.

An effective way to explore this distinction between wants and needs is to first make a list of everything that you want in life right now. Don't filter—just write away, listing all that you want. Within five minutes you might produce a list of a dozen or more things. Once you have your list, pause and, for each thing on your list, allow yourself to really feel how much you want it. Then, for each item ask, "What is the deeper need below this want of mine?" So, for example, if "I want my principal to give me a raise" is on your list, ask yourself, "What is this really about deep down?" Is it recognition? Security? Fairness?" As you ask this question for each of your wants, it is likely that you will discover that below each one there will be a deeper core need—the need for love, the need to be of service, the need for recognition, and so on.

ultimately, harmful—it results in separation. Nonviolent speech, by contrast, is open, compassionate, life-affirming (relational). Nonviolent Communication is based on observations, not judgments; feelings, not thoughts; core needs, not superficial desires; and carefully framed requests, not demands. Rather than leading to separation, NVC (both our speaking and our listening) connects us to each other.

Let's first explore a general example of NVC in action. Then we'll move to several, more specific, school-based examples.

A General Case

Imagine a mother who has just opened the door to her home after a long day of work. Stepping inside, she immediately sees her teenage daughter's dirty clothes strewn about on the living room floor, along with a half-finished bowl of cereal on the coffee table, surrounded by blobs of jelly. Meanwhile, her daughter is sprawled out on the couch filing her nails, with the stereo going full blast.

In this scenario, the mother arrived feeling glad to be home after a long day at work. Then, she opened the door and everything changed. Within seconds the hairs on the back of her neck were, literally, standing up. Meanwhile, two glands nestled on top of her kidneys began to shoot adrenaline into her bloodstream. She didn't ask her glands to do this—it's just what happens when we human beings become upset; it's how we prepare our bodies to respond to danger. So, at the very moment when this mother needed access to her full intelligence, her body was busy diverting the flow of blood away from her brain (compromising her ability to think) and toward her muscles, preparing her to fight or to flee.

Put yourself in this mother's place. Given these physiological events, all occurring within a matter of seconds, is it any wonder that you sometimes find it challenging to communicate effectively in stressful situations? Allow yourself to go further by picturing the mother raging at her daughter: "I am sick and tired of coming home to this pigsty. Get your lazy butt off the couch and clean up this mess immediately!" Then, visualize the daughter—jolted out of her reverie—stomping off, yelling over her shoulder, "I didn't ask to live in this hell hole, and I hate it here!" Slam.

Let's apply NVC to this scenario. The starting point in NVC is the simple question: "What is alive for me right now?" Again, imagine the mother has just returned home to her daughter. This time, rather than exploding, the mother, skilled in NVC, has the presence of mind to ask herself: "What is alive for me right now?" She knows that to access the answer to this question she must combine her (1) observations, (2) feelings, and (3) needs.

Observation. The mother addresses her daughter in objective terms, stating what she sees. Rather than issuing a judgment ("When I see this pigsty . . . "), the mother simply observes. ("I see clothes on the floor and unwashed dishes and several blobs of jelly on the table.") There is no embellishment, no hyperbole. She is simply stating what anyone, including her daughter, in looking around the room, would see.

Feeling. The mother's second step in accessing "what is alive for her" is to simply state how she feels in response to what she has just observed. She might say, "When I see clothes on the floor, I feel agitated or upset or ruffled." If the mother's intent is to truly let her daughter know what is alive for her, it will be necessary for her to name her feelings as accurately as possible. To simply say, "When I see clothes on the floor, I feel bad" would not be helpful. "Bad" could mean sad, upset, afraid, agitated, suspicious, nervous, heavy, fatigued, disgusted, vexed, and many, many other things. Also, attempting to speak her truth, the mother must be careful not to confuse her actual feelings with any judgments that she might have. For example, if she were to say, "When I see clothes on the floor, I feel that you should know better," she would be expressing a judgment (rather than a feeling) and this, inevitably, would create a distance between herself and her daughter.

Needs. In the third step, the mother recognizes that any time she observes something that leaves her feeling upset, it is not what the other person has done that is the cause of her upset; rather, she is upset because some need of hers is not being met. This is key. To really get at "what's alive for her," the mother has to dig deep and discern the need below her upset. Perhaps she is upset because she has a need for order. So, it is not her daughter that has upset her; it is her internal need for order that has been upset.

Now, combining steps 1, 2, and 3, the mother is able to say to her daughter: "When I come home and see clothes on the floor and unwashed dishes and blobs of jelly on the table, I feel upset because I have a need for order." With this statement the mother has conveyed what is alive for her, in terms of what she observes, feels, and needs, without mentioning her daughter, much less judging or attacking her.

The Request. The last step in NVC is to make a request. In preparing to make her request, the mother asks herself: "What would make life more wonderful for me?" Notice that the key question is not, "What should my daughter do?" There are no *shoulds* in NVC. The mother, having clearly expressed her observations and associated feelings and needs, now makes a request and, in so doing, creates the conditions for her daughter (should she choose) to contribute to her happiness.

To be effective, the mother's request must state what she wants in specific terms. Saying to her daughter "Would you be willing to stop making such messes?" is vague, tinged with judgment, and fails to focus on what this mother would like her daughter to actually do in the present to meet her need. By contrast, an effective NVC request might sound like: "After the next song is over, would you be willing to put away the things on the floor that belong to you, clean up the blobs of jelly on the table, and wash your cereal bowl and spoon?" Notice the specificity of this request and the inclusion of a time frame.

In the face of this request, introduced by a blame-free communication of observations, feelings, and needs, the daughter may very well do what is asked because, as Rosenberg points out, it is in our nature to want to meet each other's needs, provided we are not being bullied or cajoled to do so. It is essential that the request not be a disguised demand. To check for this, the mother would need to ask herself, "Am I willing to give my daughter the freedom to respond to my request in any way that she chooses?" In other words, "Am I OK if my daughter says 'No' to my request"? If not, the mother's request is really a demand. And, as Rosenberg points out: "Any time somebody does what we ask out of guilt, shame, duty, obligation or fear of punishment, we're going to pay for it . . . because demands are destructive of human relationships" (2005, 47).

In sum, the skillful use of Nonviolent Communication requires that speakers gain the capacity to access and speak with clarity and compassion about their feelings and their deep, heartfelt needs. These are skills that are rarely taught, much less modeled, in school settings. Rather, the prevailing message in schools is that feelings have no place, to have needs is a weakness, and that rules (and the threat of punitive reactions), rather than compassion, compel action.

NVC in the Classroom: Asking Students to Pay Attention

This capacity to speak using the language of NVC, to clearly state one's observations, and articulate one's feelings and underlying needs, and then make a clear request, is useful not only in moments of turmoil but at all times. Imagine that you are attempting to present a new concept to the students in your classroom, and you note that about one-quarter of them are not giving you their attention. You are starting to feel frustrated and upset. What might you do?

> Option 1. You could just plough ahead and try to ignore the situation.
> Option 2. You could try to suppress your irritation and attempt to politely ask the class members to give you their attention.
> Option 3. You could raise your voice (revealing your irritation) and order the class to pay attention or else they will receive extra homework.

In each of these cases, a different message is conveyed to students.

> Option 1. The message is passivity. You, as teacher, don't care enough about yourself or the material you are teaching to improve the situation.
> Option 2. The message is suppressed anger. You, as teacher, behave in a nice *dead* way, failing to reveal what you are feeling and why you would like the attention of your students.
> Option 3. The message is domination. You, as teacher, exercise power over your students by threatening to punish them if they don't submit to your authority.

These all sound like familiar teacher responses, no? Now, consider the NVC option. In this case you, as teacher, first speak what is alive for you, stating, in the moment, your observations, feelings, and needs; and then, you make your request. Your words might sound something like this:

> As I look around I see several of you talking and a few of you gazing out the window. (Note—this is an observation, absent any judgment.) This leaves me feeling discouraged and frustrated because I have a need to be able to explain this concept to you—a concept that has been useful in my own life and that I believe you will find useful too. So, would you give me your undivided attention for the final ten minutes of this class? If you can meet my request, simply nod and if you choose not to meet it, just shake your head, and I will accept that.

If there are students who do not nod their agreement, the teacher could choose to see this as a gift to her! Why? Because these students are truthspeaking, and this takes courage. Indeed, students who opt *not* to meet the teacher's request are signaling, as best they can, that *they* too have a need that is not being met, given the present arrangement. The wise teacher would see a student's refusal as an opportunity to help that student identify her needs and then to work to find a way whereby her needs could be met.

It might even be that most of the students shake their heads, instead of nodding in agreement. Such a peaceful rebellion could be the first step toward a teacher working, hand-in-hand, with her students to develop learning objectives that are mutually determined—objectives that are not arbitrary but, instead, meet the genuine needs of students. After all, "the most important aspect in learning is to choose what is worth learning. If I alone [as the teacher] make that choice, every day, I would be reserving the most important part of [someone else's] learning for myself" (Rosenberg 2005, 81). In the end, a teacher's demand to "pay attention" has a deeper meaning in so far as the wise teacher knows that learning is inevitably short-circuited when a teacher uses her own needs to trump her students' needs.

Listening in NVC

Listening is the energizer, the fuel and foundation, in all communication. In the specific context of NVC, listening entails focusing on the feelings and the needs behind the speaker's words. Rosenberg (1999, 13) tells of attending a meeting at a mosque in a refugee camp near Jerusalem when a man, learning that Rosenberg was American, suddenly stood up and cried "Murderer!" In that instant, rather than becoming afraid or defensive, Rosenberg listened beneath the man's harsh accusation and "heard" the word, "Please!" Why "Please!"?

Because, this refugee was, in effect, saying, *"Please* meet my unmet need." He was crying out to have his pain heard—this was his unmet need. Rosenberg's mental response in that instant was, "Thank you, stranger, for telling me your unmet need because this gives me the opportunity to serve life by meeting your need." Rosenberg proceeded to spend forty-five minutes simply listening to this refugee. As a result of receiving Rosenberg's attention, the man's demeanor changed, and the situation was defused of all tension.

Could it also be true that when students complain to their teachers, expressing upset and anger, that what they are really saying is "Please!" Please listen to me? And if teachers were able to truly listen to their troubled students, while also learning to cleanly express their own feelings and needs to their students, might this transform tension-filled classrooms into places of openness and trust? Rosenberg's answer is an emphatic, *Yes!* He should know—he has been coaching teachers in NVC for more than a decade in some of the most troubled schools in America.

In Rosenberg's book, *Life-Enriching Education*, a teacher—call her Helen—tells her story of how the practice of NVC transformed herself and her classroom. Helen describes her classroom as one specifically set aside "for the kids who do not fit into the regular high school program, mostly because of chronic aggressive behaviors or because they're so depressed they don't function very well. The class is a bit of a pressure cooker, with tempers often flaring at a moment's notice" (2003, 91).

Helen goes on to describe a time when she was preparing her students for a state-mandated standardized test. Her students resented these tests, most of them scoring below grade level. Before being introduced to NVC, Helen always had the attitude that the tests were "something we just need to get through and complaining about it won't help." But with some NVC training under her belt, Helen was able to empathize with her students, imagining their fear of failure, their frustration, their anger and feelings of hopelessness in the face of these tests. Opening her heart to her students' feelings and needs prepared her to respond in a new way when her students, learning of the upcoming state test, staged a kind of rebellion:

> *Student 1:* Why do we have to take this stupid test?
> *Student 2:* Yeah, give us one good reason.
> *Student 3:* It's to show who's smart and who's stupid.
> *Student 4:* Yeah, well, the ones who made up this test are the stupid ones.

Helen (listening to their feelings and needs): Are you feeling irritated because you'd like clarity about how you would benefit from taking the test?

Student 1: Yeah, why do we have to take them? We know what the results are going to be. It's a stupid waste of time.

Helen (reflecting students' needs): I guess you'd like to know the reasons behind people asking you to do things?

Student 5: Not "ask" us to do. Make us do.

Helen (hearing more feelings and needs): So you're angry, too, because you'd like to choose what you do here, and not be forced to do things.

Student 5: Yeah, here and everywhere else. What do we get to choose? We don't even get to wear the clothes we want to school.

Helen: (in a tone of voice that expresses inquiry): You're fed up with all the things that adults decide for you? You'd like more choice?

Student 5: It's stupid to even talk about it. There's nothing we can do.

Helen: (continuing to guess feelings and needs): It sounds like you're feeling pretty discouraged about even getting heard by adults?

Student 5: Yeah. Why waste my breath?

Helen: So you feel hopeless and, I'm guessing, real sad when your need for understanding isn't being met?

Student 5: (Silently, he lowers his head, his eyes filling with tears.)

Helen's commentary: Everyone was quiet for a few minutes. There was a noticeable shift in the energy of the class, from tense and angry to soft and sad. I'm sure it was because I was able to just listen to them—with no resistance, argument, or pat answer.

Then *Student 1* asked again: Why do we have to take these tests? Do you know?

Helen: The truth is, I don't really know why you have to take them. I've been told some reasons for the test, but I'm not as clear about them as I'd like to be, so I'd rather not talk more about it right now. I promise you that I will look into the reasons for these tests and get back to you. I want you to know why it is you are being asked to do things. I really want to be clear why I am asking you to do things. I also feel sad because autonomy is very precious to me and I want you to have more choice in your lives. I'd like to do something about that.

Following this exchange, Helen said to her students, "Obviously, there are a lot of painful feelings associated with taking these tests. There's also a lack of clarity about their purpose. I want to continue to address your needs and the confusion and other feelings connected to them. Is there anyone doubting my desire to do this?"

When no one spoke up, Helen continued: "In the meantime, to make things easiest for all of us right now, I'd like to begin and complete this round of testing that has already been scheduled. Is there anyone who would not be willing to go along with me on this?" (Rosenberg 2003, 91–94)

Helen felt astonished and grateful that all her students were willing to take the dreaded tests that day. And in hindsight she realized that, all along, her students had been telling her how they felt. Indeed, it was Helen who acted differently that day by taking the time to really hear what her students were saying. By deeply and compassionately listening to her students, both Helen and the classroom dynamic were irrevocably altered for the better.

Substituting Gratitude for Praise in NVC

We live in a culture where praise is emphasized as a means for supporting others—oftentimes as a way to support desirable outcomes. Parents use praise to reinforce good behavior in their children; teachers employ praise as a motivational technique; bosses use praise in hopes of raising employee performance. Praise motivates people to excel, or so we are told. But if you look at the research, this is not necessarily true. Students and employees respond positively to praise, but usually only for a short time. Once they realize that praise is being used simply as a motivational technique, the "praise effect" diminishes, if not evaporates altogether (Rosenberg 2005).

The language of NVC eschews the use of praise in so far as praise often constitutes a subtle, or not-so-subtle, form of manipulation. Praise is particularly problematic with children. For example, parents and teachers praise children, thinking they are building their self-esteem and self-confidence, when in actuality they may be fostering in children an addiction to outside sources of validation for their sense of self-worth. Once they become *addicted* to praise, children often lose the satisfaction of doing things for the sheer joy of it. Furthermore, praise actually perpetuates the world of judgment, with its divisive effects, insofar as it is parents and teachers who determine—*judge*—what is praiseworthy.

What's an alternative to the often hollow, even counterproductive, use of praise? Imagine a child who has just finished a painting. Standard praise responses from adults might sound something like: "That's beautiful!" "You are really good!" "That's the best painting you have ever done!" "You're amazing!" Alternatively, the parent or teacher could simply celebrate the joy of color and paint with words of gratitude by saying things like: "I see that you painted flowers and that you used a lot of yellow." "I feel happy just looking at your flowers." "I am grateful that I got to watch you painting." Praise is rendered superfluous when a child (or an adult) is able to see directly how his or her efforts are bringing personal happiness and contributing to the pleasure of others.

In sum, "NVC offers a new grammar with an accompanying new vocabulary. It's a way of speaking and listening and understanding, based on compassion, that honors rather than violates the relationships upon which life depends" (Rosenberg 2005, 63). Like any language, it is best learned through modeling and practice, and that's just what teachers around the world are beginning to do (see www.prescottnvc.org/related_sites.html).

Cultivating Classroom Kinship: Five Explorations

As human beings we're built for relationship. Our young remain dependent
far longer than most other creatures, and our neural systems and limbic
brains are hard-wired for empathy, compassion, and connection.

—N. SIMONS 2005

Exploration 1. Classroom Layout and Kinship

As any experienced teacher knows, the physical layout of the classroom reveals, at least in part, his or her beliefs about how learning occurs. For example, if a teacher believes that her students are "empty containers" that need to be filled with information and that the teacher is the "dispenser" of that information, then the classroom, likely, will be laid out in traditional fashion with students facing forward and the teacher standing in front in a position of authority. But if a teacher seeks to foster interdependence, collective exploration, and mutual respect (because she believes that her students hold unexplored creative and intellectual capacities), then a different, more flexible, classroom layout would be enacted.

In my experience, how furniture is arranged in a classroom goes a long way toward creating (or not!) the conditions for connection and relationship. As a way of exploring this idea with my own students, I often conduct an experiment on the first day of class. I begin by setting all the chairs and desks in carefully ordered rows before students arrive to class. Then, after everyone is present and settled into their places, I ask them to take a moment to join me in simply observing the layout of the room. After sizing up this all-too-familiar layout, I

ask everyone to silently note their overall sense of well-being, safety, and con-
nectivity, given this physical arrangement of our classroom space.

Then, we work together to rearrange the chairs so that we are all seated in
a large circle. To test for "circleness," I request that everyone look from left to
right, checking to be sure that they can effortlessly see all the others around our
ring. Next, I invite everyone to look around the circle, making eye contact with
each person as a way of acknowledging everyone's presence. Finally, I ask those
gathered to speak about how they felt before they came into a circle (when they
were seated in rows facing front) compared to how they feel now in the circle
arrangement. It never fails that everyone agrees that the experience of sitting
in rows, staring at each other's backs, is very different from sitting in a circle
with everyone in full view. Most people acknowledge feeling more available,
open, and excited seated in a circle while, at the same time, they note feelings of
heightened vulnerability, anxiety, and even responsibility. As we continue to sit
together, I offer a historical context for this act of gathering in a circle, by reading this passage from Christina Baldwin's book *Calling the Circle*:

> Many, many thousands of years ago, when we captured the spark of fire and began
> to carry the embers of warmth and cooking and light along with us from site to
> site, the fire brought a new experience into being . . . We [humans] came into circle
> because the fire led us there. Struggling to keep warm, struggling to keep safe, it
> made sense to put fire in the center. A circle allowed space for each person to face
> the flame, and as a member of a fire circle, we each could claim a place of warmth
> and a piece of food. Out of this instinctive taking of place, community developed.
> (1998, 27)

Building on Baldwin's description, I suggest that we might more accurately perceive our circle as a sphere. After all, with our breath we are linked to the air
around and above us, and through the daily act of eating we are tethered to the
land under our feet. In short, we are profoundly interconnected, above, below,
and in between.

It is widely recognized that the circle arrangement offers the opportunity
for teacher and student to share power and responsibility for learning. But a
circle is only an effective container for learning insofar as the participants assume responsibility for being fully present. Sometimes I enter a classroom, and
it seems like everyone is either physically exhausted or emotionally stressed. It's
as if the energy in the room is caught in a downward spiral. When this happens,
I might break the spell of lethargy by asking students to join me in "declaring

THE CHECK-IN

The simple act of sitting in learning circle is a call to be present. It is no longer possible to hide. As we face each other we face life. To bring awareness to this fact, I always begin a classroom circle with a *check-in*. (Thanks to my colleague Sally Maud for introducing this to me.) In a check-in people have an opportunity to express what is true for them in that moment. A check-in can be verbal or nonverbal. To illustrate a non-verbal check-in, imagine sitting in a circle and being invited to respond to the question, "How are you feeling right now?" But instead of using words, you express how you are feeling by enacting a body posture that reveals your answer. And, then, after you have struck your posture, imagine everyone else in the circle assuming your posture, as best they can. Then, the next person strikes his/her posture and, again, everyone assumes that posture, and so on, around the circle. In this particular check-in form, participants frequently discover that, though no words are used, they are able to really "hear" the condition of the "other." Why? Because when we allow our own bodies to assume the body state of another, an empathic bond is established.

presence." I model what I have in mind by standing tall, taking a deep breath, and then declaring with a clear, strong voice: "My name is Chris Uhl and I am alive, awake, and present." I then prompt everyone to say in unison: "Who says so?" to which I respond, "I, Chris Uhl, say so. I am alive, awake, and present!" Following my lead, I invite each person, one by one, to stand and declare their presence. Now, I am the first to admit that this is an odd, even goofy, dramatization, but it works! The moment when each person responds to, "Who says so?" with "I, _____, say so; I am alive, awake, and present!" that person, in effect, steps into presence, taking his or her place in our community of learning.

Sometimes I go a step further in employing goofiness to explore presence by asking my students to close their eyes and to take five long, deep breaths. In this interlude I drape a blanket over one of the students (e.g., Alex). When everyone's eyes are open again, I ask, "Who is it among us that has shown up missing today?" After they identify the "missing" person, I invite them to consider and put words to what is missing when Alex (still with the blanket over his head) is not present? This prompts Alex's classmates to think about what—thoughtfulness, friendship, humor, compassion—Alex brings to our learning circle. This simple demonstration reinforces the message that our circle grows in power and strength to the extent that each of us shows up as fully present.

Exploration 2. Cultivating Classroom Kinship Through Council

Imagine a conversation where participants gather in a circle in the spirit of truthspeaking to reveal their inner thoughts and feelings. Referred to as Council, this special way of being together is found in many cultures, tracing its origins far back into antiquity (Plotkin 2003). The intention within Council is to create space for participants to speak about matters of the heart—passions, values, soul stirrings, loves, fears—in short, to talk about questions and concerns that deeply matter. As such, Council is a way to build community and intimacy both outside and inside the classroom.

Zimmerman and Coyle (1991) lay out four principles that characterize the contemporary Council process. The first principle is to "speak from the heart." This is not as easy as it might sound, given our most common way of speaking, which is from our head—offering analysis, rationalization, judgment, and assessment. We often seek to impress those around us and to "win" the conversation (to impress or dominate another with our intellect). By contrast, when we speak from the heart, we are not trying to convince anybody of anything, nor to impress anybody. We simply put heartfelt words to our own lived and felt experience.

The second Council principle is to "listen from the heart." The intention here is to experience, as much as we can, the life of the other. To listen from the heart is to allow the other's words to penetrate one's body, to be conscious of the sensations and emotions they evoke, and to hold these in one's heart as if holding the other.

The third principle is to "exercise spontaneity." When it is our turn to speak, we give voice to what arises in that moment, without filtering: "If we speak what we have rehearsed and not what is in our hearts, those listening with their hearts will know it. If on the other hand, we speak our hearts, the others will be on our side no matter how much we might stumble. So we are called upon to practice a radical faith that, when [our turn comes to speak], we will indeed be able to access our hearts and find a way to express what's there" (Plotkin 2003, 157).

The fourth and final Council principle is to "exercise leanness of expression." The idea here is that hearts speak few words. If we speak too much—using too many words—we may inadvertently seduce those gathered to begin listening with their heads instead of their hearts.

Ideally, a Council is held within a hospitable setting—chairs or cushions set in a circle, with soft lighting. Once participants have settled in, the host (e.g., teacher) explains the focus of the Council. For example, at the end of the semester, class members might gather to reflect, in a heartfelt way, on what the significance of the class has been for them. Alternatively, if there has been an affront or a tragedy that has affected the group, healing or reconciliation could be the focus of a Council.

A Council process begins when a volunteer lights a candle set in the center of the circle and formally dedicates the Council (e.g., it might be dedicated to the search for truth and understanding). This volunteer also places "a talking object," having some symbolic significance for the group, in the center by the candle. The Council formally begins when one of the participants moves to the center and picks up the object and, then, returning to his seat speaks to the theme of the Council. The others listen from their hearts. After someone speaks, the talking object is placed back in the center for someone else to retrieve, or it might be simply passed from person to person around the circle.

Though Council might sound like an esoteric practice hardly suitable for a classroom, it bears noting that it is now being practiced in many settings, including schools, corporate boardrooms, families, churches, and community groups. As Plotkin observes:

> The magic of council arises from field dynamics. When we speak and listen with our hearts for a sustained period, a group field emerges . . . We come to see that each person holds a piece of the truth. Like a circle of mirrors, each person ends up reflecting a part of everyone else, and everyone sees that. The group field grows in this way and transforms everyone in it, and everyone's heart opens more. The rigid boundaries between ourselves and others dissolve or at least become more fluid and dynamic. This is what anthropologist Victor Turner referred to as "communitas"—true communing between souls. (2003, 158)

In sum, Council has the capacity to bring out the best in each one gathered. Indeed, it is amazing to witness the depths of honesty, suffering, empathy, gratitude, and love that emerge from the human heart once a safe and accepting context is established.

Exploration 3. Cultivating Classroom Kinship through Dialogue

> In our modern culture men and women are able to interact with one another in many ways: They can sing, dance or play together with little difficulty but their ability to talk together about subjects that matter deeply to them seems invariably to lead to dispute, division and often to violence.
>
> —D. BOHM, D. FACTOR, AND P. GARRETT 1991, 1

Physicist and philosopher David Bohm saw "our inability to talk together" as a kind of defect in the process of human thought. Most participants in conversation—whether in classroom discussions, political debates, or talk show diatribes

—fail to recognize that what are actually being exchanged are opinions. Furthermore, most fail to recognize that the opinions they espouse and express aren't so much their own as they are the results of events, circumstances and people (parents, authorities, coaches, elders) that have influenced them over the years. When we make the mistake of over-identifying with our opinions and then assume defensive postures, as so often happens in discussions and debates, there is little hope for gaining understanding and genuine connection with others.

As a kind of remedial response, David Bohm set about the task of developing a form of dialogue that fosters relationship rather than separation. The participants in Bohmian Dialogue are not there to bat opinions and ideas back and forth; nor do they gather to dissect and analyze an issue with the intent of solving a problem. Instead, they share a commitment to broaden understanding by opening to diverse perspectives.

The successful enactment of Bohmian Dialogue requires that participants give even more attention to their "inner" dialogue than the "outer" dialogue of the circle. DeMello (1992, 71) describes it this way:

> Of course, it's important to listen to you but it's more important that I listen to me. Otherwise I won't be hearing you. Or I'll be distorting everything you say. I'll be coming at you from my own conditioning. I'll be reacting to you in all kinds of ways from my insecurities, from my need to manipulate you, from my desire to succeed, from irritations and feelings that I might not be aware of. So it's frightfully important that I listen to me when I'm listening to you.

De Mello's point is that once we become *aware* of our own thoughts in the midst of a dialogue, they loosen their grip on us. Our thoughts are still there, but they no longer control us. In Bohmian Dialogue, participants take delight in discovering the shortcomings/wrongness of their own thinking, not someone else's thinking. These discoveries are revealed (and possibly shared) as individuals observe their reactions to each other's statements. For example, whereas in a discussion you might react with vehemence to somebody else's opinion, in Dialogue you understand your strong reaction as pointing to the fact that you, too, hold a strong opinion—otherwise, you wouldn't be having such a strong reaction.

Instead of defending opinions, participants in Bohmian Dialogue appreciate the meanings of diverse opinions, without attaching to a single view. The point is this: If each person is defending a point of view, there is no opportunity for learning. However, if everybody is suspending judgment and manifesting curiosity, then suddenly we are all looking at the same thing together, and we have opened the door to relational consciousness rather than separation consciousness.

Bohmian Dialogue, to be successful, must be conceived as a gathering of equals. In fact, Dialogue is not possible when there are overt power differentials in a group. Why? Because when hierarchies exist, those below are not free to say what they think or feel. When all gathered hold each other as equals, it is possible to act collectively in co-creating understanding.

The subject for a Bohmian Dialogue can be anything that a group agrees on. Often one person will present a question that genuinely stumps her insofar as it defies a single, self-evident answer. For example, participants in a recent Dialogue that I hosted focused on the question "How does forgiveness happen?"

After the group has selected a question and before the Dialogue begins, there is usually a period of silent reflection. Intervals of silence are also common during the Dialogue itself because participants, rather than responding quickly, often sit quietly reflecting on questions like: Given this issue, what's true for me? Why do I think that way? What am I feeling right now? How can I add to the whole?

Once the Dialogue begins, everyone sits in a circle and offers their comments to the space at the center of the circle—not to specific individuals. The idea is to create a situation similar to people sitting around a fire, with voices arising out of the darkness. The space needs to be empty of expectation to ensure a maximum of freedom.

After engaging in their first Bohmian Dialogue, several beginning teachers in my class had this to say:

Annamarie DiRaddo: As the Dialogue progressed, I constantly felt pushed to delve deeper and really figure out what was true for me . . .

Bobbie-Jo Stehle: Bohmian Dialogue opened my eyes to an entirely different way of communicating that is respectful, truthful, and soulful . . . I allowed myself to slow down and listen openly to the words of others while tuning into my own thoughts. When I spoke, I found that the fewer words I used, the more powerful my conviction became.

Erin Elias: When others in the circle spoke, I wasn't listening with the intent to reply; I was simply listening. This deeper form of listening allowed me to truly take in what was being said, rather than hearing bits and pieces and trying to think of ways to reply. This also made it easier

Since Bohmian Dialogue is such a different way of communicating, first-time participants often find it helpful to employ two filters—one for listening and one for
speaking.

The Listening Filter. As you listen: ask the question: What stirs in me as I listen? Do
I have a need to control? A need to set someone straight? A need to press a point? In
short, ask: What am I learning about myself from that person over there who seems
to see the world so differently from me? Just watch, pay attention, and learn.

The Speaking Filter. Before speaking, consider what you have to offer. Will it add
to the whole? If you are preparing to respond as you typically would in a regular
conversation, remain quiet. On the other hand, if you can reveal something of your
internal mullings to the group, proceed. You will know you are ready to share when
you feel somewhat vulnerable in making your offering. Remember that your voice is
important. Make sure it is a voice from your depths—the voice of your truth in the
moment.

> to speak when I finally decided to do so . . . Oddly, the conversation
> seemed to be one of the most natural I have ever been a part of, even
> though we were sort of following a set of rules.
>
> *Megan Weidenhorf:* I long for Bohmian Dialogue. I want to live it, I want to
> be it, and I want to share it.

At present, U.S. culture is deeply fissured. Its lack of coherence is tragically
manifest in the way we talk with each. In the case of school classrooms, talking
most often occurs in the form of lecturing, discussion, and debate. None of
these forms is very effective at fostering wisdom or self-knowledge, much less
community. Bohmian Dialogue is a powerful antidote because it seeks to create
shared meaning and kinship.

In sum, Bohmian Dialogue is grounded in the premise that it is possible for
human beings to discover shared meaning and grow in wisdom as we learn to
set aside our egos and trust in our common intelligence. In a broader societal
context this is important because a culture has coherence and vitality to the
extent that its people share meaning and purpose.

Exploration 4. Fostering Classroom Kinship through Physical Touch

Of all the school prohibitions learned by children and, now, teachers, perhaps the
strongest of them is the prohibition against touching. It just takes an occasional
newspaper report about inappropriate or punitive touching to indoctrinate us

regularly against all manners of touch. A hand on a shoulder is ill advised. To touch another's hand becomes risky. An embrace is unthinkable. For teachers and students alike, the message is clear: "Keep your hands to yourself!"

School activities that involve touch are often dismissed disparagingly as "touchy-feely" or quite simply are "against the rules." We have allowed ourselves to ignore that we humans are, by nature, "touchy-feely" creatures. Simply, to touch is part of our biology. After all, if touch didn't feel good to us, there would be no sex, no mothering, no fathering, no human species! Case in point: We know that babies who are denied touch fail to thrive and often die. The majority of infants (less than one year old) who were cared for in orphanages in the early 1900s in the United States died, even though they received proper nutrition. Absent the presence of another person to hold them, rock them, and nurture them, these children literally wasted away. Those babies who did survive were often mentally handicapped and/or had stunted growth (Ulrich 2006).

Touch is no less important to the well-being of adults, particularly during serious illnesses. For example, the fluttering heartbeat of coronary patients in intensive care units becomes more regular when a nurse holds the patient's hand to take her pulse, only to revert to an abnormal state when the nurse leaves (Davis 1999).

Studies on animals also point to a fundamental connection between touch and well-being. Lab animals provided with regular treatments of stroking and petting develop larger brains, stronger muscles and bones, and more effective immune systems compared to lab animals that are deprived of touch when young (Field 2001; Ulrich 2006).

As humans, it is in our nature to reach out to each other, to touch, and to be touched. Of all the human senses, touch is the social sense—the sense that most powerfully invites us into relationship with each other (Field 2001). We manifest friendly intentions by touching the stranger in greeting; we comfort our children by holding them in our arms; we soothe the sick by reaching out for their hands; we celebrate success by enthusiastically giving each other high-fives. Simple acts of touch like these connect us to each other in ways that go beyond what is possible with words alone.

It is undeniable. We humans are made for touching. We are covered with skin, not a hard shell. Each of us has roughly eighteen square feet of skin embedded with some five million nerve endings, each ready to be triggered by touch. This skin of ours is ready for relationship. It allows us to experience and receive the world. However, these days, from an early age, children hear the message, "Don't touch!" This remonstration comes in many forms—"Don't touch the stove!" "Don't touch that bug!" "Don't touch your privates." Undoubtedly, many of these imperatives arise out of legitimate and well-placed concern for the safety and well-being of children and adolescents. Many schools, however, have established a wholesale ban on all forms of touch—as if to imply that if some forms of touch are "bad," then all forms of touch must be bad.

The exclusion of touch in schools comes at a price. It may very well be that the troublesome behavior evidenced among some kids today—including precocious sexual activity, eating disorders, episodes of violence, and depression—would diminish significantly if children received a steady diet of loving touch at home and in school. Field (2001) reports that when adolescents with a history of aggressive behavior were given regular massages, their level of anxiety and aggression declined. Furthermore, Field cites studies showing that regular massage can reduce the symptoms of Attention Deficit Disorder, enabling a hyperactive child to concentrate better.

Giving Ourselves Permission to Touch

Teachers can take the lead, helping colleagues and students overcome the crippling taboos around touch. For example, pre-school and elementary school teachers can introduce children to the healing power that each of us literally holds in our hands. How? Imagine this scene: A group of small children are frolicking at recess, and a girl falls down and bangs her right knee on the pavement. Her teacher, hearing the girl cry out, goes to her and gently puts her hands on both sides of her bruised knee. She assures her that everything will be okay. Once the girl stops crying and begins to relax, the teacher explains that there is a reason why she has put her hands on both sides of her injured knee. The human hand, she explains, contains energy, and this energy can be used to heal ourselves and each other (Gordon 2006). As this scenario suggests, touch is more than mere physical stimulation. If that's all it was, we could use a machine to rock and pet an infant. However, we know that this would not satisfy the baby's craving for the life-force energy and love that are embodied in human touch.

There are also ways to help older students to thoughtfully explore the importance and power of touch. One starting place is to invite students to do a kind of inventory of their personal touch history by responding to questions such as:

What comes to mind when you think of the word "touching"?

What are your earliest memories of being touched?

What is your experience of touch with pets?

What are your favorite ways of being touched?

Do you have personal prohibitions and/or discomforts around touch?

On what part of the body do you usually touch people?

Do you remember any particular time or times when touch especially helped you?

Why do you think people don't touch more?

Why don't you touch more? (paraphrased from Davis 1999, 215–16)

Imagine, if after exploring these questions, students joined with their teachers in starting a schoolwide conversation on the topic of *touch*. Such a conversation could transform the fear that often surrounds touch with a healthy appreciation for the importance of touch in human communities, including schools.

Another way of transmuting our fear around touch in school settings into an appreciation of the gifts that touch brings is to conduct simple touch "experiments." In a workshop for teachers, I presented the following activity to help teachers explore the range of emotions and intentions that can be communicated and experienced through touch. The activity begins with teachers forming pairs and sitting facing each other. One person in each pair is designated the *toucher*, the other the *touchee*. The *toucher* uses her hand to touch her partner's forearm four times, each time endeavoring to convey one of the following four emotions: tenderness, anger, indifference, and sexual intimacy. Before initiating each touch, the *touchers* spend as much time as necessary to really feel inside themselves the particular emotion that they wish to convey through their touch to their partner. For example, if the *toucher* is struggling to evoke the emotion of "tenderness," she might need to imagine that she is getting ready to reach out to touch a sick child. After each touch, the person being touched (who sits with eyes closed) interprets the touch as coming from tenderness, anger, indifference, or sexual intimacy. Only at the end does the person doing the touching confirm or deny the *touchee's* determinations.

An amazing thing happens when people do this experiment. They come to realize that they can convey and correctly "read" a wide range of emotional states delivered through touch. Indeed, it's virtually impossible to give a perfunctory touch while saying you care, or an angry touch while saying you are sorry. Both the one touching and the one being touched will know the difference (Davis 1999).

With courage and love, we can reclaim our birthright to touch, making class-rooms hospitable places for the wholeness—the body-mind-spirit—that is each student.

Exploration 5. Creating Classroom Kinship through Shared Agreements

Invariably, successful companies, government agencies, churches, and foun-dations, have a clear sense of mission as well as a set of shared agreements. What about educational institutions? How many schools ground their work in an inspiring mission statement? How many teachers, in collaboration with their students, create a set of shared agreements to ensure that their mission is achieved?

Teachers in search of shared agreements capable of ensuring a vibrant and healthy classroom community may need look no further than the human body for inspiration. Deepak Chopra in *The Book of Secrets* describes how the com-munity of cells making up our bodies exhibits the core qualities necessary for the flourishing of human beings, be it in families, schools, cities, or entire nations. These qualities include:

1. *Acceptance.* Cells "recognize" each other as equally important. Going it alone is not an option for cells.
2. *Awareness.* Cells manifest awareness by flexibly responding to sur-rounding conditions from moment to moment. Getting caught up in rigid habits is not an option for cells.
3. *Communion.* Through messenger molecules, cells keep in touch with one another. Withdrawing or refusing to communicate is not an option for cells.
4. *Giving.* The primary activity of each cell is giving. Hoarding is not an option for cells.
5. *Higher Purpose.* Every cell "agrees" to work for the welfare of the whole community of cells. "Selfishness" is not an option for cells. (2004, 9).

Using the community of cells in the human body for inspiration, I invited the students in my teacher-formation course to join me in creating a mission statement and accompanying shared agreement for our course. Here is what we came up with.

A ONE-WORD MISSION STATEMENT

My friend Anita Wells, who teaches seventh grade, reminds me that middle-schoolers are "all over the board." Some days they are angels, other days they are dragons. In the midst of this firestorm of energy and emotion, Anita is committed to creating a classroom culture grounded in deep respect and kindness. When I asked her how she does this, Anita told me a story about how, at the beginning of the school year, she put the word NAMASTE, in giant letters, across the front of her classroom. At first, her students didn't comment on the sign. But, after a few days, a boy called out, "Hey Ms. Wells, what's that word up there on the wall mean?" She responded, "*Namaste* refers to the fact that we all have inside us, at our core, a *spark* of pure goodness. You do too!" Anita went on to explain, "Some days it may be hard for me to see your spark or for you to see my spark, but it's there. So *Namaste* reminds me that, no matter what happens, my job is to see that spark of purity and goodness that dwells in you and in everybody."

Hearing this, the boy asked, "Does this mean that you'll like me no matter what I do?" to which Anita responded, "That's right! No matter what you do, I will do my best to see through it to that magnificent spark of light and goodness that is you!" Anita's story illustrates that it is possible for a single word (in this case, *Namaste*) to encapsulate a mission statement and code of conduct, thereby shaping the culture of a classroom.

Mission Statement: To create a learning field marked by openness, integrity, acceptance, curiosity, courage, playfulness, kindness, and compassion so that we might come more fully to life, thereby serving the community of life.

Shared Commitments: Our shared intention is to foster personal and collective empowerment. It is in this spirit that we commit, both individually and collectively, to becoming ever more skillful in the following realms of human beingness:

- *Presence:* We have come together with a shared commitment to transformative education—to *live* rather than to merely exist. So it is that I give my word to myself and to each of you that I will offer my wholehearted presence each time we gather.
- *Fearlessness:* So that I, as an individual, and each of you as colleagues, may grow each day in strength, courage, and compassion, I commit to live from my growing and fearless edge!
- *Truthlistening:* As a member of this learning circle, I give my word that I will listen to each of you with empathy and with an open heart and mind. Specifically, when I am both internally and externally confronted

with new ideas and opinions—instead of being reactive—I commit to exercising open-mindedness.

- *Truthspeaking*: In this learning circle, I commit to fearlessly and thoughtfully speak what is true in my heart of hearts, while avoiding speech that is negative, rehearsed, petty or hurtful. Recognizing that the spoken word is a gift, I am committed to sharing my gift in a manner that benefits this circle and, in so doing, myself.

- *Mutual Trust:* Recognizing the openness and vulnerability that is called for as each of us strives to grow into our full selfhood, I give my word that whatever is shared in this circle I will hold with honor and deep respect.

- *Directness:* I give my word that, when something goes awry between myself and any one of you in this circle, I will muster the integrity and strength to speak directly to you in a manner that earnestly seeks resolution. In the event that we need help resolving our misunderstanding or conflict, I commit to seek another from this circle to serve as our facilitator in peace making.

- *Self-Acceptance:* I pledge to extend kindness and compassion to myself, affirming that I am lovable just as I am. I do this knowing that as I grow in self-love, I grow in my capacity to love each of you.

May our enactment of these shared commitments honor Earth, respect the ancestors, and serve the future ones.

These shared agreements incorporated the core elements of the human body's code of conduct—namely, acceptance, awareness, communion, giving, and higher purpose.

In sum, this approach, where a teacher joins with students to co-create a statement of purpose and intention, is emblematic of what it means to teach as if life matters.

Wrap-up

If we are to be free we must make each person we meet our ultimate object of reverence.   —BUDDHIST PROVERB

There is a wonderful parable—provided in the book *The Art of Possibility*, by Rosamund and Benjamin Zander—that beautifully captures the core message of this chapter.

A monastery has fallen on hard times. It was once part of a great order which, as a result of religious persecution in the seventeenth and eighteenth centuries, lost all its branches. It was decimated to the extent that there were only five monks left in the mother house: the Abbot and four others, all of whom were over seventy. Clearly it was a dying order.

Deep in the woods surrounding the monastery was a little hut that the Rabbi from a nearby town occasionally used for a hermitage. One day, it occurred to the Abbot to visit the hermitage to see if the Rabbi could offer any advice that might save the monastery. The Rabbi welcomed the Abbot and commiserated. "I know how it is," he said, "the spirit has gone out of people. "Almost no one comes to the synagogue anymore." So the old Rabbi and the old Abbot wept together, and they read parts of the Torah and spoke quietly of deep things.

The time came when the Abbot had to leave. They embraced. "It has been wonderful being with you," said the Abbot, "but I have failed in my purpose for coming. Have you no piece of advice that might serve the monastery?" "No, I am sorry," the Rabbi responded, "I have no advice to give. The only thing I can tell you is that the Messiah is one of you."

When the other monks heard the Rabbi's words, they wondered what possible significance they might have. "The Messiah is one of us? One of us, here, at the monastery? Do you suppose he meant the Abbot? Of course—it must be the Abbot, who has been our leader for so long. On the other hand, he might have meant Brother Thomas, who is undoubtedly a holy man. Certainly he couldn't have meant Brother Elrod—he's so crotchety. But then Elrod is very wise. Surely, he could not have meant Brother Phillip—he's too passive. But then, magically, he's always there when you need him. Of course, he didn't mean me—yet supposing he did? Oh Lord, not me! I couldn't mean that much to you, could I?"

As they contemplated in this manner, the old monks began to treat each other with extraordinary respect, on the off chance that one of them might be the Messiah. And on the off-off chance that each monk himself might be the Messiah, they began to treat themselves with extraordinary respect.

Because the forest in which it was situated was beautiful, people occasionally came to visit the monastery, to picnic or to wander along the old paths, most of which led to the dilapidated chapel. They sensed the aura of extraordinary respect that surrounded the five old monks, permeating the atmosphere. They began to come more frequently, bringing their friends, and their friends brought friends. Some of the younger men who came to visit began to engage in conversation with the monks. After a while, one asked if he might join. Then another, and another.

Within a few years the monastery became once again a thriving order, and—thanks to the Rabbi's gift—a vibrant, authentic community of light and love for the whole realm. (2000, 52–53)

It took a shift in consciousness—a shift in seeing—for these monks to enter into an entirely new reality. This reflects the age-old truth that when we change how we see the *other*, *we* change. Might such radical change in seeing—in consciousness—be unfolding right now in the world at large? Indeed, it is believed in many quarters that humankind is in the throes of a massive paradigm shift—from separation consciousness toward the realization that we are all profoundly interrelated with each other and with the entirety of creation. If we are to teach as if life matters, it is this understanding of our essential unity with each other that we must give expression to—for it is in our speaking, listening, and acting that we can create the new world that in our hearts we know is possible.

CHAPTER SIX

We Are Expressions of Everything

Relationship with Earth and the Cosmos

> There is nothing of me that is not earth, no split instant of separateness,
> no particle that disunites me from the surroundings. I am no less than the
> earth itself. The rivers run through my veins, the winds blow in and out
> with my breath, the soil makes my flesh, the sun's heat smolders inside me
> ... The life of the earth is my own life. My eyes are the earth gazing at
> itself. —R. NELSON 1991, 249

I came of age in the 1960s, a time when people were waking up to how the world's forests, rivers, air, and oceans were being recklessly exploited, contaminated with pollutants, and, in some cases, outright destroyed. Alarms were sounding. Rachel Carson (*Silent Spring*, 1962) warned Americans of the harm caused by pesticides and other toxic substances released into sky and water, and Donella Meadows (*The Limits to Growth*, 1972), foretold of disastrous consequences if population growth, rampant pollution, and unbridled consumption were not put in check. These new awarenesses eventually prompted me to pursue a graduate degree in environmental science and to focus my doctoral research on the ecological healing of deforested lands in the Amazon Basin.

Shortly after receiving a Ph.D. from Michigan State University, I hired on at the Pennsylvania State University. My first teaching assignment was an environmental science course specifically targeted to nonscience majors. At the outset, my dismay with the deteriorating condition of Earth infused every aspect of my teaching—lectures, assignments, readings, assessments. If students received anything from my course, it was the "preaching" that humans are greedy, that we, absurdly, cause the environmental destruction that imperils us all, and that we seem to be powerless to do anything about it. My offering to these young undergraduates was nothing less than a prescription for helplessness and despair if ever there was one!

It took many years of subpar teaching and low-grade depression for me to recognize that separation was at the root of my darkness. I was at odds with myself, which manifested in my addiction to work. I was separate from others, which was revealed in my harsh judgment of those who didn't see the world just as I did. And I was divorced from nature, as evidenced in my constant rushing—never stopping long enough to "smell the roses." All of which is to say that I was separate from—at odds with—life itself!

As years passed, feeling the full weight of my separation and the full magnitude of my ineffectual teaching efforts, I eventually stopped to reflect on what had brought me to ecology and environmental science in the first place. It was then that I recalled my awe in the face of Earth's landforms; my curiosity about the lives of plants, animals, and insects; my longing to live close to the land; and my exhilaration when wandering in wild places. My deep affection for the natural world had first drawn me to ecology and now, in coming to know something about Earth's declining health, my affection had transformed into grief, anger, indignation, and, finally, melancholy.

When I encountered Parker Palmer's adage—"We teach who we are"—I was stunned silent, knowing instantly that I had been given a great truth. When, as a teacher, I was guilt ridden, I was teaching guilt. When I was separate, I was teaching separation. When I was indignant, I was teaching indignation. In other words, I was modeling a way of being marked by guilt, separation, and indignation. Afflicted as I was, I could not but extend the same to the young people innocently poised in front of me. It's as if my students were being blamed for the exploits of a time period, a culture, a worldview—all through me. At some point, recognizing my own complicity with the very "problems" causing me so much grief, I woke up, knowing that young people (and all people) deserved better. So began a concerted effort to invite myself and my students into a different way of being. In this book I call this different way of thinking-seeing-feeling-knowing *relational consciousness*. This consciousness, I believe, provides a path out of our current confusion.

Nowhere, perhaps, is relational consciousness (or its opposite, separation consciousness) played out in a more visceral and profound way than in our relationship (or lack thereof) with planet Earth and, specifically, with the actual bioregion—the physical place—where we live. Whether we are aware of it or not, we all are physical expressions of Earth. Each of us *is* Earth breathing, eating, walking, seeing, being. This is not metaphor, this is reality. Minus our awareness of this truth, we live doomed to inflict harm on our home places and more generally on Earth, which is to say, doomed to *self*-abuse.

Sadly, as Dana and I can attest, most school settings do little to help young people understand and experience, in an embodied way, their relationship to the specific "real" places where they live. In other words, for lack of knowing and directly experiencing their utter embeddedness in Earth, young people matriculate without knowing, in a most fundamental sense, who and what they are.

What we are talking about here is a knowing and an embodiment of relatedness to "place" that extends far beyond common pedagogical exercises like classroom aquariums and insect farms, far beyond field studies of stream pollution and migratory bird counts, and far beyond recycling and litter removal campaigns. What is needed is an approach to education that encourages young people to develop a relationship—a deep bond with their home places—characterized by a profound sense of belonging. Ultimately, our hope is for education as loveship—love for the specific Earth bioregions in which we are embedded—a love that catapults teachers and students alike into relational consciousness.

The Roots of Separation from Earth and the Cosmos

The trauma endured by technological people, like ourselves, is the systemic and systematic removal of our lives from the natural world: from the tendrils and earthly textures, from the rhythms of sun and moon, from the spirits of the bears and trees, from the life force itself.   —C. GLENDINNING 1995, 51

We human beings are increasingly separate—physically, psychically, emotionally, and spiritually—from the generative cosmos that has brought us into being, the exuberant Earth that sustains us, as well as the specific bioregions within which each of us lives, learns, grows, and one day will die. Here we explore four roots of separation consciousness while, at the same time, offering ways of cultivating relational consciousness.

Separation Root 1. Our Indoor Lives Separate Us from the Natural World

During childhood, human beings have their first opportunity to experience nature. In urban settings, the experience of the natural world may be reduced to a moth in lamplight, a solitary tree, or a raindrop on a bedroom window. In suburbia, nature might be experienced as manicured lawns, pine bark–mulched gardens, or birds gathering at a feeder. For a child in the country, the experience of nature might include tomatoes in the garden, worms in the manure pile, chickens in the yard, and hideouts in the woods.

The frequency and richness of our childhood encounters with nature determine, to a significant degree, the affinity for nature that we have as adults. An adult who loves being in the woods likely remembers a childhood filled with opportunities to do things such as climb in trees, dig in the dirt, pick wild berries, chase after butterflies, and play "Pooh Sticks" in the neighborhood stream.

In recent decades, however, the wild world of stream, forest, and field has become "terra incognita" for many children. This is, in part, the result of the allure of indoor electronic stimuli. We've all heard the litany: Children between the ages of six and eleven now spend, on average, thirty hours a week in front of screens—watching TV, viewing videos, playing computer games and/or surfing the Internet.

This separation from the "real world" is exacerbated by recent school policies such as banning live animals from classrooms, shortening or eliminating recess, and banishing school trips. The whole idea of teaching children about nature within schools is severely flawed insofar as such teaching takes place within structures—school buildings—where the living Earth barely shows up at all.

The sobering truth is that these days children and their teachers live almost their entire lives within "boxes." We wake up in a box (bedroom), we rush off to work in a box (car or school bus), and then we proceed to spend our days in classrooms and offices (more boxes). Remarkably, it is possible for teachers and students—for each of us—to pass entire days without making direct contact with the real world—dwelling from morning to night in human-created environments that exclude unfiltered sunlight, fresh air, free-running water, pungent earth, native plants, and wild animals (Van Matre 1990).

For children and young people, in those increasingly rare instances when they do venture outside, they are often told that they must defend themselves against nature by bundling up to avoid a stray puff of fresh air that may cause a shiver or by wearing raincoats and rain hats to ensure that not a single drop of rain touches their bodies. Meanwhile, our efforts to keep our houses completely dirt- and germ-free further reinforce our removal from the natural world. Such fanaticism bespeaks our fear-based separation from all things natural and earthy.

The profound separation from nature experienced by most "educated" people is utterly new and unprecedented. Our understanding of what it means to be "outside" (to leave our houses and walk out the door) is directly opposed to native people's understanding of "outside." For them, if you are indoors you are actually outside of the real world and when you venture outdoors you are actually inside—you are dwelling within what is real, alive, and true.

The boxes that school is enacted in, with their geometric, recto-linear forms, artificial materials, and climate control are a far cry from the richly organic mix of forms, sounds, smells, and textures that make up the natural world. Dwelling in sanitized boxes surrounded by human sounds, children get the message, loud and clear, that the only world that matters—*the only world that is*—is the human-centered one.

Living lives restricted to boxes means that all of us—teachers and students alike—lack a fundamental understanding of where we are, who we are, and of what we are made. Think about it: Most schools all but ignore the geography of their students' home place—opting instead for the study of distant and exotic places. The implication, of course, is that somewhere else—somewhere far away—is more interesting and more worthy of consideration and care than the unique place that is right here! The result: Young people, all too often, grow up absent a sense of belonging to and being nurtured by the particular living place that is their home.

There is a simple test (from Brian Swimme's *The Hidden Heart of the Cosmos*) that you can take to gauge the level of intimacy you have (or lack) with your home place:

> It is easy to do. You simply invite someone to visit you who lives at least twenty miles away and who has never visited you before. You can give verbal instructions on how to get to your abode over the telephone, but the one rule is this: In your directions you may refer to anything but human artifice. You may refer to hills, oak trees, the constellations of the night sky, the lakes or ocean shores or caves, the positions of the planets or any ponds, trails, or prairies, the Sun and Moon, cliffs, plateaus, waterfalls, hillocks, estuaries, bluffs, woodlands, inlets, forests, creeks, swamps, bayous, groves, and so on. Whenever your friend gets stuck, she is free to phone you for more directions, but the rule for her is that she must describe her location without referring to any human artifice. (Swimme 1996, 56)

Though this test asks a very basic question (Do you know where you are?), most of us would flunk it. However, native peoples who dwelled on the North American continent before European settlers arrived—the so-called savages and uneducated—would, no doubt, have had little difficulty with such a test.

Because we enact our lives mostly indoors, we have little knowledge about the sources of the water, food, energy, and clothing that we depend on for our survival. Nor do we have much knowledge or interest regarding what happens to these things after we are finished with them. Here is a second quiz for gauging your basic awareness of those matters that sustain your very life.

Where does your water—this most basic of substances that you use by the tens of gallons each day—come from?

Where does the water that washes down the drains and toilet bowls in your home go?

What about the origins of the solids entering your home—especially food, clothes, and furnishings? Where do these come from?

What about the solid waste that leaves your home? What happens to it after it is picked up by garbage collectors?

Finally, what type of energy (solar, coal, nuclear, etc.) do you use in your home for electricity, heating, and cooling, and what is the source of this energy?

Tragically, many young people today, despite the best efforts of environmental education standards and curricula, have been conditioned to believe that water simply comes from the tap, food from the supermarket, and energy from the plug. As for trash, well, it simply goes "away." End of story.

And how might we overcome such hubris? A metaphorical war against ecological illiteracy? More educational reform? An ecological literacy Olympiad? No. How about simply a step outside of the boxes—both the physical boxes that restrict us and the mental boxes that condition our thinking—and a step into a genuine, visceral relationship with the unique bioregions in which we dwell.

In the end, entering into relationship with the natural world is really not that complicated. For kids, all that is required are small patches of "wildness" right where they live—little nooks and crannies where they can come and go as they please with a minimum of adult supervision. Such a "nook" might be nothing more than a single hemlock tree with low branches that forms a natural hideout, or it could be just a spot of rough ground in the backyard that is not manicured or protected—a place stockpiled with no more than some lumber scraps, logs, shovels, sand, watering cans, and a few hand tools. In short, a place for kids to dig and build, to be bumped and scraped, to get wet and muddy (Finch 2003). In such places children can engage in free-spirited play—the kind of genuine play that is open-ended and creative. Nature provides the toys—the sticks and mud, puddles and shadows. Kids bring their imagination and their narratives.

Under such conditions, anything can happen: They might cake their faces with clay masks, transform into salamanders, stalk beetles, befriend ants, ride out thunderstorms high in a tree, howl at the moon. Far from weird or abnormal, these kinds of spontaneous actions bring children into relationship, into oneness, with life.

Make no mistake: It not too late for all of us—adolescent kids, college kids, teacher *kids*—to grow into intimate relationship with the wild Earth that has birthed us (see the explorations section later in the chapter). Simply by leaving the great indoors behind and stepping jubilantly, with our students, into the juicy shapes, sounds, smells, colors, textures, and movements of the natural world, we create the ground conditions for relationship with life, eventually coming to realize that: We *are* Earth, and Earth *is* us. No separation, only relatedness.

How can such teaching be done, recognizing all the limitations to taking young people outside—weather, safety, curricular obstacles, and so on? Well, simply begin with the question: What am I teaching that could be enhanced by being outside? Observation? Quantification skills? History and the relationship of events to a physical place? Language or sensory capacities? Once relationship consciousness becomes a priority—recognizing that we are always teaching relatedness (either positively or negatively)—then apparent obstacles in our thinking about curriculum or specific context begin to dissolve. The first step is to let go of the crippling conditioning that would have us accept living within indoor boxes as normal, and that would have us believe that entrance into authentic relationship with the exuberant Earth that has birthed us can happen with an inside-only existence. In letting go of such beliefs, we can find the wild, the awesome, the mysterious—in essence, the seamless unity that binds all things.

Separation Root 2. The Way We Use Language Separates Us from Earth

The way we use language shapes the way we see and understand our relationship to Earth. Take the word *environment* that we frequently use to refer to Earth. Strictly speaking, environment means "surrounding." When we use it to refer to planet Earth, we place ourselves at the center of things—that is, we are the ones surrounded and so we conclude that Earth is *our* environment. From here it is just a short step to believing that we are at the center of things—that Earth is here for us. This is, of course, ludicrous. However, human hubris, it seems, knows no bounds.

The very way that we use the word *Earth* in English reveals something of our

✿ LANGUAGE CONSTRUCTION CAN AFFECT OUR RELATIONSHIP TO EARTH

The way a culture constructs its language is related to how its people perceive the world. Consider that the Mayan tongue, *Tzutujil,* spoken in Guatemala, does not have the verb "to be." To grasp the significance of this, note that in English we use the verb "to be" to strengthen our *separate* identity, expressing who we are and who we are not. In *Tzutujil,* absent the verb *to be,* there is a built-in tendency to understand oneself as in relationship with other people or things.

As a way of grasping the significance of this, imagine what it would be like to express yourself without the use of the verb *to be*—that is, without the means to say: "I am," "He is," or "It is." Given this limitation, how would you express the fact that the newspaper (it) is on the kitchen table? Think about it. Without the verb *to be,* your way of understanding reality would be jolted. At the very least, you would no longer experience the newspaper (it) as a separate, discrete object existing on top of another separate, discrete object (the table). Indeed, without the verb *to be* our whole understanding of reality might begin to crumble because things would no longer be defined by their separateness. In this new world, it is likely that boundaries would begin to blur and definitions would become more porous. This thought experiment invites us into a more mysterious and intimate relationship with the world.

orientation to *it*. To appreciate how this is so, read the following statement and fill in the blank: " _____ is the third planet out from the sun?" If you are like most people, you answered, "*The earth* is the third planet out from the sun—you put the definite article "the" in front of an uncapitalized "earth."

Consider, now, how it would be if you dropped *the* and simply said "Earth (with a capital E) is the third planet out from Sun." After all, when referring to Mars, you wouldn't say "*The* mars is the fourth planet out from the sun." This may seem like a trivial distinction, but saying "the earth" implies that Earth is something that is separate from us—that is, we are here and "the earth" is there. As Michael Dowd points out, "To refer to the literal ground of our being, the source and substance of our life, as 'the earth' is to objectify it. Such objectification encourages us to continue seeing Earth merely as a resource for human consumption" (1991, 1). In contrast, when we use our planet's proper name, Earth, we honor its integrity as a creative, self-organizing, living presence.

I experienced this objectification of Earth in a visceral way recently when I saw a welcome sign at the entrance to a national forest that read, "Land of Many Uses." I was disturbed by this "Land of Many Uses" phrasing because it reinforced the anthropocentric notion that Earth exists solely for human use and enjoyment. Then, I considered how differently I would have felt if this national forest welcome sign had read "Land of Many Beings." That would have felt like an invitation to see the forest I was entering as animate and beckoning relationship.

Another illustration of how words can act to separate us from Earth comes in the use of the word *on*, which is frequently placed before the word *Earth* as in, "We humans live *on* Planet Earth." Although saying that we live *on* Earth may sound right, actually it is more accurate to say that we live *in* Earth. If you doubt this, go out in the afternoon, lie on your back, and look up at the sky. Observe the clouds and consider that Earth (in the Temperate Zone) spins at roughly a thousand miles per hour in an easterly direction. So why aren't those clouds up there racing across the sky toward the West at a thousand miles per hour? The answer is that all the stuff up there that we human beings blithely refer to as *sky* or *atmosphere* is part of Planet Earth. Yes, that's Earth up there, too. If you still doubt this, hold your breath! Just as a fish is utterly dependent on water for life, our support medium is atmosphere (Abram 1997). When our aquatic ancestors moved from the ocean onto dry land, hundreds of millions of years ago, they transferred their allegiance from a watery ocean below to a gaseous ocean above (Weston 1994).

Today, our prevailing consciousness leads us to simply see atmosphere (air) as empty space or, if you are of a scientific disposition, to define atmosphere as a complex mixture of gases. Caught in this limited and objectifying worldview, we say things like, "Humans can only pump so many tons of greenhouse gases into the atmosphere each year without disturbing Earth's climate." Sadly, this way of speaking (and perceiving) fails to acknowledge that each of us is intimately entangled with the living atmosphere. Our body-mind-spirit is imbued with atmosphere and inseparable from it.

The point here is that the words that we use (even the prepositions!) in talking about Earth and its inhabitants can shape our perceptions, engendering separation. This is equally true when it comes to the animals with whom we share Earth. When we refer to other animals as "its" (like pieces of furniture), as is so often the case, we reduce them to objects. Once they are rendered objects, we feel justified in treating them as we wish. Alternatively, seeing animals as they are—co-inhabitants of a shared world—engenders respect, even reverence.

As we come to see Earth and its inhabitants in a more relational context, the expression *Mother Earth* becomes a compelling descriptor for what Earth is—the womb of life—all life! As theologian Thomas Berry reminds us: "The human is derivative; Earth is primary."

By calling attention to how our language informs either our relatedness to or separation from Earth, we seek to cultivate ways of speaking that remind us that Earth doesn't belong to us but, rather, we belong to Earth. We are part of Earth's living body, so anything we do to Earth, we do to ourselves!

Separation Root 3. Our Dominant Worldview Separates Us from Earth

Now that almost every aspect of Earth has become objectified or "thing-ified," what remains is for all to be priced and tagged. Indeed, even our most intimate *Earth*—the human body—is now being commoditized. Men sell sperm; women rent out their uteruses; global markets trade in human organs. Meanwhile, a new class of scientists—genetic engineers—busily mine and recombine the genes of plants and animals—raw materials for the manufacture of new "products" in this brave new world.

This utility-based worldview—utterly new within the history of humankind and spreading virally across nations and cultures—is what Barbara Brandt (1995) calls "economism." Adherents of economism believe that our primary purpose in life is to work hard at a job to make money in order to buy the things that will bring happiness—that is, they promote the life equation: Work = Money = Things = Happiness! Most people blindly accept this view of life as simply the way things are—end of story.

That Americans are more commonly referred to as *consumers*, rather than as *citizens*, in public media discourse is a measure of economism's power to affect perception. A further indication of economism's effectiveness has been its ability to co-opt the original purpose of many societal institutions and functions. So it is that many Americans have now come to see schools as places where teachers help kids get ahead so that they can compete and make money in a dog-eat-dog world. Lost, or anachronistic, is the view of education as the process through which young people are helped to identify and creatively pursue their passions, all the while cultivating civic responsibility and relational intelligence. In a similar vein, under the spell of economism, the main purpose of government these days is to promote, unabashedly, policies that encourage perpetual growth and consumption, as opposed to promulgating democratic ideals that lead to peace and justice for all of Earth's inhabitants.

Recognizing that economism has all the trappings of a religion—deities, high priests, missionaries, places of worship, commandments—helps explain its power to influence our thoughts and actions. Among *economism*'s "deities" are: *money*, the ultimate source of security; *science*, the ultimate source of knowledge;

and *technology*, the ultimate source of power. Indeed, this is the trinity that many in Western culture now trust in for earthly salvation. It follows that the "high priests" of economism—those who are closest to the gods—are economists, scientists, and technologists.

Other parallels between religion and economism are easily recognized. For example, economism's missionaries are the minions of transnational corporations seeking to convert all nations to free-market capitalism; economism's "churches"—the places where the faithful hear about the power of money and hard work to bring them happiness—are the outlets of the corporate-controlled media. Finally, economism, just like a bona fide religion, has commandments: Work long hours, and you will be judged worthy! Shop, and you will happy! Trust in technology, and you will be saved! So institutionalized have these commandments become that most people see them as basic tenets of life (Uhl 2004).

The tragedy of economism—its dark underbelly—is that it leads neither to happiness nor freedom. The National Opinion Research Center reports that although Americans almost doubled their expenditures on goods and services between 1970 and 2000, there is no evidence for an increase in happiness during that period. In fact, the freedom that money buys—fancy cars, trophy houses, exotic vacations—tends to yield its opposite, entrapment. Rather than genuine freedom, people become entrapped by their trappings. Will Rogers famously captured the essence of this entrapment and the tragedy of economism when he said, "Too many people spend money they haven't earned, to buy things they don't want, to impress people they don't like."

At Penn State and other universities, it seems that economism is a prominent ideology guiding many (but by no means all) young people on their career paths. Conditioned by economism, these students understand college as an economic transaction, a business deal, and they wager that their monetary investment in college tuition will yield good financial returns in the workplace. This has not always been the case. In the 1960s fully 80 percent of college freshman registered their primary college concern as "developing a meaningful philosophy of life" (reported in Pope 2001).

As we see it, economism has become such a seductive belief system, in large part, because it caters to our adolescent self—the child in us who wants everything *now*. In this sense, economism is actually an adolescent religion, drawing out our greed and small-mindedness while precipitating separation from our higher, more actualized self, as well as separation from the living Earth that sustains us.

THE *GOD* OF TECHNOLOGY

Neil Postman, in his book *The End of Education,* describes posing the following question to students in a college graduate seminar: "If someone you love were desperately ill and you had to choose between praying to God for his recovery or administering an antibiotic as prescribed by a competent physician, which would you choose?" Some chose the antibiotic, justifying their choice with the belief that "God helps those who help themselves." Postman countered that one might just as readily say that "God helps those who express their faith through prayer." In the end, when really pushed to the wall, most students chose the antibiotic. The point of this exercise, Postman is quick to point out, was not to "prove" anything. Rather, he used it to invite students to consider how technology acts as a kind of "God" in our culture—"in the sense that people believe technology works, that they rely on it . . . that they are bereft when denied access to it, that they are delighted when they are in its presence, that for most people it works in mysterious ways, that they condemn people who speak against it, that they stand in awe of it, and that, in the *born-again* mode, they will alter their lifestyles, their schedules, their habits, and their relationships to accommodate it. If this be not a form of religious belief, what is?" (Postman 1996, 38).

In the final analysis, economism is simply a *story*—one that many people have chosen, unwittingly or otherwise, to organize their lives around. In accord with this story, we humans are greedy, competitive, and materialistic by nature. However, another, more life-affirming story is possible. We might choose a story like:

> We humans are born to connect, to learn, and to create in ways that respect and honor Earth; it is our very nature to seek to create a world of cooperation, sharing, justice, beauty and peace.

If we were to assign our allegiance to this alternative story, our *gods* would not be Money, Science, and Technology but, instead, Community (the genuine source of security), Love (the all-powerful force that connects us to each other and to the whole of life), and Spirit (the all-knowing, self-organizing, generative energy that serves as the ground of existence). This is the kind of story that would be worthy of our lives.

Separation Root 4. Speciesism Separates Us from Earth

It appears that many of us living today suffer, to varying degrees, from a kind of inferiority complex. We feel as if we don't quite measure up and that no matter what we do, it is never quite good enough. To escape our feelings of inadequacy we sometimes seek scapegoats—in the form of ethnic groups, races, social classes—"others" who we disparage in an effort to quell our own feelings of unworthiness. Our insecurity might also manifest as speciesism—the belief that we, Homo sapiens, are superior to all other life forms and that we are, therefore, justified in treating Earth's myriad species as we please.

But just because we human beings happen to have big brains and the ability to communicate complex messages and make tools doesn't necessarily mean that we are *superior* to the millions of other species that inhabit Earth along side of us. One could as easily make the claim that plants are far superior to us. How so? Because the ability of plants to snag light photons moving at speeds of almost 200,000 miles per second and then to use those photons to transmute water and carbon dioxide into food, is a feat far beyond anything our human bodies are capable of! In a similar vein, bats could easily be judged as superior to us, if the capacity for flight and echolocation were criteria for superiority. Or how about elephants? Their ability to sense danger was well documented during the 2005 tsunami that struck Indonesia. In advance of the arrival of the tsunami wave, elephants were observed to move to high ground, literally scooping up humans on the way. But wait, how about the "lowly" horseshoe crab, a species that has managed to survive the rigors of Earth's changing conditions for more than 100 million years? If longevity were the primary criterion, humans—who have not yet survived for a million years—would be clearly inferior.

Even in the realm of cognitive intelligence, there is no guarantee that we are top dog. So far as we know, intelligence is correlated with brain structural characteristics such as the area and layering of the neocortex, the degree of regional brain specialization, and the folding of the brain's cortical surface. In all of these realms, the brains of dolphins surpass those of humans. The implication: We may simply not yet be "smart" enough to understand and appreciate the nature of dolphin intelligence (Weston 1994).

The larger truth that we have been slow to grasp is that evolution has produced a "tree" of life. This tree has myriad branches, each its own evolutionary line. The "buds" along each of these branches are species. Our species, Homo sapiens, is simply one bud on one branch. We are certainly different from, but not necessarily better or worse than, the millions of other buds strung along the tree's other branches. It is the totality of species—the vast range of life strategies and competencies—that constitutes the wonder and magnificence of life on Earth and not the particular attributes of any one species.

By opening ourselves to live encounters with other species, the hubris and ignorance of speciesism is exposed. One such opening is told about a man hiking in the desert. He stopped to rest.

> Glancing idly around, he saw that his foot had dislodged a stone, beneath which an earthworm lay in the moist indenture, half concealed. He plucked the worm from the soil and held its small coolness in the palm of his hand.
>
> "Lowly earthworm," he addressed the creature, "I am no more important in the scheme of things than you." He said this in mock drama, not realizing that the common creature he thus addressed was, in fact, a being of great consequence. And though the worm neither saw nor heard him, it certainly sensed him—with an ancient wisdom of his kind that no human could ever fathom.
>
> For this worm's [lineage dated back] hundreds of millions of years. And the [earthworm] stands out through history as the single creature most responsible for the survival of all living things. A master alchemist, the earthworm performs the magical function by which death and decay are transformed into fertile earth . . . This it does by eating, digesting, and excreting its food in the form of castings. These castings have buried the Earth many times over in richness . . .
>
> A denizen of the underground, the worm has blue, photosensitive cells in its head to bend its course always away from the sunlight and down into cool, moist, dark, ravenous byways, where, starving and with nothing to eat, it performs its [magic] . . .
>
> Of course the man did not know or think of this, or he would not have absentmindedly tossed the earthworm beyond the lifesaving shade of the mesquite. There, in the full sunlight, it died within sixty seconds. It might have died forgotten. But the man . . . spied the lifeless form of the creature on a rock. He saw that it was dead and realized that he had killed it.
>
> He picked it up again. The corpse had begun to smell. He had murdered the worm . . . He had not intended to kill an innocent creature and thus spoil the perfection of the place where he had found peace. He had kicked the door ajar and was now powerless to close it.
>
> "How many times have I done this?" the man thought wearily. "How many times have I destroyed life around me?" His heart throbbed in his throat . . . (Foster and Little 1992, 182–83).

At the beginning the man speaks to the earthworm in jest. By the end of the story, things have changed; the man's heart, in some measure, has been cracked open. Where there was once indifference, there is now a softening—a place where relationship can take hold. At its core, this is a story about "biophilia" (Wilson 1984), the innate affinity that life has for life. Recognizing this innate affinity—that is, allowing ourselves to experience our natural biological orientation toward relationship—we are able to transcend specieism and respectfully join Earth's family of life, absent hubris. Indeed, the time has come to discover and embody our beingness *in* Earth. To teach as if life matters requires nothing less.

A *New* Story: Returning to Our Home in the Cosmos

It's all a question of story. We are in trouble just now because we do not have a good story. We are in between stories. The old story, the account of how the world came to be and how we fit into it, is no longer effective. Yet we have not learned [a] new story . . . We need a story that will educate us, a story that will heal, guide, and discipline us.   —T. BERRY 1988, 123–24

Ever since (and probably before!) our full emergence as a species some seventy thousand years ago, we have been stargazers. It has been said that our human ancestors saw the stars in the night sky as the campfires of *their* ancestors. Later, with the rise of Christianity in the West, people imagined that starlight was the eminence of God shining down onto Earth. In our time, the human hunger to understand the conundrums of existence—Where did we come from? Why are we here?—is still evoked, unabated, when we gaze into the abyss that is the night sky.

The world's religious traditions provide many examples of how humans, in their quest for meaning and purpose, have attempted to answer life's eternal questions. Within individual faith traditions, the answers have been tweaked and modified over the centuries, invariably with the intent of constructing a compelling narrative—a story—that touches, moves and inspires people.

In the West, the Christian Bible offered the dominant cosmology for thousands of years. According to biblical cosmology, though God created Earth, *He* resided in a realm separate from Earth; and though we, humans, were created in God's image, we were born with Original Sin, besmirched, as it were, due to the Fall of Adam and Eve. The great sin of Adam and Eve was curiosity—their desire to know—their hunger for knowledge. This story was crafted long ago when Earth was understood as a flat surface existing at the center of a universe that extended only a short distance up into the night sky. Although much has happened in the last two thousand years in the realm of scientific inquiry to expand our understanding of the cosmos, we have (at least in the West) remained mired in an antiquated cosmology. Now this is beginning to change; a new story is being born.

As a result of the diligent observations of the heavens by generations of scientists—motivated by an insatiable desire to know (to eat from the tree of knowledge)—we in the twenty-first century now know that stars, like our sun, are actually fiery balls of burning hydrogen. We also know that hydrogen is the most common element in the human body because 70 percent of our bodies are water, and each water molecule contains two atoms of hydrogen and only one of oxygen.

By looking deeply into the origins of the hydrogen and oxygen that make up our watery bodies, we find clues to the origins of the cosmos and, by extension, ourselves. To make this less abstract, fill a glass with water and set it in front of you. Take a sip and consider: Where did the hydrogen in this water come from in the first place? If you don't know, you are not alone. Most people have no idea how hydrogen, the most abundant element comprising their very bodies, originated. So get this: Modern science reveals that all the hydrogen on Earth—including all the hydrogen comprising your body—was formed some 14 billion years ago when the Universe burst into being. Hydrogen was *only* created in that primordial flaring forth—known as the Big Bang—never again since then.

Consider the implications of this. If all the hydrogen in that glass of water in front of you is 14 billion years old and if you are mostly water, then how old are you? Your human age might be twenty or fifty or eighty, but the stuff of you is 14 billion years old! You are ancient; you have emerged through the generative creativity of the cosmos. As we see and come to understand ourselves through this larger lens, our sense of ourselves can't help but be enlarged and deepened.

And what about that atom of oxygen that completes the water molecule? How did oxygen come into being in our cosmos? Just as with hydrogen, the answer to this question holds clues to our origins. During the first several billion years of our universe's existence, there was no oxygen, no carbon, no potassium. These and all the other elements making up our bodies were created when the first stars of the cosmos—so called "first generation stars"—came to the end of their lives and, in so doing, produced the heavier elements of which our bodies are now made. Yes, we owe our existence, the very elements of our bodies, to the generation of cosmic dust produced in star "death." So, we are stardust, not in a metaphorical sense, but in a literal sense; the stuff of us is the stuff of the cosmos. And, really, how could it be otherwise?

GRAVITY OR EROS?

Every evening each of us has an opportunity to reinforce our connection to the cosmos. Just go out after dark, lie down, and gaze up at the night sky. Behold the stars! As you lie there, it is natural to assume that you really are looking "up" at the stars. But as Swimme (1996) reminds us, "up" is just a cultural construct. When you stand on Earth you are not standing up but sticking out into space!

So, instead of thinking of yourself as looking up at the stars, visualize it so that you are on the underside of the Earth looking down into the inky night sky. It may take a while, but eventually you will experience all the stars as way down there below you, and you will be surprised that you are not falling down there to join them. Of course, you don't fall because the Earth's gravitational pull holds you. But were this powerful hold on you to suddenly vanish, you would, in fact, fall down into the dark chasm of stars below. It bears noticing that this mutual attraction between two bodies—your body and Earth's body—fits the definition of *eros*—the Greek word for "love."

In this New Story, we learn that the Big Bang (or, if you prefer, *The Great Radiance*) at the beginning of time led to the *Great Bloom*. "Bloom" here refers to the innate tendency of the universe to become, over time, more complex, more highly organized, more conscious, and more fully alive. In contrast, our Old Story perceives the cosmos as static, unchanging, dead.

Swimme, offers this one-sentence summary of the New Story of creation: "Take hydrogen and wait for 14 billion years and what you get is roses, gazelles and Mozart symphonies." Loyal Rue (1997, 12) provides a complimentary way to think of the emergence of the universe: "Matter was distilled out of radiant energy, segregated into galaxies, collapsed into stars, fused into atoms, swirled into planets, spliced into molecules, captured into cells, mutated into species, compromised into ecosystems, provoked into thought, and cajoled into cultures. All of this (and much more) is what matter has done as systems upon systems have emerged over the past 14 billion years."

This New Story of creation has profound theological implications. For example, rather than understanding "God" as a being, a noun, as is the case with the Old Story, the New Story invites us to understand "God" as more akin to a verb—an action or process—the beingness infusing all: human being, animal being, plant being, atmospheric being, geologic being. Catholic priest Diarmuid O'Murchu echoes this understanding when he writes: "The creative energy which makes all things possible and keeps all things in being is within and not outside the cosmos. [After all,] the notion of an external creator is a construct of the human mind, a projection initially adopted to assuage our fears of threat and possible annihilation . . . In itself, the evolutionary process is the greatest proof of a divine creative energy at work in our world" (1997, 57).

Embodying the wisdom within both science *and* religion, this New Story provides an opportunity to end the tiresome sparring that pits science *against* religion. Said differently, it is an invitation to live in the expansive reality of "both-and" rather than in a constrictive dualistic reality of "either-or."

When we realize and hold in our consciousness the idea that we are here through the creativity of stars, our lives and world look very different. And what truly stretches our cognitive powers beyond their limits is the idea that this stardust—embodied in our beings—has gained through us the capacity of consciousness, of self-reflection.

In the end, the New Story is a narrative of *relationship*. No longer do we see ourselves as separate beings born *on to* Earth but rather as part of a greater whole—beings born *out of* the cosmos—out of Earth. This new self-understanding challenges us to abandon the alienating old belief that "the world was made for us," substituting instead the view that "we were made for the world." In other words, it is not the world that belongs to us, but we who belong to the world.

In sum, everybody—from kindergartners through college students to professional teachers—yearns for a compelling story that explains how we got here, a story that ennobles and inspires us and fills us with wonder, delight, and meaning. This New Story, born of ancient wisdom and modern science, is a step toward filling this void. Infusing this new cosmological knowledge into educational curriculum will help schools fill a core purpose in society—to be places for inspiration, exploration, discovery, and the making of meaning. Our times call for no less.

Embodying the New Story: We *Are* Earth and Cosmos

Why not let awe and wonder be the first goals of education? Why not let our teachers be judged on how successful they are at generating students who can respond to the universe, each other and their own bodies with awe, wonder, and radical amazement at the miracles that are daily with us? . . . Why not declare the person who is most grateful and most awe-filled as the person most likely to succeed in building a fulfilling life . . . ?

—ADAPTED FROM LERNER 2000, 243

What does it mean to *be* Earth? What does it mean to *be* Cosmos? There is no need to be theoretical. Let's cut to the chase. Simply point, with your finger, to the natural world. Where in space is that place that you refer to as Earth... as Cosmos? If you are like most people, you are pointing to some place outside yourself. But, at the same time as you do this, three of your fingers will be pointing right back to you. This is fitting in so far as your pulsating, breathing, life-filled body is an inseparable part of the natural world. Earth and Cosmos are just as much inside you as outside you! In fact, there is really no boundary separating You, Earth, and Cosmos.

This is not something that we need to be taught. We know it deep in our bones; we are born with this knowledge. Think of it as *original wisdom*. If you are skeptical though, simply pay attention to children.

> Mark and his eight-year-old daughter, Miranda, were at a quiet beach one warm, sunny day. Miranda soon sauntered into the soft and steady waves pulsing against the beach. She stood in the water up to her waist, just moving back and forth with the waves. Ten or fifteen minutes passed, and Mark thought that her eyes were closed. Thirty minutes went by, and she was still swaying in the gentle surf in the same spot. After an hour, he found himself swaying with her as he sat and watched from the beach. It was as if she were in a trance. He wanted to make sure she was all right. Is this some kind of seizure? Does she have enough sunscreen on? he wondered, but he managed not to intrude.
>
> It was nearly an hour and a half before she came out of the water, absolutely glowing and peaceful. She sat down next to him without a word. After a few minutes, he managed to gently ask what she had been doing. "I *was* the water," she said softly. "The water?" he repeated. "Yeah, it was amazing. I *was* the water. I love it and it loves me . . . " They sat quietly until she hopped up to dig in the sand a few minutes later. (Hart 2003, 47)

What Mark witnessed and Miranda experienced is open to us all—it is part of our birthright to know that we are one with all that is. But this *right* is not always easy to reclaim, especially when we have been conditioned to see ourselves as *apart from* rather than *a part of* Earth and Cosmos.

In the interest of engendering relational consciousness, Dana and I are always on the lookout for activities that might give young people, as well as teachers, a sense of connection and intimacy with Earth, and by extension, Cosmos. Here we showcase six such explorations, acknowledging at the outset that you may find parts of this material a bit out there or weird. Yet, in our experience, when engaged in with an open and inquisitive spirit, each exploration holds the potential to open up tender places within our hearts and minds, offering insight into what it could mean to teach and to live as if life matters.

Exploration 1: Our Hands Connect Us with Earth and Cosmos

The famous inventor Buckminster Fuller used to hold up a hand during public lectures and ask, "What is this?" Someone would invariable call out, "It's a hand." Fuller would then point out that the entire universe is manifested in the human hand. Indeed, when we look at our hands, what you really see is "the universe's capacity to create hands" (Senge et al. 2004, 4).

In the classroom, I take advantage of the fact that humans have hands to help me and my students hone our observation skills while also exploring our animal nature. I begin by directing my students' attention to their hands, studying the texture and suppleness of their skin, the lines on their palms, the contours of their knuckles, the hardness of their fingernails, the mechanics of their hand's movements. Next, I coach my students to read the history of their hands. What stories are encoded in their scars . . . their calluses? Finally, I guide them to look at the general features of their hands—the "paw" nature of their hands; their grasping fingers and opposable thumbs, the webbing at the base of their fingers. Each of these attributes bespeaks of our kinship with other animals— many other mammal species have "paws" for clutching, other primates have fingers and an opposable thumb, and our webbed finger bases bear similarity to the webbing in the feet of ducks.

With this initial series of observations, the stage is set for having students compare their own hands to those of a partner (in terms of shape, feel, dimensions, thickness, temperature, pulse, color, smell, and so forth.) Before they know it, and largely absent the shackles of self-consciousness, students are holding hands, learning things through direct observation. Most importantly, they are reawakening to their animal nature—their hands show them how they are related to each other and the whole of life (Weston 2004).

Sometimes, depending on the readiness of the class, I go a step further and ask students to stand and find a new partner. When everyone is ready, I instruct them to close their eyes so that they can bring all their attention to the sensation of touch. Next, I ask them to reach out and make contact with their partner's hands. Then I guide them with these words:

What is this object you are holding? There is life in it. If you were anywhere in outer space, in the intergalactic reaches, and you were to grasp this object, you would know that you were home. It is only made here. This is the human hand of Planet Earth and it has taken five billion years of conditions particular to this planet to shape it. Take both your hands now and turn it, feeling it, flexing it. Explore it with great curiosity as if you have never known one before, as if you are on a research mission from some other solar system. Please note the intricacy of the bone structure. Note the delicacy of the musculature, the soft, sensitive padding on palm and fingertips. No heavy shell or pelt encloses this hand. It is vulnerable; it is easy to break or burn or crush. It is an instrument of knowing as well as doing.

Open your awareness to this hand's journey through time. It was a fin once in the primordial seas where life began . . . Countless adventures since then have shaped it . . . This hand connected with tree and wind as it refined its intelligence. This hand: the ancestors are in it, ancestors who learned to push up on dry land, to climb, to reach, to grasp, to chip rocks, to gather weeds and weave them into baskets, to gather seeds and harvest them and plant them again; to make fire and carry it, banked, on the long marches through the ages of ice. It's all in this hand from an unbroken succession of adventures.

Similarly, open your awareness to this hand's journey through this particular lifetime, ever since it opened like a flower as it came out of its mother's womb. Clever hand that has learned so much: learned to reach for breast or bottle, learned to tie shoelaces, learned to write and draw, learned to wipe tears, learned to give pleasure . . .

Experience how much you want this hand to be strong and play its part in the building of a culture of sanity and decency and beauty. Without words, express your appreciation for this hand, and your blessing for it.
(adapted from Macy and Brown 1998, 96–97)

In the debriefing that follows, it is not uncommon for participants to observe that it has never occurred to them that their own hands embody the story of evolution from the ancient past to the present. Indeed, we all owe our existence to a remarkable sequence of cosmological and biological events that occurred in the distant past. To ignore or dismiss our past as inconsequential diminishes our consciousness, circumscribing our experience of what it means to be human.

Exploration 2: Opening Our Senses to Earth

Stop for a moment and look down at your body. You stand upright; your chest and belly are open and vulnerable to the world. Your flesh is not covered by thick fur or scales or a hard shell. Instead you are swathed in soft, sensitive skin; you have eyes to see, ears to hear, a nose to smell, and a mouth to taste. It is self-evident that you are designed to take in the world, to be in relationship with Earth.

To help students exercise their senses and in so doing to experience their kinship with Earth, I employ a simple activity called the Mirror Walk. The procedure is simple. In an outside setting (it could be a field or forest or playground) participants form pairs. One person serves as guide and leads the other, who is blindfolded, by the arm or hand on an excursion, offering a medley of sensory experiences—smelling a flower, tasting a blueberry, touching tree bark, sucking on a twig of sassafras, hearing the sound of leaves being crumpled, touching running water, feeling the gritty texture of soil—in short, engaging with anything that stimulates the senses, tickles curiosity, or brings delight.

The entire walk is conducted in silence, except at certain moments when the guide takes the head of her partner and points it in a certain direction—for example, directly at a large boulder or a spider web—and then says, "Open your eyes and look at yourself in the mirror." The person being guided then opens his eyes and allows for the possibility that he, literally, is looking at himself. After about ten minutes, roles are switched (Macy and Brown 1998).

The activity concludes with participants talking to one another about their experience. I have facilitated the Mirror Walk many times—in the swirling snow of winter and the sizzling heat of summer—and always the outcome is the same: Delight! Participants are touched and moved! They are like children enchanted by wild nature, having been invited, in effect, to come home to themselves—to rediscover their primordial bond with the more-than-human world!

For many participants, the Mirror Walk underscores how grossly they tend to underestimate their sensory capacities. In this vein, Colorado State professor Temple Grandin describes a dyslexic student, Holly, who "has such acute auditory perception that she can actually hear radios that aren't turned on . . . She'll say, 'NPR is doing a show on lions,' and we'll turn the radio on and sure enough NPR is doing a show on lions. Holly can hear it. She can hear the hum of electric wires in the wall. [Grandin believes] the potential to be able to hear the radio when it's turned off is already there inside everyone's brains; we just can't access it" (2005, 63).

It turns out that some noteworthy Western scientists owe their success, in part, to their capacity to *hear* in extraordinary ways. Barbara McClintock, Nobel Prize recipient for her discovery that segments of genes in corn plants actually "jump" from place to place along chromosomes, did not hold her beloved corn plants at a distance—rather, she was in relationship with them. Her biographer Evelyn Fox Keller relates that "over and over again [McClintock] tells us one must have the time to look, the patience to *hear* what the material has to say to you," and the openness to "let it come to you." Above all, one must have "a feeling for the organism." McClintock, in her relation to corn plants, achieved "the highest form of love, love that allows for intimacy without the annihilation of difference" (Keller 1983, 164, 198). McClintock's genius lay, I believe, in the fact that she was part traditional scientist, working with logic and data, and part seer (one endowed with profound intuitive powers), using her full sensory capacities to "look" deeply into corn plants, partially dissolving the boundary between observer and subject.

It is possible for us, like McClintock and others, to also be in genuine relationship with the wild plants and animals that we live among. For starters, rather than being largely oblivious to the sounds of birds, we can really stop and pay attention, recognizing that what we are really hearing are *voices*. Though the sounds aren't words that we can understand, we are witnessing a form of meaningful *speech*. By simply acknowledging this, our capacity to *hear* the world might expand and deepen. And we can wake up our other senses, as well, simply by pausing to remember that everything on this glorious planet is alive; everything moves. Some things like rocks, move more slowly, but everything has its movement and, as such, everything has the potential to move us, provided we are open to relationship.

Exploration 3: Bonding with the Life We Call Food

The act of eating provides an unparalleled opportunity to cultivate intimacy with the particular Earth bioregions within which we dwell. After all, when we eat, we literally take parts of the living Earth into our bodies. Few things are more sensuous than eating wild berries in a mountain meadow, crunching on a carrot freshly plucked from a backyard garden, savoring a pan-fried fish caught in a nearby pond, or sampling wild mushrooms while hiking in the woods. It is food that is our umbilical cord to both Earth and Sun. When we walk, it is Earth's energy—bequeathed from the sun—that walks us! *Mother Earth* and *Father Sun* participate in a cosmic marriage, and each of us, in a very real sense, is the progeny of their union.

All too often these days we eat absent a conscious connection to the "ground" of our being. Much of what arrives on our plates barely resembles food—in the sense that our great-grandmothers would recognize it. In becoming ever-more distant and separate from food, the act of eating is rendered increasingly abstract, banal, a "fueling" activity, akin to stopping at a gas station to put gas in our car. As both food and body are rendered objects, the sacred communion of subject with subject is diminished. And yet, this need not define our relationship to food. Our connection to food is elemental. When we pay attention, it has the capacity to bring us back to our senses, to wake us up.

One way I bring food into my teaching at Penn State is by taking students (or teachers, as the case may be) on an afternoon field trip to our household vegetable garden. In the carrot patch, I present each student with a vegetable-flavored cracker (common to cheese plates). Once everyone has their cracker in hand, I ask them to examine it, noting the color, feel, smell, and so on, and then, when they are ready, to slowly taste it and to register how they feel. Next, I have them reach down and pluck a fresh carrot from the ground, and—just as with the cracker—to look at it, smell it, touch it, and, then, to eat it slowly, really taking time to taste it and to note how they feel. In the case of the cracker, students are quite literally eating *dead* food; in the case of the carrot, they are placing food that is alive, filled with vitality, into their mouths. It is easy to *feel* the difference. Vitality is not something that we need to measure; we all have the innate capacity to detect it, unmistakably, with our senses.

While class members forage and munch their way through our garden, I invite them to pause and to imagine that they are in the supermarket looking at all the brightly festooned food packages filled with nutritional claims—*no* introduced salt, *no* artificial colors, *no* pesticides, *no* cholesterol, *no* growth hormones, *no* saturated fat, *no* MSG, *no* genetically modified components, and on and on. Then, I remind them that all the vegetables they have been munching on have *no* added salt, *no* artificial colors, *no* pesticides, *no* growth hormones, *no* MSG, *no* additives, *no* saturated fats, *no* cholesterol, and *no* genetically modified components, *no* additives of any kind! The point: If you want health and well-being, eat real food—not foodlike substances.

The highlight of this garden field trip comes when I invite students to join

Consider this: Most schools have three important and complementary assets: kitchens, cafeterias, and land. What's missing? How about food growing on school land? Imagine how it would be if school grounds were transformed into diverse and beautiful vegetable gardens and orchards, if school kitchens became health and nutrition centers, and if school cafeterias became places where the school community gathered for the sharing of wholesome school-grown food.

This vision is actually being realized at Martin Luther King Middle School in Berkeley, California, through a program called "The Edible Schoolyard." Established on a one-acre plot (formerly black-topped until pick-ax armed junior high schoolers were given a mission), students tend organic gardens—planting, nurturing, and harvesting vegetables. Along with the garden is the kitchen-classroom where the garden's produce is prepared, served, and eaten fresh.

Rather than bullying kids by lecturing to them about what they should and shouldn't eat or preaching to them about connecting to the natural world, this project invites kids into an intimate relationship with food and soil. Chef Alice Waters, the fountainhead of this project, believes that "we must teach the children that taking care of the land and learning to feed yourself are just as important as reading, writing, and arithmetic" (www.schoollunchinitiative.org).

me in making vegetable soup. We start by harvesting the carrots, onions, garlic, Brussels sprouts, cabbage, squash, beets, kale, beans, peppers, and potatoes growing in abundance in the garden. After cutting up the vegetables, we place them in a big soup pot with some spring water. Then we build a fire and place the soup on to cook. This is a radically different way of eating for most class members. Why? Because there are no intermediaries between them and their dinner. There is nothing coming out of boxes or the freezer; they are the ones harvesting the food, preparing it, and cooking it. When it comes to the actual eating, participants are always effusive, some even professing that it is the best food they have ever eaten. No wonder!

Exploration 4: Bonding with the Trees

Most of us are quick to note how we are different from trees: We can walk and they can't; we have a brain and they don't; we can talk and they can't, and so forth. But if you stop to think about it, we actually share a great deal with trees. We are made up of the same chemical elements in roughly the same proportions, we share many of the same metabolic pathways, our cells contain a nucleus with DNA just like theirs, we reproduce sexually just like they do, and we are air breathers just like them.

I help students to directly explore their vital connection to trees by taking them into a patch of forest and telling them to consciously breathe *with* a tree. It is easy to do.

> Simply take hold of a leafy tree branch and bring your attention to your breath. Breathe out in such a way that the leaves on the branch that you are holding are bathed with your exhalations. As you do this, be mindful that the carbon (as carbon dioxide molecules) leaving your body is entering the tree leaves. Fired by solar rays, this carbon is being forged into sugars in each leaf's interior. In other words, the carbon that seconds ago was part of you is literally becoming part of these leaves as you stand there. That's not all. Each time that you breathe in, oxygen, the byproduct of the leaves' solar forging, is finding its way into your lungs and thence, by way of your blood, into the very cells of your body.
>
> Breathe in and out with full consciousness of the exchange that is taking place. Now, slowly let go of the branch and, as you do so, hold your breath. That's right— stop breathing! Sense the discomfort as your body clamors for oxygen. Then, when you can stand it no more, grasp the tree branch again and breathe in deeply.
>
> Yes! Life-giving connection restored!
>
> Next, slowly release your hold on the tree branch and, without touching, simply cup your hands around a single leaf. Continue to breathe, giving your breath to and receiving breath from this leaf. Then, open your arms to embrace, figuratively, the whole tree, breathing in and out, experiencing your breath going out to the tree and the tree's breath entering you. This sharing of breath between you and tree is truly a kind of holy communion (adapted from Uhl 2004).

As we come to recognize the many commonalties between ourselves and trees, we can slowly build the scaffolding for a relationship with trees and in the process discover that a tree is much more than an isolated brown and green object sticking out of the ground. Like us, the tree is part of a larger whole. The gases that move in and out of its leaves and roots, the water coursing through its vessels, the sunlight penetrating its chloroplast-studded leaves, the insects fertilizing its flowers, and the specialized fungi shunting nutrients to its roots are all integral parts of the tree.

Our relationship with trees, and the plant world more generally, expands and deepens as we acknowledge that it is through the prowess of the plant kingdom that all animals on Earth, including ourselves, are ultimately sustained.

Exploration #5: Bonding with the Insects

What are the first words that spring to mind when you hear the word *insect*? When I pose this question to my students, they often respond with words like: *gross, buzzing, biting, annoying, creepy*. Rarely does someone say: *beautiful, remarkable, helpful, cool, friendly*. I sometimes quiz my students further, in multiple-choice format, by asking, "What would you do if you discovered an ant crawling across your bedroom floor?"

A. Shriek and run out of the room?
B. Squash it or zap it with insecticide?
C. Capture it and place it outside?
D. Step around it, allowing it to go on its way?
E. Greet the ant with kind words and wish it well?

The option a student chooses points, in some measure, to his alienation (or not) from the world of insects.

I believe that befriending insects can expand compassion and with it, relational consciousness. I first came to this view when reading *The Voice of the Infinite in the Small* by Joanne Lauck. Lauck tells a story about Joanna Macy, a teacher-activist, who traveled to a village in Tibet to help the people there start a craft cooperative. One day during her visit Macy met with a group of Buddhist monks. During the meeting, a fly fell into Macy's tea. Though this was not a matter of concern for Macy, the young lama who was sitting beside her leaned over and asked her if she was OK. Macy responded that she was fine. After all, it was only a fly. A moment later the monk again expressed his concern, and she reassured him that she was fine and he need not concern himself with her. Finally, the young man, overcome with concern, fished the fly out of Macy's tea and disappeared. Out of sight, he gently placed the tea-soaked fly on a bush until it had revived. When he returned to the meeting a few minutes later, he was beaming as he assured Macy that the little fly was going to be OK. For Macy, this was a watershed moment, as she came to see that the young man's compassion extended not just to her—in that she had observed the suffering fly—but also to the fly, the lowly fly!

In interpreting this story, Lauck writes: "If something sputters inside us in indignation at the thought of helping a fly, it may only be self-importance arising out of a narrow band of awareness. Our sense of self expands when we extend our compassion to insects. It is an appropriate response to our interdependence.

The question is not how to connect with a fly—we are already connected. The question is how to translate that connection into appropriate behavior. Helping one in need is always a good place to start" (2002, 42).

Lauck's story suggests that in extending kind regard to insects we might actually become more peaceful and loving. In a related vein, when the Dalai Lama was asked what he thought was the most important thing to teach children, he responded, "Teach them to love the insects!" When he might have called attention to any aspect of human existence—compassion, justice, hope, duty—the Dalai Lama focused on the importance of loving the insects!

So, taking this spiritual leader seriously, how might we come to love—to be open to and accepting of—insects? It begins with an invitation to be in relationship with them. To this end, Anthony Weston (2004) instructs his students at Elon College to search their classroom for insects and, when they find one, to carefully observe what the insect is doing, endeavoring, all the while, to see the world from the insect's perspective. Weston sometimes goes a step further and actually releases Daddy Longlegs spiders into his classroom. He informs his students of this fact and then challenges them to find them by *thinking* like a spider—by imagining where you would go if you were such a creature. This is a striking and important departure from standard environmental education pedagogy in so far as Weston is not bringing creatures into the room as exhibits for inspection. Instead, his aim is to help his students realize that there are other beings, other awarenesses, living with them—foraging, resting, making a home, laying eggs, nurturing young—all the time!

Like Weston, I also help my students overcome their separation and/or indifference regarding insects by inviting them to hold a live cockroach in their hands. For many, this is an enormous challenge. Indeed, a Yale University study cites that of all insects, the cockroach is the one that most evokes terror in Americans. We see them as sinister creatures, crawling around behind our walls, operating in darkness, spreading disease and filth. Our beliefs about cockroaches evoke fear in us—even terror!

The cockroaches I bring into my classroom are known as Madagascar Hissing Cockroaches. Adults of this species are about two inches long with a lustrous deep-brown carapace. While holding one of these handsome cockroaches in my hand, I tell students about the fascinating biology of this species. My intent is to offer information that will help them question common myths about cockroaches being dirty, dangerous, icky, and so forth. After hearing these myths debunked, some class members are willing, for the first time in their lives, to hold a cockroach in their hands. This act of extending one's hand to—what for many may be—the "ultimate other" represents a giant step away from fear and toward relationship with the natural world.

Exploration 6: Communicating *across Species Boundaries*

The preceding sequence of explorations has the power to soften our boundaries, opening the lines of communication between ourselves and those wild beings that live around us. Rainer Maria Rilke (1957) refers to the ability to deeply presence the other—be it a tree or spider or cockroach—as "in-seeing."

Having a willingness to sense the world the way another organism might experience it sets the stage for exploring the possibility of communicating across species boundaries. Though this might seem daunting, it does not call for any specific training—just curiosity and a willingness to suspend limiting beliefs. For example, Dossey (2006) reports that local healers in Madagascar, when asked how they know which of the some fifteen thousand species of native plants is the best for treating a certain disease, reply that they wait for the plants to tell them. In practice, they walk about in the forest with an open mind, humbly asking the plants for assistance. Eventually, a certain plant captures their attention—in effect, calling out to greet them—declaring itself to be the proper remedy. Although this seems bizarre from a Western scientific perspective, many of these indigenous practitioners are highly successful healers.

I introduce my students to "in-seeing" by sending them off to simply wander anywhere outside without a set destination. I advise them to simply go where your feet take you until you have the experience of being called or attracted to something—it might be a leaf dangling on a tree, a spider web, a moss-covered rock, an anthill, a rotting stump, a mouse . . . Whatever it is, settle down and prepare to spend time together with this "other."

Begin, as you might any life encounter, by speaking out loud, telling this *being* about yourself. Speak what is true for you, explaining why you are wandering, what it is that attracts you to this "other," including a description of the "other's" salient features, especially those that seem to call out to you. Articulate, as best you can, what you see as the common ground between both of you. If it turns out that words are not the best way to communicate, employ other modes of communication—nonverbal sounds, body language, movement.

Proceed in this manner until you are "interrupted"—until you sense that it is your turn to listen—and then listen with your whole being: eyes, ears, flesh, heart, intuition, emotions. Listen absent expectation. You are not waiting for this "other" to necessarily tell you anything; rather, you are simply present, open to relationship in whatever form it may take. You may learn something about yourself or something about this "other" or something about your kinship or who knows what else. The net result of this practice is that you will be in the world in a more wild, authentic, and wholesome way simply because you will be becoming relational with more of the world (Plotkin 2003).

As we break free of the culturally transmitted hubris of speciesism, we are better able to dissolve the conceptual boundaries that create walls, distinctions, and separation among species, thereby enabling deeper kinship with the entire community of life. As with all facets of teaching as if life matters, the work starts with the teacher—her example, not her words. A teacher who is willing to openly explore interspecies relatedness and to then share her experiences will, in effect, give her students permission to do the same. This is tantamount to giving her students permission to be more expansively human.

Healing Earth, Healing Ourselves

Earth, which is synonymous with me . . . you . . . we . . . is sick. For most of my career as an ecologist and teacher, I simply couldn't figure out why the human response to all the environmental disruption and upset of our times is so tepid. After all, we have been hearing about the so-called ecological crisis for decades. But information alone is not enough to induce action. The missing ingredient is care. When we care deeply about something, our whole being is engaged, not just our minds. But care is only possible when we allow ourselves to feel. Perhaps this is why the Buddhist monk Thich Nhat Hanh, when asked what can we do to heal the world, responded: "What we most need to do is to hear within us the sounds of the Earth crying" (www.ashokaedu.net/coursesM/34/ecologyjm5.htm).

When we allow ourselves to feel the world's pain, we feel pain. This pain has the power to motivate us to respond as compassionate healers. In this state, we no longer engage in environmental acts such as recycling plastic or conserving water or reducing our material consumption because we feel guilty or afraid. Instead, we are moved to act because the *beloved* is ill, and we cannot but act to hold, to help, to heal. Said differently, we don't act because we should or because we need to; rather, we act because we want to, because it pleases and gratifies us to act. In short, we act because we are in love.

When we understand that what we do to Earth's body we do to our own body, we become connected selves (rather than separate selves)—realizing that we are, nothing more nor less than the sum total of our relationships. In this state of comprehensive relatedness, a profound sense of gratitude and love motivates us to act as Earth healers. Our acts become gifts through which we manifest and celebrate our relationship in Earth.

Wrap-up

You live in delusion when you regard all the stuff that happens on or within your body as "you" and all the stuff occurring outside the membrane of your skin as "not you." After all, what about the oxygen your body breathes in and the carbon dioxide it breathes out? Is this you or not you? What about the water you drink? Or the ocean, the source of all water? You or not you? What about the plants or the animals that produce the proteins and the minerals that make up your blood and bone? You or not you? Or the sun that fuels it all, or the elementary particles, spread through the Universe that make up the Cosmos and make up you . . . or not you? What about the vast expanses of empty space between stars, or the silence between thoughts? You or not you? Where does your body begin and where does it end? Where do you begin? Where do you end? Who are you, in reality, as opposed to the whole shopping-cart load of who or what you think you are or think you should be? If you come to this point, realizing that what you have always accepted as "you" is just a deeply habitual thought pattern, a limited framing of reality, what happens? Find out!   —ADAPTED FROM J. CROCKETT 2008

Though we are one with Earth, all too often we live in isolation from Earth— separated into boxes, conscripted to the hollowness of "economism," deadened by objectivism, deluded by speciesism. In short, we live blind, deaf, and mute to the wonders of life. It is as if we have lived our entire lives in isolation, never having had the opportunity to meet the source of all life—the generative, profligate Earth and Cosmos that have brought us, and all things, into being. Though we have lost our way, the call to awaken is palpable.

This is not a time for fretting or complaining. Such actions are an abnegation of life. Rather, our call is to live life deeply, consciously, relationally. It is a call to seethe with passion, to bubble with curiosity, to gurgle with open-heartedness;

it is a call to marinate in life's wonders with fearlessness. In so doing we become juicy and succulent—beings oozing with vitality. We become ourselves—fully human.

Yes, in the final analysis, teaching as if life matters is teaching in the service of awakening! It is not enough to just read about the stars or to merely imagine what it would be like to breathe with a tree or to welcome a cockroach onto your hand. Much more is required. The way to begin is to unlock the doors of our "boxes" and to be deeply present to the myriad manifestations of life, knowing that we *are* Earth and Cosmos incarnate—Earth and Cosmos becoming!

Epilogue

When it's over, I want to say: all my life
I was a bride married to amazement.
I was the bridegroom, taking the world into my arms.
When it's over, I don't want to wonder
if I have made of my life something particular, and real.
I don't want to find myself sighing and frightened,
or full of argument.
I don't want to end up simply having visited this world.

—FROM "WHEN DEATH COMES," M. OLIVER 1992, 10–11

Some years back, standing on a street corner talking with my friend Kersey, I asked, "Is this it? Is this all there is?" I was referring to my life as university professor: teaching classes, conducting research, writing articles for academic journals, going to meetings, sending and responding to e-mails. It had been pleasant enough but, surely, there must be more, I thought. The "more" I was seeking was "more" purpose, "more" meaning. I was seeking an answer to the question: What really matters? With the passing of time, I have arrived at a succession of answers, each one, in its own way, offering temporary solace.

Now, in my early sixties—no longer deluded by the fantasy of my immortality—the question, "What really matters?" continues to stalk me. It often arises as I listen to tributes or eulogies that attempt to sum up a person's life. I note in these moments that one's lasting legacy seldom has much to do with one's career accomplishments.

Physician and author Rachel Naomi Remen tells a story about a special dinner she attended when she was still a medical student. It was a black-tie affair to honor a Nobel laureate on the medical faculty. The man, at age eighty, was approaching the end of his life. After the dinner the esteemed doctor gave a wonderful speech describing all the astounding medical advances that marked his fifty-year career. When he finished he was greeted with a standing ovation. Then a remarkable thing happened. After everyone sat down, the man remained at the podium for a long moment, casting his eyes around the room. He then directly addressed Remen and the other doctors-to-be in the audience, saying: "I have been a physician for 50 years and I don't know anything more about life now than I did at the beginning. I am no wiser. It slipped through my fingers" (Remen 1994, 29).

This man, in spite of his fame, was admitting publicly that he had, by his own measure, failed to live his life as deeply, expansively, and wisely as he might have done. His failure? The pursuit of something other than what mattered most! Remen, in recalling this moment writes, "We were stunned into silence. I remember thinking that perhaps he was senile. In retrospect, it was a very remarkable thing he did. He took an opportunity to warn us about the cage of ideas and roles and self-expectations that was closing around us, even as he spoke to us—the cage that would keep us from achieving our good purpose, which is healing" (Remen 1994, 29).

This story has relevance for teachers insofar as we, too, run the risk of becoming "caged" by the constrictions of role expectations and the spirit-diminishing effects of limiting beliefs—separated from our creativity, goodness, and compassion—left disillusioned and diminished. And it is no different for the students in our classrooms. "Caged" in the web of compulsory schooling, young people are cajoled, year after year, to comply with others' agendas and to respond and seek answers to questions not their own. Just like the famous doctor in the story, today's young are conditioned, more often than not, to understand *success* in terms of the acquisition and accumulation of status, power, money, and fame—all won primarily through competition with fellow human beings.

What really does matter for a successful life? The answer—to know and to have manifested one's soul—what Parker Palmer (1998) expresses as to "live divided no more." Palmer calls this soul manifestation the "Rosa Parks Decision" after the black woman who, living in Alabama in the 1960s, decided one afternoon that she would no longer pretend to accept what she knew, in her heart and soul, to be fundamentally wrong. By taking a seat in the front of the bus (instead of in the designated zone in the back), Parks stood up with her whole, undivided being.

What Parks did within the movement for justice for people of color and all people was remarkable. What's more remarkable, though, is how we all endure

(to our soul's impoverishment) injustice. Parks became fearless when she realized that there was no punishment—not public criticism, not jail, not physical
beating—that could come close to equaling the punishment suffered through
collusion in her own diminishment, through living separately from her own
soul's deep truth. This "truth" is what really matters, this truth is what I long
to live out in my own teaching life, this truth is what will heal children, young
people and their teachers alike.

More than anything, what the world needs now is people (and especially
teachers) who align themselves with life, people who are committed to *living
divided no more*, people who have *come alive*.

To *come alive* is to *feel* alive. Aliveness is felt! It is felt in our bellies when our
purpose is clear and our direction known. Aliveness is felt as a tingling in our
arms and legs as we move to fulfill our heart's deepest yearnings. To be truly
alive is to be fully aware of the unique miracle that is our life's unfolding, now.

Surely, before we meet death, each of us would like to know and to feel that
we have come fully to life. Yet, where in our culture—where in our schools—are
young people receiving the encouragement and support necessary to discern
their path and to nurture those qualities of heart, body, and mind that would
bring them fully to life?

For too many young people, the answer is nowhere. If this seems harsh, consider the results of the recent National High School Survey of Student Engagement (Yazzie-Mintz 2008), which reveals that:

- Two-thirds of high school students in the U.S. are bored in class
  every day.
- One-third report that they have *no* day-to-day interaction with
  teachers.
- Sixty percent say they see little *value* in the work they are being asked
  to do.

Disturbing, yes! But should we really be surprised? The sad truth is that school,
with few exceptions, is enacted in such a way that it mostly distracts young people from what is compelling, immediate, motivating, and engaging—thereby
undermining self-discovery in any significant sense. Indeed, the idea that young
people should have a significant say in their lives—that a ten-year-old should
have the freedom to choose whether to go to school or not, as well as what to
learn and how—is regarded in many quarters as terribly naive. But the truth is
that when we accord deep respect to young people, when we believe uncondi-

tionally in their innate intelligence and goodness, and give them a significant say in their lives, what happens is that they shine, growing daily in brilliance, self-respect, creativity, and power (Cameron and Meyer 2006).

Teachers, in the final analysis, possess the overarching solution to the deadening relational separation handicapping themselves, limiting their students, and crippling their workplaces. The answer is to provide openings for life, for *anima* (soul)—openings for relationship in all its forms—to thrive in classrooms and beyond. There is no mystery in how to do this, for it is life that is all around us, present in all the relationships that constitute our individual lives.

How might one begin? First, by honoring the sacred bond we have with ourselves, which is to say by loving ourselves unconditionally. Then, grounded in self-love, we can bring acceptance and love into all our human relationships, bowing to the myriad forms our *neighbor*—the "other"—takes. And then we can extend this understanding of the good, the true, and the beautiful into our relationships with the living Earth that sustains us. It's just that simple; it is just that wondrous. May we all come alive! May we all awaken to what truly matters!

The breeze at dawn has secrets to tell you.
Don't go back to sleep.
You must ask for what you really want.
Don't go back to sleep.
People are going back and forth across the doorsill
where the two worlds touch.
The door is round and open.
Don't go back to sleep.   —J. RUMI

Bibliography

Abram, D. 1997. *The Spell of the Sensuous: Perception and Language in a More-Than-Human World*. New York: Vintage.

Aldort, N. 2006. *Raising Our Children, Raising Ourselves*. Bothell, WA: Book Publishers Network.

Arney, W. www.academic.evergreen.edu/curricular/awareness/newlectio.htm.

Bacci, I. 2000. *The Art of Effortless Living: Simple Techniques for Healing Mind, Body and Spirit*. New York: Vision Works, Croton-on-Hudson.

Baldwin, C. 1998. *Calling the Circle*. New York: Bantam.

Beck, M. 2001. *Finding Your Own North Star: Claiming the Life You Were Meant to Live*. New York: Three Rivers.

———. 2008. *Steering by Starlight*. New York: Rodale.

Berry, T. 1988. *The Dream of the Earth*. San Francisco: Sierra Club.

———. www.earth-community.org/quotes.htm.

Berry, W. 1987. *Home Economics*. New York: Northpoint.

Boal, A. 2002. *Games For Actors and Non-Actors*. New York: Routledge.

Bohm, D., D. Factor, and P. Garrett. 1991. "Dialogue: A Proposal." www.ratical.org/many_worlds/K/dialogueProposal.html.

Bowles, S., and H. Gintis. 1976. *Schooling in Capitalist America: Educational Reform and the Contradictions of Economic Life*. New York: Basic.

Brach, T. 2003. *Radical Acceptance: Embracing Your Life with the Heart of the Buddha*. New York: Bantam.

Brandt, B. 1995. *Whole Life Economics: Revaluing Daily Life*. Gabriola Island, BC: New Society.

Brown, J. 2001. *The World Café: Living Knowledge through Conversations That Matter*. Santa Barbara, CA: The Fielding Institute.

Bryson, K. 2004. *Don't Be Nice, Be Real*. Santa Rosa, CA: Elite Books.

Buechner, F. 1993. *Wishful Thinking: A Theological ABC*. San Francisco: Harper.

Caine, R. N., and G. Caine. 1997. *Education on the Edge of Possibility*. Alexandria, VA: Association for Supervision and Curriculum Development.

Cameron, B., and B. Meyer. 2006. *Self Design: Nurturing Genius Through Natural Learning*. Boulder, CO: Sentient Publications.

Childre, D., and H. Martin. 1999. *The Heartmath Solution*. San Francisco: Harper.

Childre, D., and D. Rozman. 2005. *Transforming Stress: The HeartMath Solution for Relieving Worry, Fatigue, and Tension*. Oakland, CA: Harbinger Publications.

Childs, A. 2008. "Birthing Ourselves, Our Children, and Our World." In *Life Learning*, edited by W. Preisnitz. Toronto: Alternative Press.

Chopra, D. 2004. *The Book of Secrets: Unlocking the Hidden Dimensions of Your Life*. New York: Harmony Books.

Connelly, D. 1993. *All Sickness Is Home Sickness*. Columbia, MD: Traditional Acupuncture Institute.

Crockett, J. 2008. "Of War and Whales: A Personal Journey from Nicaragua to Nova Scotia and Beyond." Lecture presented 3 April. Antioch University New England, Keene, NH.

Crowell, S., R. N. Caine, and G. Caine. 1998. *The Re-Enchantment of Learning*. Tucson, AZ: Zephyr.

Cummings, E. E. 1966. *A Miscellany*. Edited by G. J. Firmage. London: Peter Owen.

Davis, P. K. 1999. *The Power of Touch*. Carlsbad, CA: Hay House.

DeBono, E. 1994. *DeBono's Thinking Course*. New York: Facts on File.

DeMello, A. 1992. *Awareness: The Perils and Opportunities of Reality*. New York: Doubleday.

Dossey, L. 2006. *The Extraordinary Healing Power of Ordinary Things*. New York: Harmony.

Dowd, M. 1991. Earth or "the earth." www.thegreatstory.org.

Farhi, D. 1996. *The Breathing Book*. New York: Henry Holt.

Field, T. *Touch*. 2001. Cambridge, MA: MIT Press.

Finch, K. 2003. "Extinction of Experience: Challenge to Nature Centers." *Directions: Journal of the Association of Nature Center Administrators*, special issue, 1–8.

Finkel, D. 2000. *Teaching with Your Mouth Shut*. Portsmouth, NH: Boynton/Cook Publishers.

Ford, D. 1998. *The Dark Side of the Light Chasers*. New York: Riverhead.

Foster, S., and M. Little. 1992. *The Book of the Vision Quest*. New York: Simon and Schuster.

Freire, P. 1970. *Pedagogy of the Oppressed*. New York: Continuum.

"From the Editors." 1997. *Orion*. Autumn.

Gatto, J. T. 1992. *Dumbing Us Down: The Hidden Curriculum of Compulsory Schooling*. Gabriola Island, BC: New Society Publishers.

Ginott, H. G. 1993. *Teacher and Child: A Book for Parents and Teachers*. New York: Scribner.

Glendinning, C. 1995. "Technology, Trauma, and the Wild." In *Ecopsychology: Restoring the Earth, Healing the Mind*, edited by T. Roszak, M. E. Gomes, and A. D. Kanner, 41–54. San Francisco: Sierra Club Books.

Goleman, D. 1995. *Emotional Intelligence: Why It Can Matter More Than IQ*. New York: Bantam.

———. 2006. *Social Intelligence*. New York: Bantam.

Gordon, R. 2006. *Quantum Touch: The Power to Heal*. Berkeley, CA: North Atlantic Books.

Grandin, T. 2005. *Animals in Translation*. Orlando, FL: Harcourt.

Greenberg, D. 1987. *Free at Last: The Sudbury Valley School*. Framingham, MA: Sudbury Valley School Press.

Halifax, J. 2009. *Being with Dying*. Boston: Shambhala.

Hanh, T. N. 1991. *Peace Is Every Step: The Path of Mindfulness in Everyday Life*. New York: Bantam.

Hart, T. 2003. *The Secret Spiritual World of Children*. Novato, CA: New World Library.

———. 2004. "Opening the Contemplative Mind in the Classroom." *Journal of Transformative Education* 2 (1): 28–46.

———. 2007. *From Information to Transformation: Education for the Evolution of Consciousness*. New York: Peter Lang.

Harvey, O. J. 1961. *Conceptual Systems and Personality Organization*. New York: Harper and Row.

HeartMath Research Center. 2001. *Science of the Heart*. Boulder Creek, CA: Institute of HeartMath.

Hern, M. 2003. *Field Day: Getting Society Out of School*. Vancouver, BC: New Star Books.

Holden, R. 2005. *Success Intelligence*. New York: Hay House.

Holt, J. 1976. *Instead of Education*. New York: E. P. Dutton.

Huber, C. 1995. "Unconditional Self-Acceptance." 6 CDs. Boulder, CO: Sounds True.

———. 1999. *The Depression Book*. Murphys, CA: Keep it Simple Books.

———. 2000. *How to Get from Where You Are to Where You Want to Be*. Carlsbad, CA: Hay House.

———. 2007. *Making a Change for Good: A Guide to Compassionate Self-Discipline*. Boston: Shambhala.

Illich, I. 1971. *Deschooling Society*. New York: Harper and Row.

Jensen, D. 2000. *A Language Older than Words*. White River Junction, VT: Chelsea Green.

———. 2004. *Walking on Water: Reading and Writing and Revolution*. White River Junction, VT: Chelsea Green.

Judith, A. 2004. *Eastern Mind Western Mind*. Berkeley, CA: Celestial Arts.

Katie, B. 2002. *Loving What Is*. New York: Three Rivers Press.

———. 2005. *I Need Your Love—Is that True?* New York: Harmony.

Kegan, R., and L. L. Lahey. 2001. *How the Way We Talk Can Change The Way We Work*. San Francisco: Jossey-Bass.

Keller, E. F. 1983. *A Feeling for the Organism: The Life and Work of Barbara McClintock*. New York: Freeman.

Kumar, S. 2002. *You Are Therefore I Am*. Foxhole, England: Green Books.

Lauck, J. E. 2002. *The Voice of the Infinite in the Small: Re-Visioning the Insect-Human Connection*. Boston: Shambhala.

Lerner, M. 2000. *Spirit Matters*. Charlottesville, VA: Hampton Roads.

Levoy, G. 1997. *Callings: Finding and Following an Authentic Life*. New York: Three Rivers.

Lewis, T., F. Amini, and R. Lannon. 2000. *A General Theory of Love*. New York: Vintage.

Lichtmann, M. 2005. *The Teacher's Way: Teaching and the Contemplative Life*. New York: Paulist.

Limmer, E. 1995. *The Body Language of Illness*. Liberty Lake, WA: Freedom Press.

Macy, J., and M. Y. Brown. 1998. *Coming Back to Life*. Gabriola Island, BC: New Society Publishers.

Mander, J. 1991. *In the Absence of the Sacred*. San Francisco, CA: Sierra Club Books.

McTaggart, L. 2007. *The Intention Experiment*. New York: Free Press.

Merton, T. 1985. *Love and Living*. New York: Harcourt Brace Jovanovich.

Miller, J. 1996. *The Holistic Curriculum.* Toronto: The Ontario Institute for Studies in Education.

Miller, J. P. 2006. *Educating for Wisdom and Compassion.* Thousand Oaks, CA: Corwin Press.

Miller, R. 1997. *What Are Schools For?* Brandon, VT: Holistic Education Press.

———. 2005. *Yoga Nidra.* Boulder, CO: Sounds True.

———. 2008. "Five Principles of the Coming Education Revolution." *Green Money Journal* 17, no. 2: 17.

Nelson, R. 1991. *The Island Within.* New York: Vintage.

O'Sullivan, E., and A. Morrell, eds. 2002. *Expanding the Boundaries of Transformative Learning: Essays on Theory and Praxis.* New York: Palgrave.

O'Murchu, D. 1997. *Quantum Theology.* New York: Crossroads.

Oliver, M. 1992. "When Death Comes." *New and Selected Poems.* Boston: Beacon.

Olsen, K. 2009. *Wounded by School.* New York: Teachers College Press, Columbia University.

Orr, D. 1994. *Earth in Mind: On Education, Environment and the Human Prospect.* Washington, DC: Island Press.

Palmer, P. 1998. *The Courage to Teach.* San Francisco: Jossey-Bass.

———. 2004. *A Hidden Wholeness.* San Francisco: Jossey-Bass.

Peavy, F. 2001. *Strategic Questioning.* San Francisco: Crabgrass Organization.

Pert, C. 1997. *The Molecules of Emotion.* New York: Touchstone.

Phillips, C. *Socrates Café.* 2001. New York: W. W. Norton and Co.

Plotkin, B. 2003. *Soulcraft: Crossing into the Mysteries of Nature and Psyche.* Novato: New World Library.

Pope, D. C. 2001. *Doing School: How We Are Creating a Generation of Stressed Out, Materialistic, and Miseducated Students.* New Haven: Yale University Press.

Postman, N. 1996. *The End of Education: Redefining the Value of School.* New York: Vintage.

Postman, N., and C. Weingartner. 1969. *Teaching as a Subversive Activity.* New York: Delta.

Prakash, M. S., and G. Esteva. 1998. *Escaping Education: Living as Learning within Grassroots Cultures.* New York: Lang.

Remen, R. N. 1994. "The Recovery of the Sacred." *Context,* no. 39, 28–31.

Rilke, R. M. 1957. *New Poems.* Translated by J. B. Leishman. New York: New Directions.

———. 1993. *Letters to a Young Poet.* Translated by M. D. Herter. New York: Norton.

Rosenberg, M. 1999. *Nonviolent Communication: A Language of Compassion.* Encinitas, CA: PuddleDancer Press.

———. 2003. *Life-Enriching Education.* Encinitas, CA: PuddleDancer Press.

———. 2005. *Speak Peace in a World of Conflict.* Encinitas, CA: PuddleDancer Press.

Rue, L. 1997. "Going Deeper: Spiritual Dimensions of the Epic of Evolution." *Earth Light,* no. 26 (Summer): 12–13.

Rumi, J. 1984. "The Breeze at Dawn." In *Open Secret,* translated by J. C. Barks. Putney, VT: Threshold Books.

Sachar, L. 2003. *Stanley Yelnats Survival Guide to Camp Green Lake.* London: Bloomsbury.

Saint-Exupéry, A. de. 1943. *The Little Prince.* New York: Harcourt.

Schachter-Shalomi, Z. 1995. *From Ageing to Sage-ing.* New York: Warner.

Schmier, L. 2005. *Random Thoughts III: Teaching with Love.* Stillwater, OK: New Forums.

Schultz, B. D. 2008. *Spectacular Things Happen Along the Way.* New York: Teachers College Press.

Segal, J. 1997. *Raising Your Emotional Intelligence.* New York: Henry Holt.

Senge, P., C. O. Scharmer, J. Jaworski, and B. S. Flowers. 2004. *Presence: Human Purpose and the Field of the Future.* Cambridge, MA: Society for Organizational Learning.

Simons, N. 2005. "Cultivating Relational Intelligence." *EarthLight* 14, no. 3. www.earthlight.org/2005/essay53_simons.html.

Song, T. 2004. *Sacred Speech: The Way of Truthspeaking.* Three Lakes, WI: Teaching Drum Outdoor School.

Stern, F. 2000. "The Importance of 'Why.'" *World Policy Journal,* Spring, 1–8.

Stoddard, L. 2004. *Educating for Human Greatness.* Brandon, VT: Holistic Education Press.

Swimme, B. 1996. *The Hidden Heart of the Cosmos.* New York: Orbis.

Targ, R., and J. J. Hurtak. 2006. *The End of Suffering.* Charlottesville, VA: Hampton Roads.

Tolle, E. 1999. *The Power of Now.* Novato, CA: New World Library.

———. 2005. *A New Earth.* New York: Dutton.

Uhl, C. 2004. *Developing Ecological Consciousness: Path to a Sustainable World.* Lanham, MD: Rowman and Littlefield.

Ulrich, C. 2006. "The Power of Touch." *Body Sense Magazine,* Spring/Summer, 17–19.

Van Matre, S. 1990. *Earth Education: A New Beginning.* Cedar Cove, Greenville, WV: The Institute of Earth Education.

Vogt, E., J. Brown, and D. Isaacs. 2003. "The Art of Powerful Questions." Mill Valley, CA: Whole Systems Associates.

Walsh, R. 1999. *Essential Spirituality: The 7 Central Practices to Awaken Heart and Mind.* New York: John Wiley and Sons.

Wellwood, J. 1983. *Awakening the Heart.* Boston: Shambhala.

———. 1996. *Love and Awakening: Discovering the Sacred Path of Intimate Relationship.* New York: Harper Collins.

———. 2002. *Toward a Psychology of Awakening: Buddhism, Psychotherapy, and the Path of Personal and Spiritual Transformation.* Boston: Shambhala.

———. 2006. *Perfect Love Imperfect Relationships.* Boston: Trumpeter.

Weston, A. 1994. *Back to Earth.* Philadelphia: Temple University Press.

———. 2004. "What if Teaching Went Wild?" *Canadian Journal of Environmental Education* 9:31–46.

Wilson, E. O. 1984. *Biophilia.* Cambridge, MA: Harvard University Press.

Wu Wei Wu. 2002. *Ask the Awakened.* Boulder: Sentient Publications.

Yazzie-Mintz, E. 2008. "Voices of Students on Engagement: A Report on the 2006 High School Survey of Student Engagement." Available at http://ceep.indiana.edu/hssse/pdf/HSSSE_2006_Report.pdf

Zander, R. S., and B. Zander. 2000. *The Art of Possibility.* New York: Penguin.

Zimmerman, J., and V. Coyle. 1991. "Council: Reviving The Art of Listening." *Utne Reader,* March/April, 79–85.

Zull, J. E. 2002. *The Art of Changing the Brain.* Sterling, VA: Stylus.

Index

individual and collective, 65; relational, xvii, 162; schooling as undermining, 6; and speciesism, 165; trust in common, 144. *See also* mind

interdependence, 13, 137

Internet, 48

IQ (Intelligence Quotient), 14, 17

job/occupation, 27. *See also* career

Judaism, 101. *See also* religion

judgment, xv; and Council process, 140; and fear, 33, 113; fear-induced, 113; and feeling, 25; and feeling of inadequacy, 39, 44; and labels, 118, 119–20; and love, 37, 76; as mental construct, 120; and mind chatter, 79; and Nonviolent Communication, 129, 130–31, 133, 136; of other, 36, 100; and praise, 136; and separateness, 117, 120, 126, 154; and shadow, 89, 90, 92; and stories, 94; suspension of, 142–43; transcendence of, 98, 99, 100, 119–20, 122, 124, 126, 127

Jungian psychology, 88

Kabbalah, 101

kindness, 44, 46, 89, 91, 109, 127, 149, 150. *See also* compassion

kinship: and classroom layout, 137–39; through Council, 139–41; through dialogue, 141–44; through physical touch, 144–48; through shared agreements, 148–50

knowledge: acquisition of personal, 9; assessment of, 8; of bioregion, 154, 155, 157–58; as collection of facts, 8; and economism, 162; and not knowing, 86; and objective verifiability, 8; as separation, 4; and students as empty containers, xv; teacher-student transfer of, 5, 8–9, 12. *See also* learning; self-knowledge

label, xv, 12, 38, 117–20, 126

Labeling Game, 119–20

language: as cheapened, 68; of common values vs. difference, 126; and compassion, 127, 128; of complaint and blame, 121; and dualism, 116, 118; of fear, 127; and Non-

violent Communication, 132, 136, 137; and perception, 160; of relationship, 126–27; and separation from Earth, 159–62; and violence, 127, 128. *See also* communication

learning: banking model of, 8, 17; as best in school setting, 5–7, 12; and check-in, 139; comparison of, 9; and discipline, 5, 9–10, 12; feeling as hindrance to, 16; as fun, 9–10; independent, 9; innate desire for, 53; as interesting and important to lives, 6; midwife to, 109; motivation of, 5, 9–10, 12; and objectification, 5, 10–12; question-centered, 58–61; question concerning, 2; as separated from life, 7; social, 17; and students as empty containers, xv, 10, 17, 61, 137; as synonymous with living, 6; and teacher-student knowledge transfer, 5, 8–9, 12; transformative, xvi, xvii. *See also* knowledge; self-knowledge

Lectio Divina, 68–70

Levi, Primo, 65

life: community of, 182; expansion and openness to, 36; fullness of, 36; moment-by-moment acceptance of, 108; and objectification, 12; openings for, 188; as precious, xiii–xiv; as relationship, 3, 13; separation of learning from, 7; service, honor, and respect for, 13; well-lived, 13

life calling, 73

life force, 13, 113

listening: and Bohmian Dialogue, 144; deep, 72–73; from heart, 140, 141; and Nonviolent Communication, 133–36; shared agreement about, 149–50; and Strategic Questioning, 73

love, 3; as antidote to fear, 38–40; for bioregion, 155; completeness of, 40; as conditional, 21; conditional vs. unconditional, 38–39; and consciousness climate, 44; cultivation of, 15; desire for, 105; for Earth, 14, 15; experience of, 105; extension of, 83; and fear, 21, 22, 35; for feeling body, 18; and good vs. bad, 39; grounding in, 14; and healing of Earth, 182, 183; and heart awareness, 42–43; and heart disease, 23; as inexhaustible fount within, 108; for insects, 180; and intrinsic goodness, 40;

love *(cont.)*
  and learning to let go, 106–8; and loving-
  kindness meditation, 45–46; motivation
  through withdrawal of, 21; nature as being,
  105; need for, 106; and need for other, 40;
  and obligation, 106; of other, 15, 100; as
  permeating whole of existence, 104–5;
  and possessions, 84; for questions, 52;
  search for, outside of ourselves, 104; for
  self, xiv, 15, 39, 76–77, 100, 107, 188; self
  as, 14; separation from, 105; and separation vs. relational consciousness, 14; and
  shadow, 89, 91; student as manifestation
  of, 113; teaching of, 40–41; as transfor-
  mational, 32; unconditional, 40, 81; as
  universally acknowledged virtue, 46. *See
  also* unlove
loving kindness meditation, 45–46

manipulation, 40, 78, 87, 91, 106, 128, 136
media, 44, 74, 80, 162. *See also* culture
meditation, 44, 45, 46, 68, 101, 102, 104
Merton, Thomas, 88
metaphysical reflection, 101
mind, 5, 17–18, 48, 116. *See also* dualism;
  intellect/intelligence; knowledge
mirror neurons, 31
Mirror Walk, 174
mission statement, 148–50
money, 4, 9, 14, 162, 163
motivation: by desire, 10, 11; and emotional
  intelligence, 17; and fear, 21; to heal
  Earth, 182; of learning, 5, 9–10, 12; outer
  directed, 18; and praise, 136; of self, 9;
  through withdrawal of love, 21

Namaste, 149
Nasrudin, 92
native people, 157
nature, removal from, 155–59. *See also* Earth
need, 107; and body, 128; and compassion,
  128; as confused with want, 128, 129;
  innate desire to meet, 128, 131; learning
  objectives for genuine, 133; for love, 106;
  and Nonviolent Communication, 129, 130,
  131, 132, 133, 134; shared, 128; unmet,
  131; as weakness, 132

Nonviolent Communication, 127, 128–37;
  and judgment, 129, 130–31, 133, 136;
  and language, 132, 136, 137; and observation, 129, 130, 131, 132, 133; and request,
  131–32. *See also* communication

objectification, xv; and dualism, 114; of Earth,
  160, 161; grounding in, 10–12; institutionalization of, 12; and learning, 5; and
  separation, 4
objectivity, 8, 17
observation, 159; as foundation for questions,
  63–65; and Nonviolent Communication,
  129, 130, 131, 132, 133; and stories, 94
occupation/job, 86–88
oneness, 122–23, 159
opinion, 142. *See also* belief
Oppenheimer, Robert, 54
original sin, narrative of, 79–80
other: ability to deeply presence, 181; business of, 96; compassion for, xv; as extension
  of self, 113; fear of, 33, 123–24; love of, 15;
  relationship with, 13, 111, 113
oxygen, 168, 178, 183

parents: and emotional development, 20–23;
  and fear, 21; and love as conditional, 38;
  and questions, 51; and unlove, 80
Parks, Rosa, 186–87
Peavy, Fran, 70–71, 73
perception, 126; and economism, 162; and
  labels, 118; and language, 160; and relationship, 2
plants, 162, 165, 169, 175, 176, 178, 181, 183
Plutarch, 76
PMI approach, 67–68
possessions, material, 84–85, 88
praise, 136–37
progress, 17
Project Citizen, 55–56
projection, 39, 90, 93, 96–100

questions/questioning: art of asking, xiv;
  aspects of good, 57–58; and assumptions,
  60, 66; audacity of, 75; avoidance of, 6;
  construction of, 56–58; correct answers to,
  50; to create community, 62–63; critiquing

self-esteem, 35, 36
selfishness, 89
self-knowledge, 13, 43, 109; and emotion, 47;
    journey toward, 81; through others, 123; as
    priority, 109; and shadow, 88; and success,
    87; and time for self, 101. *See also* knowl-
    edge; learning
self-reliance, 9
self-worth, 125, 126, 136
sense perception, 174–75, 181
separation, 154; and blame and complaint,
    122; through cultivation of helplessness, 4;
    and dialogue, 142; and dualism, 114; early
    enactment of, 4; from Earth, 155–67; from
    ennobling work, 4; and fear, 34, 123–26;
    identification of causes of, 126; and judg-
    ment, 117, 120, 126, 154; and knowledge,
    4; and language, 159–62; from love, 105;
    and manipulation, 40; mending of, 13; of
    mind and body, 17–18; from natural world,
    155–59; as nonexistent, 2; in school, 4;
    teaching of, 154; and transcending dualism,
    117; and violent speech, 129
separation consciousness, 152; and dialogue,
    143; and Earth, 154; and education myths,
    5–12; love as transforming, 14; movement
    away from, 113–26; and schooling, 7; trans-
    formation from, 3–5
September 11 attacks, 71, 123
sexuality, 146
Shackles Test, 27
shadow, 88–93
Shaler, Nathaniel, 63
shame, 89
silence, 32, 34
Sisyphus, myth of, 109
social change, 4
social class, 4
socialization, 14, 20–21, 22, 25, 51. *See also*
    children; conditioning; culture
society, 76, 80, 87
sociobiology, 19
Socrates, 56–57
Socratic tradition, 124
soul, manifestation of, 186
species, 181–82

speciesism, 164–67, 182, 183
spontaneity, xii, 140
stars, 167, 168, 169, 170
Stern, Fritz, 65
story: construction of, 94; as interpretation
    generated from observations, 94; personal,
    93–100; questioning of, 94–100; and sepa-
    ration from self and others, 96
Strategic Questioning, 70–74
stress: and consciousness climate, 44; and
    heart, 42; and HeartMath techniques, 43
success, 109, 186; and full humanity, 2; genu-
    ine, 86–88; and IQ, 17; and mind-body
    separation, 18; and mistrust of emotion, 17;
    and relationship, 13
Sudbury Valley School, 11
Sufism, 101

technology, 3, 4, 13, 14, 17, 163, 164. *See also*
    science
testing, 4, 8, 9, 14, 17, 48, 81
touch, 144–48, 172–73
Toyota, 65
Transcendental Meditation, 44
trees, 177–78
trust: and acceptance of responsibility, 121;
    and authority, 59; and Byrd Elementary,
    54–56; in common intelligence, 144; and
    democratic classroom, 55; and dualism,
    116; need for, 128; and Nonviolent Com-
    munication, 134; and questions, 53–54;
    shared agreement for, 150
truthspeaking, 124–26, 127, 133; and Council,
    139–41; shared agreement about, 150

unlove, 78–81, 104, 105
unworthiness, xiv, 81; trance of, 79, 93, 109

violence, xvii, 4, 76, 80, 127, 128. *See also*
    aggression

warfare, 4
WE consciousness, 116, 117
worldview, 3, 14, 39, 162–64
woundedness, 104